D1070762

3

STRATEGIES FOR writers

Senior Author

Rebecca Bowers Sipe, Ed.D.
Eastern Michigan University

Consulting Authors

Julie Coiro, Ph.D.
University of Rhode Island

Amy Humphreys, Ed.M., NBCT
Educational Consultant

Sara B. Kajder, Ph.D.
Shady Side Academy, Pittsburgh, Pennsylvania

James Scott Miller, M.Ed.
National Writing Consultant

Mark Overmeyer, M.A.
Cherry Creek School District, Colorado

ZB Zaner-Bloser

Program Reviewers

Zaner-Bloser wishes to thank these educators who reviewed portions of this program and provided comments prior to publication.

Joe Anspaugh
Shelbyville Middle School
Shelbyville, IN

Michele Barto, Ed.D.
Fairleigh Dickinson University
Madison, NJ

Jackie Blosser
Lima City Schools
Lima, OH

Kim Bondy
South Arbor Academy
Ypsilanti, MI

Kelly Caravelli
Meadowbrook Middle School
Poway, CA

Cathy Cassy
St. Louis Public Schools
St. Louis, MO

Penny Clare
Educational Consultant
Lee, NH

Mary Dunton
Literacy Consultant
Sparks, NV

Emily Gleason
Beaverton School District
Beaverton, OR

Denise Gray, Ed.D.
Whiteriver Elementary School
Whiteriver, AZ

Laura Hall
Walton Charter Academy
Pontiac, MI

Donna Jett
Rockwood South Middle School
Fenton, MO

Christine Johnson, Ed.D.
Boonton Public Schools
Boonton, NJ

Dr. Roma Morris
Columbia School District
Columbia, MS

Rosanne Richards
Southern Nevada Regional
Professional Development Program
North Las Vegas, NV

Sharlene E. Ricks
Alpine School District
American Fork, UT

Debbie Rutherford
Independent National Consultant
Omaha, NE

Melinda Springli
Lawton Public Schools
Lawton, OK

Kerry Stephenson
Pendleton County School District
Butler, KY

Photography: Cover © Exactostock/SuperStock; Interior models, George C. Anderson; Stopwatch image © Royalty-Free/Corbis; p. 3 © Prisma/SuperStock; p. 123 © Sheldan Collins/Corbis; p 176 © Jeff Topping/Stringer/Getty Images; p. 213 © John Wang/Photodisc/Getty Images; p. 235 © Sandy Felsenthal/Corbis; p. 268 © Rubberball/Corbis; p. 290 © John Parker/Getty Images; p. 307 © Joe Raedle/Getty Images; p. 308 (top and bottom left) Plimoth Plantation; p. 308 (bottom right) © Michael Springer/Stringer/Getty Images; p. 327 © Visions of America/SuperStock; p. 328 (left) © George H.H. Huey/Corbis, (right) © David Muench/Corbis; p. 329 (top) © Ed Darack/Sciene Faction/Corbis, (bottom) © Corbis; p. 353 © Rudy Sulgan/Corbis; p. 445 © Shobeir Ansari/Flickr/Getty Images

Art Credits: pp. 4, 26, 48, 124, 146, 168, 236, 260, 282, 354, 376, 400 Paul Montgomery; pp. 76, 97, 99, 190, 304, 422 Chris Vallo; pp. 51, 52, 53 Anthony Davila; p. 75 Karen Stormer-Brooks

Literature Credits: pp. 104–105 *Our American Flag* by Mary Firestone © 2007 by Picture Window Books, an imprint by Capstone. All rights reserved; pp. 216–217 Excerpted from The Underground Railroad for Kids by Mary Kay Carson. Copyright © 2005 by Mary Kay Carson. Used with permission of Chicago Review Press; pp. 334–335 From "Reading In Mongolia" by Dashdondog Jamba. Copyright ©2011 Highlights for Children, Inc., Columbus, Ohio. All rights reserved. Used by permission; pp. 336–337 From *My Librarian is a Camel* by Margriet Ruurs. Copyright ©2005 by Margriet Ruurs. Published by Boyds Mills Press, Inc. Used by permission.

ISBN 978-1-4531-1221-2

Zaner-Bloser, Inc.
1-800-421-3018
www.zaner-bloser.com
Printed in the United States of America 14 15 16 17 18 25170 5 4 3 2 1

Hi, there! **We're your *Strategies for Writers* Writing Partners!**

We're here to guide you step-by-step through the stages of the writing process: Prewrite, Draft, Revise, Edit, and Publish.

In each unit, we'll focus on one text type: **narrative, informative/explanatory,** or **opinion**.

Have you ever wondered what makes a good friendly letter? Or what the elements of a problem-solution essay are? How about some reasons for writing an opinion paragraph? We'll answer those questions and more.

We'll focus on these six traits of effective writing: **Ideas, Organization, Voice, Word Choice, Sentence Fluency,** and **Conventions**. We'll explain how to apply the traits to each genre of writing, and we'll show you how the traits work together.

In each chapter, we'll first review a model writing sample. Then we'll use a rubric to score the model. Rubrics are a great way to know exactly what is expected as you plan and evaluate your writing. After that, it's your turn to write!

Narrative writing

Optional Revising Lessons available at **www.sfw.z-b.com**

Table of Contents

Informative/Explanatory writing

Optional Revising Lessons available at **www.sfw.z-b.com**

Table of Contents

Opinion writing

Optional Revising Lessons available at **www.sfw.z-b.com**

Table of Contents

More Writing Practice

Descriptive Elements in the Text Types

Optional Revising Lessons available at **www.sfw.z-b.com**

Table of Contents

Appendices

Appendix A: Grammar Practice

Table of Contents

Appendix B: Rubrics

Narrative writing tells a story about real or imaginary events.

Hi! My name is Marina, and I love to use my imagination, especially when I write stories. In the morning when I wake up, I like to listen to the birds chirping. I try to imagine what they might be saying. Sometimes I draw pictures of the birds and tell stories to go along with my drawings. When I write letters to my grandmother, I tell her stories of things that happen in my life. I also like to write science and social studies stories at school. Now I want to learn strategies to turn my stories into good pieces of writing.

IN THIS UNIT

- Personal Narrative
- Friendly Letter
- Folktale
- LITERATURE CONNECTION ▶ Fable
- Next Generation Narrative Assessment

Name: Marina
Home: Illinois
Favorite Activities: drawing and playing the piano
Favorite Food: tamales
Favorite Book: *Charlotte's Web* by E. B. White

What's a Personal Narrative?

It's a true story that I write about something I saw or did.

What's in a Personal Narrative?

A personal narrative answers some important questions.

Who
It tells *who* the story is about. It can be about me, or I can also put other people in my story if I want to.

Where
That's the place *where* my story happened. It could be at my house or on a beach at the lake.

What
It tells *what* happened to me. Maybe I saw a storm at the beach or maybe I found some interesting shells.

When
That's the time *when* my story happened. It could be yesterday, on a holiday, or after a thunderstorm.

Why
That's the reason *why* the event happened. It could be because I wanted to learn something or to have fun.

Why write a Personal Narrative?

There are lots of reasons to write a personal narrative. Here are two reasons I can think of for writing about something that happened to me.

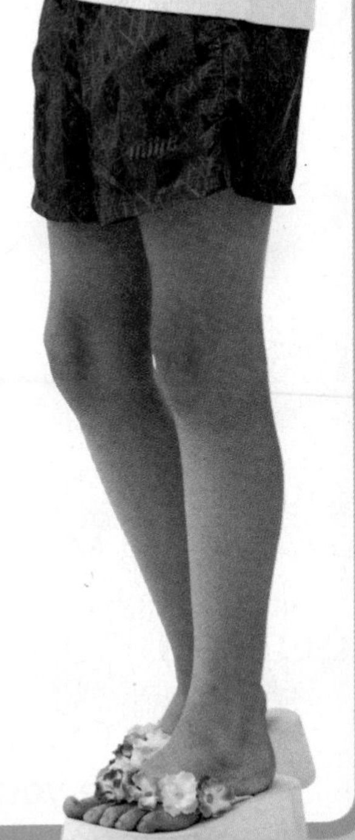

To Entertain
Sometimes it's fun to tell a friend about something that happened to me. If my friend has had something similar happen, we can talk about how our experiences were the same or different. If she hasn't, she may ask me a lot of questions to learn about what I did.

To Inform
I like to share stories about trips I take with my family. My friends always want information about what it was like to visit someplace different. They often think they would like to go to the same place after they hear my story. I also like to think about what I learn on my trips.

Linking Narrative Writing Traits to a Personal Narrative

In this chapter, you will write a story about an experience you want to share. This type of narrative writing is called a personal narrative. Marina will guide you through the stages of the writing process: Prewrite, Draft, Revise, Edit, and Publish. In each stage, Marina will show you important writing strategies that are linked to the Narrative Writing Traits below.

Narrative Writing Traits

	• a topic that is just the right size, not too big or too small • descriptive details that answer the reader's questions (such as *who, what, where, when,* and *why*)
	• a logical sequence of events • a strong beginning and a satisfying ending • temporal words/phrases to signal order of events
	• a voice that is friendly and speaks directly to the audience • dialogue that, if used, fits the characters
	• exact words that tell the story
	• a variety of sentence lengths that makes the story flow smoothly
	• no or few errors in spelling, punctuation, and capitalization

Before you write, read Luis Delgado's personal narrative on the next page. Then use the personal narrative rubric on page 8 to decide how well he did. (You might want to look back at What's in a Personal Narrative? on page 4, too!)

A Whole Bat-talion

by Luis Delgado

Did you know that bats have lived in Carlsbad Caverns for more than 5,000 years? That is what the park ranger told us as I sat in the outdoor theater with my brother Mario. Our parents had just driven us across the desert to see an amazing event. Now, as we waited, we listened to the ranger at Carlsbad Caverns National Park. She explained that more than 300,000 Mexican free-tailed bats live in the cave. "During the day, the bats sleep," she said, "but they get hungry, and at night they come out to eat. Every night they eat tons of insects!" The sun went down as the ranger finished talking, and then it happened. First it looked like a puff of smoke coming from the cave. Then it seemed more like a spinning black tornado. Waves of bats poured out of the cave. As the bats flew in circles, darting and looping higher and higher, we could hear the humming of their wings. I never knew there were so many bats living so close to my home. I'm glad they are all eating harmful insects while we sleep!

who

where

what

when

why

Personal Narrative Rubric

Use this rubric to analyze the model. Then use it to plan and score your own personal narrative.

	6	5	4
Ideas	The topic is just the right size. The details are surprising or interesting.	The topic is the right size. A few details are surprising or interesting.	The topic is the right size, but most details are not interesting.
Organization	The beginning establishes the situation and grabs the reader's attention. The ending provides a sense of closure.	The beginning is interesting and establishes the situation. The ending provides some closure.	The beginning is somewhat weak. It does not grab the reader's attention. The ending may be weak.
Voice	The writer uses first-person point of view and questions to speak to the audience.	The writer usually uses first-person point of view and questions to speak to the audience.	The writer sometimes uses first-person point of view and questions to speak to the audience.
Word Choice	The writer uses exact nouns and strong verbs.	The writer usually uses exact nouns and strong verbs.	The writer sometimes uses exact nouns and strong verbs.
Sentence Fluency	A variety of sentence lengths makes the story flow smoothly.	A variety of sentence lengths makes the story flow smoothly most of the time.	The writer attempts to vary sentence lengths but story flow is not present.
Conventions	Spelling, punctuation, and capitalization are correct. There are no sentence fragments.	Spelling, punctuation, and capitalization are almost all correct with no sentence fragments.	There are a few errors in spelling, punctuation, and capitalization, and a few sentence fragments.

+Presentation The narrative is legible and neat. The title and writer's name are at the top of the page.

	3	2	1	
	The topic is too big or too small. The details do not support the topic.	The topic is somewhat unclear. The details are confusing.	The reader can't tell what the topic is. Details are rambling and vague.	Ideas
	The beginning is very weak. The ending does not provide a sense of closure.	The narrative is difficult to follow. There is no clear beginning or ending.	The writing is not a narrative. There is no clear beginning or ending.	Organization
	The writer attempts to present a first-person point of view but does not connect to the audience.	The writer never speaks directly to the reader and does not have a clear sense of audience.	The writer is not "present" anywhere in the writing.	Voice
	The writer uses general nouns and weak verbs.	The writer's nouns and verbs are frequently misused.	The writer does not seem to have given any thought to the choice of words.	Word Choice
	Too many sentences of the same length make the story sound boring.	There is little or no variety in sentence structure.	The piece is challenging to read due to poor sentence structure.	Sentence Fluency
	There are many errors in spelling, punctuation, and capitalization.	There are so many errors in spelling, punctuation, and capitalization that the writing is difficult to understand.	The writing has not been edited.	Conventions

See Appendix B for 4-, 5-, and 6-point narrative rubrics.

Using the Personal Narrative Rubric to Analyze the Model

Did you notice that the model on page 7 points out some key elements of a personal narrative? As he wrote "A Whole Bat-talion," Luis Delgado used these elements to help him describe a personal experience. He also used the 6-point rubric on pages 8–9 to plan, draft, revise, and edit the writing. A rubric is a great tool to evaluate writing during the writing process.

To get started, look at the top score for each trait as you study the model. Do you agree that Luis has earned a 6 for each trait?

- **The topic is just the right size.**
- **The details are surprising or interesting.**

In the story, Luis tells about one experience he had. His topic is just the right size. He also includes surprising or interesting details that help me understand his topic. Look at how he answered one of my questions about the number of bats.

> Now, as we waited, we listened to the ranger at Carlsbad Caverns National Park. She explained that more than 300,000 Mexican free-tailed bats live in the cave.

- **The beginning establishes the situation and grabs the reader's attention.**
- **The ending provides a sense of closure.**

Starting the story with a question grabs my attention. Then Luis answers my questions, such as *who, what, when, where,* and *why*. Reading for answers kept my interest. I especially like the way the ending wraps up the story.

Did you know that bats have lived in Carlsbad Caverns for more than 5,000 years?

I'm glad they are all eating harmful insects while we sleep!

- **The writer uses first-person point of view and questions to speak to the audience.**

Luis sounds like he is speaking directly to me. He uses first-person point of view to share his story. I can also tell that he wants me to understand what he heard and saw at the cave.

Now, as we waited, we listened to the ranger at Carlsbad Caverns National Park.

Using the Personal Narrative Rubric to Analyze the Model

- **The writer uses exact nouns and strong verbs.**

The author uses many exact words to help me see clear pictures. For example, he uses the word *poured* instead of a less exact word like *came*. The word *looping* is a better choice than the word *going*.

> Waves of bats poured out of the cave. As the bats flew in circles, darting and looping higher and higher, we could hear the humming of their wings.

- **A variety of sentence lengths makes the story flow smoothly.**

Luis uses both long and short sentences. If the sentences were all short, the writing would be choppy. If they were all long, the writing would be confusing. In this example, Luis writes a variety of interesting sentences that flow well. I especially like the way he includes the park ranger's words in his story.

> "During the day, the bats sleep," she said, "but they get hungry, and at night they come out to eat. Every night they eat tons of insects!" The sun went down as the ranger finished talking, and then it happened.

- **Spelling, punctuation, and capitalization are correct. There are no sentence fragments.**

I checked Luis's story and I can see that he doesn't have any errors in spelling, punctuation, or capitalization. Every sentence has a subject and a verb, which means that there are no sentence fragments. When he includes the ranger's words, he uses quotation marks correctly.

"During the day, the bats sleep," she said, "but they get hungry, and at night they come out to eat. Every night they eat tons of insects!"

Presentation The narrative is legible and neat. The title and writer's name are at the top of the page.

My Turn!

I'm going to write my own personal narrative. Follow along to see how I use the rubric and good writing strategies.

Prewrite

Focus on **Ideas**

The Rubric Says The topic is just the right size. The details are surprising or interesting.

Writing Strategy Jot down notes about an interesting personal experience.

My teacher asked everyone to write a personal narrative. I tried to think of an experience I have had that I really enjoyed. I knew I needed to have enough information about my idea to keep my classmates interested. I decided to write about my trip to the beach to collect seashells. I love to collect shells. Last winter, my aunt took me to Sanibel Island to find some. Sanibel is in Florida on the Gulf of Mexico. It is famous for having the most beautiful seashells. The trip was so much fun! I thought my friends might enjoy reading about it, too. I'll start by jotting down some notes about what happened that day.

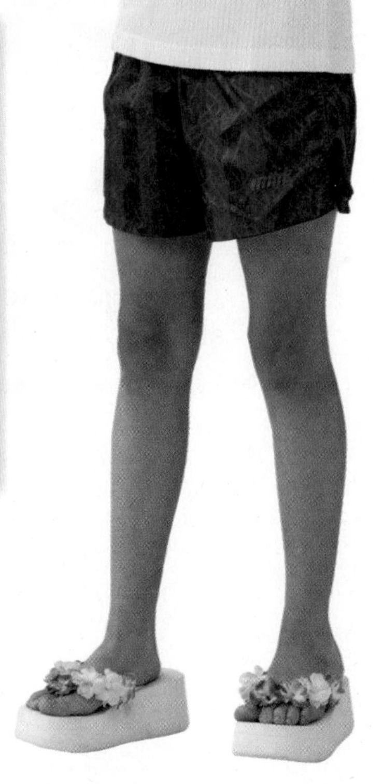

My Notes About Finding Shells

- ✔ went with Aunt Angela to Sanibel Island
- ✔ big storm washed up lots of shells
- ✔ looked on beach for shells for my collection
- ✔ found many kinds

Write

Think about an interesting experience you had. Jot down notes about what happened.

Prewrite

Focus on **Organization**

The Rubric Says The beginning establishes the situation.

Writing Strategy Make a 5 W's Chart to ask and answer questions.

I know from the rubric that my personal narrative should share something I saw or did. I want to let my readers know that my story is about my trip to Sanibel Island. I also want to answer the *who, what, where, when,* and *why* questions for the reader. So I'll use my notes and a 5 W's Chart to organize my story.

Writer's Term

5 W's Chart

A **5 W's Chart** helps organize information. A writer can use the chart to ask and answer these questions: **Who? What? Where? When? Why?**

5 W's Chart

Who was there?	Aunt Angela and I
What happened?	found lots of seashells
Where did it happen?	a beach on Sanibel Island
When did it happen?	after a big storm
Why did it happen?	wanted to find shells for my collection

Analyze

Is there enough interesting information for Marina to write her personal narrative? What could she add?

Write

Make your own 5 W's Chart. Put information from your notes on the chart.

Draft

Focus on **Ideas**

The Rubric Says The details are surprising or interesting.

Writing Strategy Keep the reader's attention with interesting details.

Now I'm ready to write. I will include interesting details to make the reader want to learn more. I'll also add unusual details to surprise the reader. I hope I put in enough information to answer the reader's questions!

Writer's Term

Details

The **details** in a story help answer important questions. Interesting details hold the reader's attention. Good details might be surprising, funny, or informative.

Surprising detail: A good time to look for shells on the beach is after a big storm.

Funny detail: You might find a lion's paw or a buttercup on the beach!

Informative detail: My aunt likes to press one type of shell against her ear. Can you guess why?

I'll use my 5 W's Chart to help write the rest of my draft. I'll do my best with grammar and spelling, but I can check for mistakes later. I'll just write to get my ideas down now.

Proofreading Marks

⊐ Indent	Take out something
≡ Make uppercase	⊙ Add a period
/ Make lowercase	¶ New paragraph
∧ Add something	(sp) Spelling error

[DRAFT]

Going on a Treasure Hunt

Aunt Angela took me to a beach on Sanibel Island after a big storm. It was a great time to hunt for nice shells for my collection. The wind and waves from the storm made the shells on the ocean floor loose. Then the shells washed up on the beach. Carefully near the water she walked. The wet sand went between her toes. Sometimes the shells were on the sand. Sometimes thay were buried a little. Then I would dig them up and take off the sand. Found many shells. Aunt Angela told me their names. Some of them had funny names. Aunt Angelas favorite is a konch shell We love all the seashells, though. A special kind of treasure!

an interesting detail

a funny detail

Analyze

Read the draft. Which details answer the questions in the 5 W's Chart?

Write

Use your 5 W's Chart to write a draft of a personal narrative about something you saw or did.

Revise

Focus on **Organization**

The Rubric Says The beginning establishes the situation and grabs the reader's attention.

Writing Strategy Keep the reader's attention with interesting details.

I finished my draft. Then I checked the rubric. It tells me that my story needs a beginning that will catch the reader's attention. It also gives an idea of what the story will be about. It might tell a surprising fact or ask a question. My friend Joselito likes my story but asked if I could write a more interesting beginning. So here's how I revised it.

Going on a Treasure Hunt [DRAFT]

Is it a good idea to go to the beach after a storm? It is if you want to find seashells!
^Aunt Angela took me to a beach on Sanibel Island after a big storm. It was a great time to hunt for nice shells for my collection.

added interesting beginning

Write

Read your draft again. Try writing different beginnings to see which one you like best.

Revise

Focus on 

The Rubric Says The writer uses first-person point of view and questions to speak to the audience.

Writing Strategy Write as if you were talking to your readers.

The rubric reminds me to use a first-person point of view. A friendly voice also helps me connect with readers. When I use natural language, I help readers feel like I am speaking just to them. I looked for formal sentences that I could make more personal.

Writer's Term

First-Person Point of View

A **first-person point of view** uses the personal pronouns **I, me, mine,** and **my** to connect with the reader.

[DRAFT]

used a first-person point of view

I walked carefully near the water.
beach. ~~Carefully near the water she walked.~~ The wet
my I found
sand went between ~~her~~ toes. Sometimes the shells
~~were~~ on the sand. Sometimes thay were buried a
little. Then I would dig them up and take off the sand.

Analyze

Look at the revisions. Does Marina use a friendly voice and a first-person point of view?

Write

Read your draft again. Add or replace words to give your writing a friendly, personal tone.

Revise

Focus on **Word Choice**

The Rubric Says The writer uses exact nouns and strong verbs.

Writing Strategy Use specific nouns and verbs.

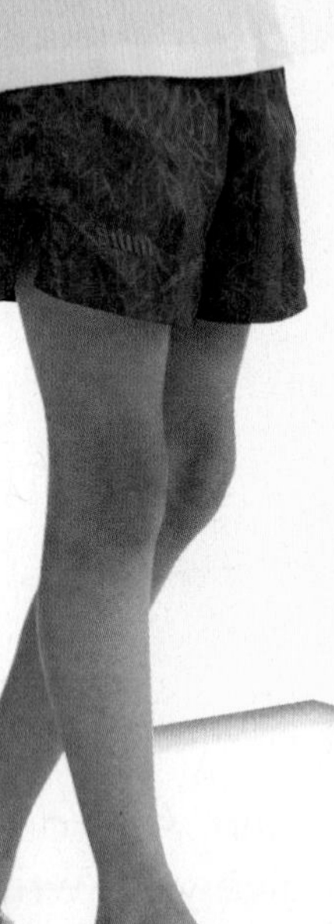

The rubric reminds me to use specific nouns and verbs. Specific words create a clear picture for the reader. As I read my draft again, I found a few vague words that I can replace with vivid ones. Do you think my changes give my reader a better picture of me on the beach?

used exact words

beach. ~~I walked~~ tiptoed carefully near the water. The wet sand ~~went~~ oozed between my toes. Sometimes I found the shells on the sand. Sometimes thay were buried a little. Then I would dig them up and ~~take~~ brush off the sand.

[DRAFT]

Write

Read your draft again. Replace vague words with exact nouns and strong verbs.

Edit

Focus on **Conventions**

The Rubric Says Spelling, punctuation, and capitalization are correct. There are no sentence fragments.

Writing Strategy Make sure there are no sentence fragments.

The rubric reminds me to check my spelling, capitalization, and punctuation. I will also fix any sentence fragments I may have written.

Writer's Term

Sentence Fragment

A **sentence fragment** does not express a complete thought. It is missing either a subject or a predicate.

[DRAFT]

fixed sentence fragment

~~Angelas~~ Angela's favorite is a ~~konch~~ conch shell. She likes it best ~~becawse~~ because she hears the sound of the ocean when she presses it to her ear. We love all the seashells, though. ~~A~~ They are a special kind of treasure!

Analyze

Look at Marina's editing. Did she proofread her writing carefully and fix any sentence fragments? Why do you think complete sentences are easier to read?

Write

Conventions

Edit your draft for spelling, punctuation, and capitalization. Fix any sentence fragments.

For more practice fixing sentence fragments, use the exercises on the next two pages.

Subject and Predicate

Know the Rule

The **subject** is the part of the sentence that tells whom or what the sentence is about.

Example:

Grandpa likes to row on his pond.

The subject can be one or more words.

Example:

He and I saw ducks, snakes, and a turtle.

The **predicate** is the part of the sentence that tells what the subject is or does.

Example:

Grandpa **grabbed a flashlight for a big surprise!**

Practice the Rule

Number a sheet of paper from 1–10. Read each group of words. Write **S** if the words are the subject of a sentence. Write **P** if the words are the predicate of a sentence.

1. Rowed on his pond
2. My grandpa and I
3. Slithered in the shallow water
4. The sun
5. The edge of the pond
6. Aimed the light
7. Hundreds of tiny fish
8. The ink-black pond
9. Watched for a while
10. Need some rest

Sentence Fragments

Know the Rule

A sentence tells a complete thought and needs a subject and a predicate. A **sentence fragment** is a group of words that is missing a subject or a predicate.

Examples:
Fragment: Lived in the shell. (no subject)
Fragment: A tiny hermit crab. (no predicate)
Sentence: A tiny hermit crab lived in the shell. (subject and predicate)

Practice the Rule

Number a sheet of paper from 1–10. Write **F** for each sentence fragment. Write **C** for each complete sentence. If the sentence is a fragment, write **S** if the subject is missing. Write **P** if the predicate is missing.

1. I like to build sand castles at the beach.
2. Made a big one last summer.
3. My brother, mother, and father.
4. First we made a pile of sand.
5. Shaped it into a castle.
6. Dug a moat filled with water around it.
7. Several very tall, narrow towers.
8. Used a stick with a leaf on it for a flag.
9. Stopped to look at our castle.
10. We were proud.

Publish

+Presentation

Publishing Strategy Share your story in an author's circle.

Presentation Strategy Use neat handwriting or word processing.

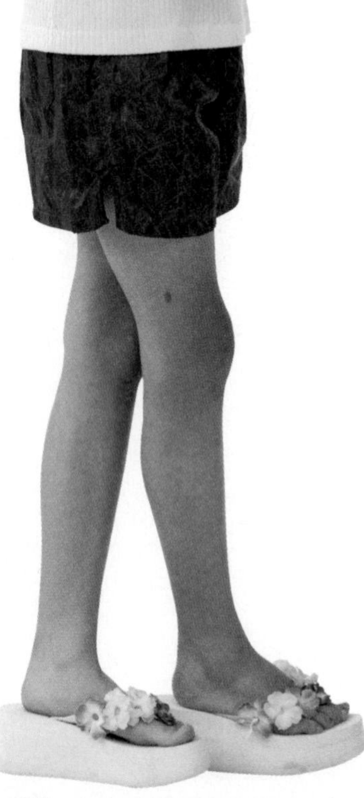

I want to share my story in our author's circle. I need to be sure to use neat handwriting or word processing so I can read my writing easily. Before I read my paper aloud, I will check it one more time. Here is the checklist I will use.

My Final Checklist

Did I—

- ✔ check the spelling, capitalization, and punctuation?
- ✔ make sure all my sentences are complete?
- ✔ make my personal narrative neat and easy to read?
- ✔ put my name and the story's title at the top of the paper?

Write

Use this checklist to prepare your final copy. Then share your story in an author's circle.

Going on a Treasure Hunt
by Marina

Is it a good idea to go to the beach after a storm? It is if you want to find seashells! Aunt Angela took me to a beach on Sanibel Island after a hurricane. It was a great time to hunt for unusual shells for my collection. The wind and waves from the storm made the shells on the ocean floor loose. Then the shells washed up on the beach. I tiptoed carefully near the water as the wet sand oozed between my toes. Sometimes I found the shells on the sand. Sometimes they were buried a little. Then I would dig them up and brush off the sand. I found many shells. Aunt Angela told me their names. Some of them had funny names like buttercup, kitten's paw, and lion's paw. Aunt Angela's favorite is a conch shell. She likes it best because she hears the sound of the ocean when she presses it to her ear. We love all the seashells, though. They are a special kind of treasure!

Analyze

How did Marina do? How well did she use the traits of a good personal narrative in her story? Remember to use the rubric to check your story, too.

What's a Friendly Letter?

A friendly letter is writing I send to someone I know well, like a friend or a member of my family.

What's in a Friendly Letter?

Heading
That's my address and the date.

Greeting
That's the part where I write *Dear* and then the person's name that I'm writing to.

Body
That's the message. Sometimes it's a story about something that happened.

Closing
That part tells my reader that I've ended the letter. It's like saying goodbye.

Signature
That's my name in cursive. I'll write a friendly letter to someone I know well, so I'll sign just my first name.

Why write a Friendly Letter?

There are many reasons for writing a letter to a friend, a family member, or someone else who's special to me. Here are some of my reasons.

To Entertain or Express

Sometimes I have a story I want to share. I wrote a letter to my friend to tell her about a book I read. Other times I want to express my feelings. I wrote to my aunt to thank her for the birthday present she sent me.

To Tell or Inform

I might write a letter to tell about something I did. I wrote to my older brother who lives in another city. I told him about an exciting visit to the zoo.

I can write a letter to tell someone what's been happening in my life. I wrote to my grandpa to tell him about an award I got at school.

Linking Narrative Writing Traits to a Friendly Letter

In this chapter, you will write to someone about a personal experience. This type of narrative writing is called a friendly letter. Marina will guide you through the stages of the writing process: Prewrite, Draft, Revise, Edit, and Publish. In each stage, Marina will show you important writing strategies that are linked to the Narrative Writing Traits below.

Narrative Writing Traits

	• a topic that is just the right size, not too big or too small • descriptive details that answer the reader's questions (such as *who, what, where, when,* and *why*)
	• a logical sequence of events • a strong beginning and a satisfying ending • temporal words/phrases to signal order of events
	• a voice that is friendly and speaks directly to the audience • dialogue that, if used, fits the characters
	• exact words that tell the story
	• a variety of sentence lengths that makes the story flow smoothly
	• no or few errors in spelling, punctuation, and capitalization

Before you write, read Katy's friendly letter on the next page. Then use the friendly letter rubric on page 30 to decide how well she did. (You might want to look back at What's in a Friendly Letter? on page 26, too!)

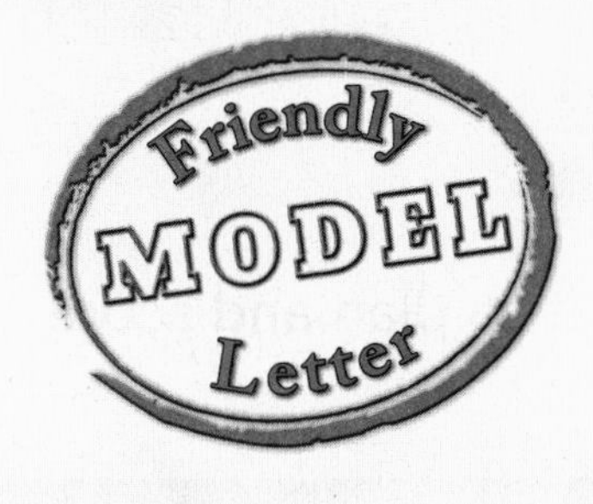

53 Ocean Ave.
Friendship, ME 04547
December 5, 20__

Dear Grandma,

greeting

When we backed out of your driveway, we thought we'd be home soon. Were we wrong! You'll never guess what happened.

At first we drove along quietly, listening to music. Then Dad suddenly shouted, "Wow!" and stopped the car. I looked up, and there was a huge moose standing in the middle of the road!

Mom thought that maybe the moose would move if we just waited for a while. We waited a few minutes. Then we waited some more. The moose stared at us. We stared at it. That moose just kept standing there.

Finally Dad turned the car around, and we took the long way home. I don't know why the moose wouldn't move. Maybe it was upset that you hadn't invited it to Thanksgiving dinner, too!

Thank you for inviting all of us, though. It was nice to visit with you.

body

Love,

closing

Katy

signature

Friendly Letter Rubric

Use this rubric to analyze the model. Then use it to plan and score your own friendly letter.

	6	5	4
Ideas	The topic of the letter is focused. Descriptions and details bring the topic to life.	The topic is generally focused. The descriptions add details about the topic.	The topic lacks focus at times. The details tend to be general.
Organization	The events are in the order they happened. The letter has all five parts.	The events are in order. The letter has all five parts.	Most of the events are in order. The letter is missing one or two parts.
Voice	The writer uses a friendly voice and personal tone to connect with the reader.	The writer uses a friendly voice and personal tone most of the time.	The writer's voice is friendly some of the time.
Word Choice	The writer uses words creatively to show rather than tell.	The writer's words create a picture for the reader.	The words are used correctly, but they are too general to create a picture.
Sentence Fluency	Useful temporal words and phrases vary the way sentences begin.	Useful temporal words and phrases vary the way most of the sentences begin.	Some temporal words and phrases vary the way sentences begin.
Conventions	Spelling and grammar are correct. All uppercase letters and commas are used correctly.	There are few errors in spelling and grammar. Most uppercase letters and commas are used correctly.	There are some errors in spelling and grammar. Some uppercase letters and commas are used correctly.

+Presentation The letter has all five parts and is legible and neat.

3	2	1	
The letter has details that do not have anything to do with the topic.	The topic is unclear. Details, when present, do not make the topic any clearer.	The letter doesn't have a clear topic.	Ideas
Some of the events are in order. There are a few parts of a friendly letter included.	Events are not in order or confusing. Parts are missing.	The writing is not in letter form.	Organization
The writer's voice comes through in the beginning but fades.	The writer's voice sounds stiff or distant.	No voice comes through in the letter.	Voice
The same words are used too many times or are too general.	Words are frequently misused and confuse the reader.	Word choice feels random and makes it difficult for the reader to understand the letter.	Word Choice
Sentence beginnings are occasionally varied with temporal words and phrases. The flow is interrupted by choppy sentences.	Many sentences share the same beginning. No temporal words and phrases are used.	Sentences are not varied. Some are incorrect or incomplete.	Sentence Fluency
There are many errors in spelling and grammar. Many uppercase letters and commas are used incorrectly.	Numerous errors in spelling and grammar make the letter difficult to read.	Serious errors in spelling and grammar make the letter almost impossible to understand.	Conventions

See Appendix B for 4-, 5-, and 6-point narrative rubrics.

Using the Friendly Letter Rubric to Analyze the Model

Did you notice that the model on page 29 points out some key elements of a friendly letter? As she wrote her letter, Katy used these elements to help her include all the parts of a friendly letter. She also used the 6-point rubric on pages 30–31 to plan, draft, revise, and edit the writing. A rubric is a great tool to evaluate writing during the writing process.

To get started, look at the top score for each trait as you study the model. Do you agree that Katy has earned a 6 for each trait?

- **The topic of the letter is focused.**
- **Descriptions and details bring the topic to life.**

The information in Katy's letter is focused. It helps her grandmother get a good picture of the family's experience. She includes descriptions to make her topic more interesting to her grandmother.

> I looked up and there was a huge moose standing in the middle of the road!
>
> Mom thought that maybe the moose would move if we just waited for a while. We waited a few minutes. Then we waited some more.

- **The events are in the order they happened.**
- **The letter has all five parts.**

Katy's letter tells steps in the order they happened. She uses words like *first* and *then* to help make the order clear. Katy also included all five parts of a friendly letter. She included the heading, the greeting, the body, the closing, and the signature.

At first we drove along quietly, listening to music. Then Dad suddenly shouted, "Wow!" and stopped the car.

- **The writer uses a friendly voice and personal tone to connect with the reader.**

Katy's letter sounds very personal. She writes as if she is speaking with her grandmother. Her voice especially comes through near the end. She has a sense of humor about the event and makes a joke about the moose. She connects that experience with the dinner her family shared with her grandmother.

I don't know why the moose wouldn't move. Maybe it was upset that you hadn't invited it to Thanksgiving dinner, too!

Using the Friendly Letter Rubric to Analyze the Model

- **The writer uses words creatively to show rather than tell.**

Katy makes her letter more interesting by using creative words and descriptions to paint a clear picture of the experience.

> The moose stared at us. We stared at it. That moose just kept standing there.

- **Useful temporal words and phases vary the way sentences begin.**

Katy's sentences flow smoothly. I noticed that she varies the beginnings of her sentences. Temporal words and phases like *At first*, *Then*, and *Finally* make her letter easy to follow and enjoyable to read.

> At first we drove along quietly, listening to music. Then Dad suddenly shouted, "Wow!" and stopped the car.

- **Spelling and grammar are correct. All uppercase letters and commas are used correctly.**

Katy uses uppercase letters in her address, in the word *Grandma,* and in the closing. She puts a comma after *Grandma* in the greeting and after *Love* in the closing. She also uses them correctly in the body of the letter.

Thank you for inviting all of us, though. It was nice to visit with you.

Love,
Katy

Presentation The letter has all five parts and is legible and neat.

My Turn!

Now it's my turn to write a friendly letter! I'll use the rubric and good writing strategies to help me. Read on to see how I do it.

Prewrite

Focus on **Ideas**

The Rubric Says The topic of the letter is focused. Descriptions and details bring the topic to life.

Writing Strategy Think about an interesting experience you would like to share. Take notes about the experience.

My teacher asked us to write a friendly letter about a weather-related experience. I decided I'd like to write to my cousin Lia, who lives in a part of California where it never snows. Here in Illinois, winter is cold and snowy. I want to tell her what happened after a blizzard we just had.

I'll begin by making a list of the things I did. Lia is my audience. I'll be sure to write things she wants to know and that will bring my experience to life.

Writer's Term

Audience

The **audience** is the person or people who will read or hear what you write. Think about what your audience will want to know. Keep your audience in mind during the writing process.

My Notes

- went snow tubing
- built a snow doghouse
- made snow people
- went for a walk

Write

Jot down some notes about your experience to share with your audience.

Prewrite

Focus on **Organization**

The Rubric Says The events are in the order they happened.

Writing Strategy Make a Sequence Chain to organize your notes.

I know from the rubric that organization is important. Telling things in the order in which they happened will make it easier for Lia to understand my experience.

I'll make a Sequence Chain to help me organize the details from my list. When I write the draft of my letter, I'll use the Sequence Chain to write the events in order.

Sequence Chain

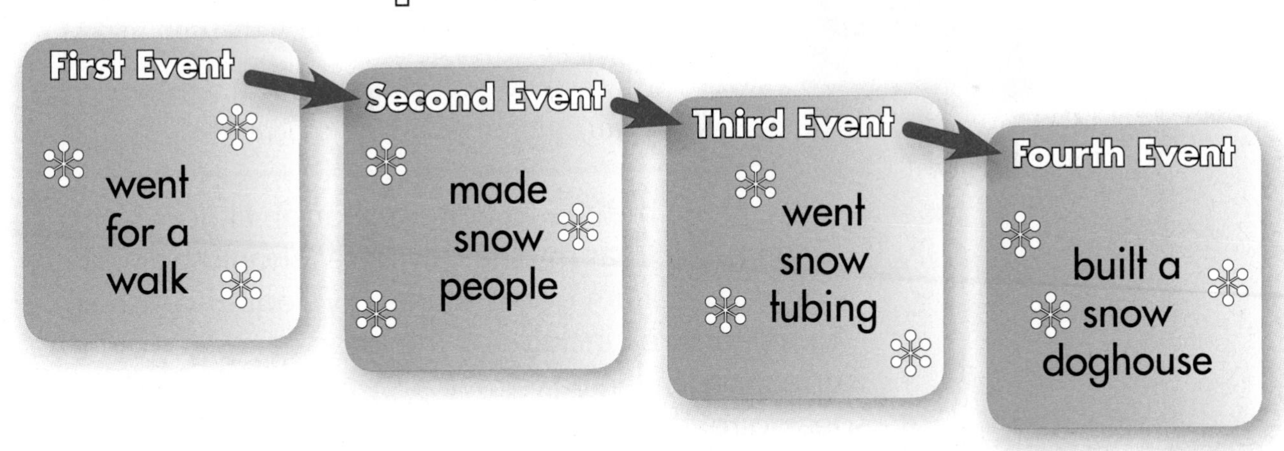

Analyze

How will the Sequence Chain help Marina organize her letter?

Write

Look at the notes you took. Choose notes that tell about the events. Then make a Sequence Chain to organize the events.

Draft

Focus on **Organization**

The Rubric Says The events are in the order they happened. The letter has all five parts.

Writing Strategy Put the information in the form of a friendly letter.

Writer's Term

Parts of a Friendly Letter

- The **heading** tells the address of the person who wrote the letter and the date it was written.
- The **greeting** gives the name of the person who will get the letter. It begins with **Dear,** the person's name, and ends with a comma.
- The **body** is the main part of the letter.
- The **closing** ends the letter. It begins with an uppercase letter. It ends with a comma.
- The **signature** is the handwritten name of the person who wrote the letter.

Now it's time to write my letter. I know from the rubric that my friendly letter should be well organized. I am going to use my Sequence Chain to make sure I include all the important events in the correct order. I'll make my letter interesting and speak directly to Lia. I want my letter to sound like me!

Right now I'm not going to worry about using uppercase letters correctly or whether everything I write is spelled perfectly. I'm just going to get my ideas down in the order in which they happened. I also need to make sure my letter includes a *heading, greeting, body, closing,* and *signature.*

Proofreading Marks

⊐	Indent	ℓ	Take out something
≡	Make uppercase	⊙	Add a period
/	Make lowercase	¶	New paragraph
∧	Add something	(sp)	Spelling error

[DRAFT]

greeting

Dear Lia

I sure wish you could have been here last week. We had a blizzard that lasted two days!

Our school was closed for a whole week, so we had lots of time to play in the snow. We went for a walk. We made four snow people in the yard.

After eating pizza, apples, and carrot sticks for lunch, we decided to go snow tubing on the big hill at the park near our house. My little dog Fluffy tried to keep up with us. We went so fast. It was a lot of fun! I don't think she liked it very much. Too chilly in there! Finally, we built a snow doghouse for Fluffy.

It would have been even more fun to have you here with us. Maybe next year. During winter break.

lots of Love

Marina

signature

Analyze

Read Marina's draft. Can you locate all five parts of her friendly letter?

Write

Use your notes and Sequence Chain to write a draft of a friendly letter. Remember to write to someone you know and to use a friendly tone.

Revise

Focus on **Voice**

The Rubric Says The writer uses a friendly voice and personal tone to connect with the reader.

Writing Strategy Write the letter as if you are talking to a friend.

After I finished my draft, I looked back at the rubric. It says that my letter should have a personal tone. Are there places where I could make my letter sound friendlier? I know! I will look for sentences where I can use the pronoun *I*. Using *I* will make the letter sound more like I am talking to a friend. For example, I think Lia would like to know what I thought about our snow people.

Writer's Term

Tone

Tone is how your writing sounds. Writing sounds friendlier when you use the personal pronouns **I** and **me.**

used a personal tone

[DRAFT]

Our school was closed for a whole week, so ~~we~~ Carmen and I had lots of time to play in the snow. We went for a walk. ~~We~~ She and I made four snow people in the yard. I thought they looked great.

Write

Read your draft. Add the pronoun *I*, if necessary, to make your letter sound friendlier.

Revise

Focus on **Word Choice**

The Rubric Says The writer uses words creatively to show rather than tell.

Writing Strategy Use clear and colorful words to create a picture for the reader.

The rubric says to use words creatively to "show" rather than "tell" the reader about my experiences.

I'll read through my draft again. Then I'll look for ways to add more descriptive words to paint a clear picture. I think Lia would like to know more about what we saw on our walk and what the snow people looked like. I will add words to show her.

added descriptive words

[DRAFT]

Our school was closed for a whole week, so Carmen and I had lots of time to play in the snow. We went for a walk around the neighborhood. The trees and bushes sparkled with snow. She and I made four snow people in the yard. I thought they looked great when we dressed them up with cheerful woolen hats and scarves.

Analyze

Look at Marina's revisions. Do they help paint a clear picture of the events?

Write

Read your draft again. Revise your writing to include more descriptive words to create an even better picture for the reader.

Revise

Focus on **Sentence Fluency**

The Rubric Says Useful temporal words and phrases vary the way sentences begin.

Writing Strategy Begin sentences with words that help the reader.

Sometimes my sentences sound choppy. My teacher suggested starting some sentences with words like *first* or *next*, or *after eating lunch*. These words smooth out my sentences and make them easy to read. They also guide the reader through my letter by telling how the sentences and ideas fit together.

I'll read through my draft again. Then I'll look for places where I can make my letter more interesting by using temporal words to vary my sentence beginnings.

added temporal words

[DRAFT]

Our school was closed for a whole week, so Carmen and I had lots of time to play in the snow. First, we went for a walk around the neighborhood. The trees and bushes sparkled with snow. Next, she and I made four snow people in the yard.

Write

Read your draft again. Add temporal words to vary sentence beginnings and guide the reader.

Edit

Focus on **Conventions**

The Rubric Says Spelling and grammar are correct.

Writing Strategy Check that uppercase letters, commas, and the words *I* and *me* are used correctly.

Now I need to check for errors. I know from the rubric that spelling, punctuation, and capitalization are important. I'll make sure that I used uppercase letters and commas correctly in all the parts of my friendly letter.

Writer's Term

Capitalize	Commas
• street	• between day and year
• city	• between city and state
• state	• after greeting
• month	• after closing
• words in greeting	
• closing	
• signature	

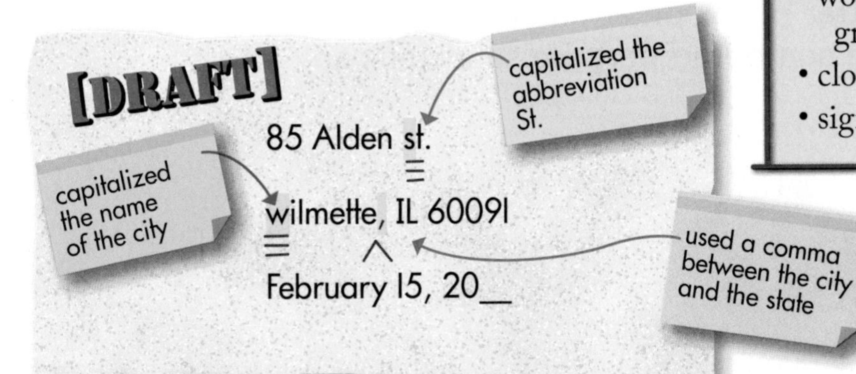

Analyze

Look at Marina's edits. Did she use uppercase letters and commas correctly? How did Marina's edits improve her friendly letter?

Write

Conventions

Edit your draft for spelling, punctuation, and capitalization. Fix all uppercase letters and commas.

For more practice using uppercase letters, commas, and the pronouns *I* and *me*, use the exercises on the next two pages.

Friendly Letters

Know the Rule

A friendly letter has five parts. Each part has special punctuation.

- In the **heading,** use a comma to separate the city and state. Use another comma to separate the day and year.
- Begin the **greeting** with an uppercase letter and end with a comma.
- Punctuate the sentences in the **body** of the letter correctly.
- Start the **closing** with an uppercase letter and end with a comma.
- Start your **signature** with an uppercase letter.

Practice the Rule

Copy the friendly letter below on another sheet of paper. Write the name of each numbered part. Be sure to fix any errors that are in the letter.

1. 90 roth avenue
Hackensack NJ 01601
January 13 20__

2. dear terry

3. What a storm we are having! I think we must have at least two feet of snow. Maybe they will call off school. Do you have snow where you live?

4. your cousin

5. pat

I or Me

Know the Rule

I is a subject pronoun. It can be used as the subject of a sentence.

Example:

I like to play in the snow.

Me is an object pronoun. It is used after an action verb or words such *as to, at, for, of,* or *with.*

Examples:

The snow tube carried **me** down the hill very quickly!

The snow days were fun for Carmen and **me**.

When you talk about yourself and another person, always name the other person first.

Examples:

Carmen and I had so much fun making snow people.

Dad fixed a healthy snack for **Carmen and me**.

Practice the Rule

Number a sheet of paper 1–10. Write the word or words in ( ) that correctly complete each sentence.

1. (Me/I) had lots of time to play in the snow.
2. A walk through the neighborhood was fun for (Carmen and I/Carmen and me).
3. (I and Carmen/Carmen and I) had so much fun dressing the snow people!
4. It was a special activity for (Carmen and me/me and Carmen).
5. (Carmen and I/Carmen and me) built a snow doghouse for Fluffy.
6. (I/Me) don't think Fluffy liked it.
7. She did not look happy to (Carmen and I/Carmen and me).
8. (I/Me) think it was too cold for her.
9. I hope you can come visit (me and Carmen/Carmen and me) soon.
10. (Carmen and I/Carmen and me) look forward to a visit.

Publish

+Presentation

Publishing Strategy Mail the letter.

Presentation Strategy Make sure the letter has all five parts.

I have finished writing my friendly letter. I am almost ready to publish it by mailing it to my cousin. First I will check to see that my letter has all five parts. Do I have a heading, greeting, body, closing, and signature? Next I will make sure I have used neat handwriting. My cousin will be excited to get a letter from me, and I want to be sure I have done my best work. Before I mail my friendly letter, I want to check it one more time. Here is the checklist I will use.

My Final Checklist

Did I—

- ✔ check to be sure my spelling, grammar, and punctuation are correct?
- ✔ use uppercase letters and commas correctly?
- ✔ include all five parts of a friendly letter?
- ✔ use my best handwriting?

Write

Make a checklist for your friendly letter. Then write a neat final copy to mail to your friend. When you get a letter back from your friend, bring it to class to share.

85 Alden St.
Wilmette, IL 60091
February 15, 20__

Dear Lia,

I sure wish you could have been here last week. We had a blizzard that lasted two days!

Our school was closed for a whole week, so Carmen and I had lots of time to play in the snow. First, we went for a walk around the neighborhood. The trees and bushes sparkled with snow. Next, she and I made four snow people in the yard. I thought they looked great when we dressed them up with cheerful woolen hats and scarves.

After eating lunch, we decided to go snow tubing on the big hill at the park near our house. My little dog Fluffy tried to keep up with us. We went so fast that I was really scared. It was a lot of fun! Finally, we built a snow doghouse for Fluffy. I don't think she liked it very much. I guess it was too chilly in there!

It would have been even more fun to have you here with us. Maybe next year you can visit during winter break.

Lots of love,

Marina

Analyze

Use the rubric to analyze Marina's letter. Are all the traits of a good friendly letter there? Don't forget to use the rubric to evaluate the friendly letter you wrote.

What's a Folktale?

It's a story that has been told many times by people from a particular culture or country.

What's in a Folktale?

Characters
Characters are the people in the story. Many folktales have animal characters that talk, act, and think like humans. The main character is the one that the folktale is about.

Dialogue
This is what the characters say. The dialogue helps tell the story of a folktale.

Setting
Setting is when and where the story happens.

Plot
Plot is what happens in the story. The plot has a beginning, a middle, and an end. Folktales describe a problem. Trying to solve the problem is what the story is about.

Why write a Folktale?

There are different reasons for writing a folktale. Here are two reasons that I can think of for writing one.

To Entertain
Folktales are great stories. That's why they are told over and over again. People love to hear them or read them, even when they already know how the stories will end. Often each person who tells a folktale changes it a little.

To Teach a Lesson
Some folktales have a message about living. One of the characters may get into trouble because of the way he or she behaves. Some folktales encourage us to be a certain way or not to do something foolish. Some folktales teach a lesson.

Linking Narrative Writing Traits to a Folktale

In this chapter, you will write a story like the ones that people have told over many years. This type of narrative writing is called a folktale. Marina will guide you through the stages of the writing process: Prewrite, Draft, Revise, Edit, and Publish. In each stage, Marina will show you important writing strategies that are linked to the Narrative Writing Traits below.

Narrative Writing Traits

	• a topic that is just the right size, not too big or too small • descriptive details that answer the reader's questions (such as *who, what, where, when,* and *why*)
	• a logical sequence of events • a strong beginning and a satisfying ending • temporal words/phases to signal order of events
	• a voice that is friendly and speaks directly to the audience • dialogue that, if used, fits the characters
	• exact words that tell the story
	• a variety of sentence lengths that makes the story flow smoothly
	• no or few errors in spelling, punctuation, and capitalization

Before you write, read Martha Sullivan's folktale that begins on the next page. Then use the friendly letter rubric on page 54 to decide how well she did. (You might want to look back at What's in a Folktale? on page 48, too!)

Why Spiders Have Thin Waists

setting

beginning

retold by Martha Sullivan

Long, long ago, a greedy spider named Anansi lived deep in the jungle in Africa. Anansi could trap his food in his web, but he also liked to eat other animals' food. His waist was fat from all his eating. He didn't know that this would soon change!

main character

One day, Anansi heard that some animals were planning to have special feasts. Mmmm, mmmm, mmmm, he thought. He asked about the feasts, but none of the animals would tell him anything. They didn't want Anansi coming to eat all their food.

problem

Anansi called his children together. He asked them what they knew about the feasts. Anansi's first son told him that Rabbit was holding a feast, but he didn't know when. Anansi quickly made a plan to find out.

middle

He took a thread from his web. He tied one end around his own fat middle and the other end around his son. He told his son to spy on Rabbit. When the feast started, all his son had to do was pull the thread. Then Anansi and his son would go to the feast.

Anansi's daughter told him that the antelopes were having a feast, but she didn't know when. Anansi made the same plan with her.

Then Anansi's second son told him that the bullfrogs were having a feast, but he didn't know when. Anansi made the same plan with him.

No one could have been more pleased with himself than Anansi! This is the smartest plan ever, he thought.

A few days later, Anansi felt the first tug on his waist. He shouted with joy. Two minutes later, though, he felt another tug. Then he felt a third tug. "Help! Help!" he screamed, but all three threads kept pulling. Anansi was pulled tighter and tighter until he almost fainted. Then suddenly the threads snapped.

After a long while, Anansi felt fine again, but his waist was never the same. All that pulling had made it much smaller. That is why spiders today have very thin waists.

dialogue

ending

Folktale Rubric

Use this rubric to analyze the model. Then use it to plan and score your own folktale.

	6	5	4
Ideas	All the description and details develop the characters, setting, and plot.	Most of the description and details develop the characters, setting, and plot.	Description and details about characters, setting, and plot are present, but the main idea is confusing.
Organization	The folktale has a clear beginning, middle, and ending. The beginning introduces the characters, setting, and plot.	There is a beginning, middle, and ending. The beginning introduces the characters, the setting, and the plot.	The beginning, middle, and ending are present. The beginning has general details about the characters, setting, and plot.
Voice	The voice clearly sounds like a storyteller telling a folktale.	The writing generally uses a tone and language appropriate for a folktale.	The writing occasionally uses a tone and language appropriate for a folktale.
Word Choice	The writer uses specific nouns and verbs to add life to the story.	The writer uses some specific nouns and verbs.	The writer occasionally uses specific nouns and verbs.
Sentence Fluency	Sentences are clear, varied, and not too wordy.	Most sentences are clear, varied, and not too wordy.	Occasional sentences are clear, varied, and not too wordy.
Conventions	There are no grammar errors. The correct forms of adjectives are used.	There are occasional grammar errors. The correct forms of adjectives are generally used.	There are a few errors in spelling, grammar, and forms of adjectives.

+Presentation Pictures support the text.

3	2	1	
Some description and details are about the characters, setting, or plot, but there may be extra, unrelated details.	Description and details about the characters, setting, and plot are weak or missing.	The characters, setting, and plot are not developed at all.	Ideas
The beginning, middle, and ending are not clear. The beginning does not introduce the characters, setting, and plot.	The folktale just begins or ends. The beginning is confusing.	The folktale is not well organized.	Organization
The voice of a storyteller is inconsistent; it appears and disappears.	The voice sounds flat or lifeless.	Little or no voice is present.	Voice
Words are used correctly, but most of them are general.	Words may not be used correctly or they may be repeated too often.	The word choice is random and makes the story lifeless.	Word Choice
Many sentences are wordy and unclear, making it difficult to understand.	Sentences are not well formed and are confusing to read.	Choppiness, run-on sentences, and wordiness make the folktale almost impossible to understand.	Sentence Fluency
There are many errors in spelling, grammar, and forms of adjectives.	There are so many errors in spelling, grammar, and forms of adjectives that the story is difficult to read.	Serious, frequent errors in spelling, grammar, and forms of adjectives prevent understanding.	Conventions

See Appendix B for 4-, 5-, and 6-point narrative rubrics.

Using the Folktale Rubric to Analyze the Model

Did you notice that the model on pages 51–53 points out some key elements of a folktale? As she wrote "Why Spiders Have Thin Waists," Martha Sullivan used these elements to help her write her folktale. She also used the 6-point rubric on pages 54–55 to plan, draft, revise, and edit the writing. A rubric is a great tool to evaluate writing during the writing process.

To get started, look at the top score for each trait as you study the model. Do you agree that Martha has earned a 6 for each trait?

- **All the description and details develop the characters, setting, and plot.**

Martha Sullivan takes ideas from an old folktale and writes it her own way. She uses descriptive details to develop her characters, especially Anansi. She also uses specific details to give a clear picture of the setting and the plot. Here's where she sets up the plot:

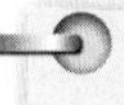

Anansi called his children together. He asked them what they knew about the feasts. Anansi's first son told him that Rabbit was holding a feast, but he didn't know when. Anansi quickly made a plan to find out.

- **The folktale has a clear beginning, middle, and ending.**
- **The beginning introduces the characters, setting, and plot.**

The writer grabs my attention with a very clear beginning. I learn in the first paragraph that the main character is Anansi and the setting is an African jungle. The writer also tells me that the problem is that Anansi likes to eat other animals' food. I couldn't wait to find out what happens in the middle and ending of the story!

Long, long ago, a greedy spider named Anansi lived deep in the jungle in Africa. Anansi could trap his food in his web, but he also liked to eat other animals' food.

- **The voice clearly sounds like a storyteller telling a folktale.**

The folktale uses natural language that makes me feel like the storyteller is talking directly to me. The tone of the folktale is natural and friendly. That really makes me want to read the story!

One day, Anansi heard that some animals were planning to have special feasts. Mmmm, mmmm mmmm, he thought. He asked about the feasts, but none of the animals would tell him anything. They didn't want Anansi coming to eat all their food.

Using the Folktale Rubric to Analyze the Model

- **The writer uses specific nouns and verbs to add life to the story.**

The writer uses the noun *tug*. It tells exactly what it was that Anansi felt. He didn't feel a touch or a push. He felt a tug. The word *tug* gives the reader an exact picture of what was happening to Anansi. The writer also uses the verb *shouted*. It shows exactly what Anansi was doing and feeling. It shows emotion.

A few days later, Anansi felt the first tug on his waist. He shouted with joy. Two minutes later, though, he felt another tug.

- **Sentences are clear, varied, and not too wordy.**

Martha Sullivan uses different kinds of sentences in her folktale. Some are longer and some are shorter. If she used all short sentences or all long sentences, the writing wouldn't flow.

He took a thread from his web. He tied one end around his own fat middle and the other end around his son. He told his son to spy on Rabbit. When the feast started, all his son had to do was pull the thread. Then Anansi and his son would go to the feast.

- There are no grammar errors.
- The correct forms of adjectives are used.

The writer uses adjectives that compare. She chooses the correct form. For example, she uses *more pleased* (not *most pleased*) and *smartest* (not *most smart*).

No one could have been more pleased with himself than Anansi! This is the smartest plan ever, he thought.

+Presentation Pictures support the text.

My Turn!

Now I'm going to retell a folktale. Follow along to see how I use good writing strategies. See how the rubric helps me write a good story.

Prewrite

Focus on **Ideas**

The Rubric Says All the description and details develop the characters, setting, and plot.

Writing Strategy Read some folktales and decide which one to retell. Make some notes.

My class has been reading folktales all month. When our teacher asked us to choose one to retell, it was easy for me to decide. I chose the one about a crocodile and a monkey. It is a folktale from India that is more than 2,000 years old. I love monkeys, and the monkey in this story is really smart and funny.

To get started, I'll jot down the main characters, the setting, and the problem. Then I'll list the plot details. I may change some in my retelling, but that's okay. Folktales can change a bit each time they are retold.

Writer's Term

Folktales

Folktales are stories that have been shared and retold by people of a particular culture or country. Folktales often tell about a culture's values.

First, I wrote down the name of the folktale. Next, I wrote down the characters, the setting, and the problem. Then, I listed notes about the events.

Folktale: Monkey Tricks Crocodile

Characters: Monkey and Crocodile

Setting: A jungle long ago

Problem: Crocodile is always hungry

Plot:

- ✔ Monkeys live in tree near river.
- ✔ Crocodile lives near happy monkeys.
- ✔ Hungry crocodile wants a monkey for dinner.
- ✔ Monkey can't swim.
- ✔ Crocodile tricks monkey into getting on his back.
- ✔ Monkey tricks crocodile and escapes.

Write

Read some folktales. Pick one you would like to retell in your own words. Jot down notes to help you remember the characters, setting, problem, and plot.

Prewrite

Focus on **Organization**

The Rubric Says The folktale has a clear beginning, middle, and ending.

Writing Strategy Make a Story Map to organize your notes.

I know from the rubric that my folktale needs a clear beginning, middle, and ending. I'll make a Story Map to organize the folktale. I think a Story Map would be the best graphic organizer to help me put my notes and the events in order.

Writer's Term

Story Map

A **Story Map** organizes the events of a story into a beginning, a middle, and an ending. The **beginning** introduces the characters and the story's problem. The **middle** tells the main events that happen because of the problem. The **ending** tells how the problem is solved.

I know the characters in this story are monkeys and crocodiles. The crocodile is always hungry, and this is the problem. I will put this information in the *Beginning* box. The crocodile makes a plan and tries to trick the monkey. The monkey has her own plan. These are the main events of the story, so I'll put them in the *Middle* box. The monkey solves her problem and escapes. This is how the story comes out in the end. I will put this in the *Ending* box.

Here is how my Story Map looks so far.

Story Map

Beginning

Characters: Monkey and Crocodile

Problem: The crocodile is always hungry.

Middle

The crocodile plans to eat the monkey.

The crocodile tricks the monkey into getting on his back.

The crocodile starts to swim across the river.

The monkey plans how to escape.

Ending

The monkey solves her problem.

Analyze

How will Marina's Story Map help her write the fable?

Write

Look at your notes and use them to create your own Story Map.

Draft

Focus on **Voice**

The Rubric Says The voice clearly sounds like a storyteller telling a folktale.

Writing Strategy Make the writing sound like a storyteller telling a folktale.

It's time to write my draft. The rubric reminds me to make my writing sound like a storyteller is telling the folktale. That means I have to use a friendly voice and descriptive language. I will start my story with words that storytellers use. I want my folktale to be so exciting that readers can't wait to see what happens! The Story Map will help me. As I write, I'll do my best with grammar and spelling, but I won't worry about mistakes. I can fix them later. Here's the first part of my draft.

Writer's Term

Voice

Voice is the sense a reader gets of the writer. A writer's voice can make you feel that a real person is speaking or reading just to you.

Proofreading Marks

⊐ Indent	Take out something
≡ Make uppercase	⊙ Add a period
/ Make lowercase	¶ New paragraph
∧ Add something	(sp) Spelling error

[DRAFT]

Smart and Smarter

storyteller voice

Long ago, in a faraway place, there were some happy monkeys and some unhappy crocodiles. The monkeys lived in the trees and ate mangoes all day. Crocodiles can live on the land or in the water. The crocodiles lived in the river. one day, a young crocodile decided to catch a monkey and eat it for dinner. He had many crocodile friends who were hungry, too.

The next day, Crocodile went up to one of the most big, most fat, cheerfulest monkeys. He said, "Those mangoes look good, but I know were you can find more big, more ripe mangoes than those."

dialogue

Analyze

Read the beginning of Marina's draft. How did she use a storyteller's voice? Does the dialogue keep your interest?

Write

Use your notes and Story Map to write a draft of your folktale. Be sure to use a storyteller's voice and some dialogue.

Revise

Focus on **Ideas**

The Rubric Says All the description and details develop the characters, setting, and plot.

Writing Strategy Take out anything that doesn't help to tell the story.

I know from the rubric that I have to take out details that don't help tell the story. My classmate Zoe read my folktale. She helped me decide which details don't belong in the story. See if you agree with us.

[DRAFT] **Smart and Smarter**

Long ago, in a faraway place, there were some happy monkeys and some unhappy crocodiles. The monkeys lived in the trees and ate mangoes all day. ~~Crocodiles can live on the land or in the water.~~ The crocodiles lived in the river. one day, a young crocodile decided to catch a monkey and eat it for dinner. ~~He had many crocodile friends who were hungry, too.~~

took out details that don't belong

Write

Read your draft again. Cross out details that don't help to tell your story.

Revise

Focus on **Word Choice**

The Rubric Says The writer uses specific nouns and verbs to add life to the story.

Writing Strategy Use exact words.

The rubric reminds me to use specific words. If I use exact words to retell this folktale, my readers will find it more lively and interesting. I'm going to read what I've written again. I'll ask myself if each word says exactly what I mean. If it doesn't, I'll try to think of a more specific word.

Writer's Term

Specific Words

A **specific word** gives more information than a general word. For example, the word **crocodile** is more specific than the word **animal**. Here are more examples.

General Words	Specific Words
food	apples
got	grabbed
went	raced
said	shouted

Just give me a ~~little time~~ minute, and I'll climb the tree and get it."

She ~~got~~ leaped off Crocodile's back and ran quickly to the top of the tree.

When Monkey reached the highest ~~part~~ branch, she laughed loudly.

"Ha! You can't eat me now, Crocodile," she ~~said~~ called.

used exact words

Analyze

Look at Marina's revisions. How do her changes make this part of the folktale more lively?

Write

Read your draft. Replace any general words with specific words. Use a print or online thesaurus to find replacement words.

Revise

Focus on Sentence Fluency

The Rubric Says Sentences are clear, varied, and not too wordy.

Writing Strategy Avoid long, confusing sentences.

The rubric says that varied sentences will help my writing flow. I know that it is especially important to check long sentences. They can be confusing sometimes. I read my draft and saw a confusing sentence. See how I fixed it.

[DRAFT]

Crocodile was almost at the island when he told Monkey that he was going to eat her for dinner. Monkey was surprised, but she was not so surprised that she couldn't think fast. She said in her most agreeable voice, "Oh, that's too bad ~~because~~ if I had known, I would have brought my heart ~~because~~ that's the most delicious part of me!"

shortened a long sentence

Write

Check your draft to be sure your sentences are varied. Try making some of your long sentences into short sentences to make your story flow smoothly.

Edit

Focus on Conventions

The Rubric Says There are no grammar errors. The correct forms of adjectives are used.

Writing Strategy Check that the correct form of an adjective is used to compare two or more things.

Next, I want to check my spelling, capitalization, and punctuation. The rubric also reminds me to use the correct forms of adjectives that compare. I'll proofread those adjectives next.

Writer's Term

Adjectives That Compare

To compare two things, add **-er** to most short adjectives. For most longer adjectives, use the word **more** before the adjective. To compare more than two things, add **-est** to most short adjectives.

[DRAFT]

The next day, Crocodile went up to one of the ~~most~~ ~~big~~ biggest, ~~most fat~~ fattest, ~~cheerfulest~~ most cheerful monkeys. He said, "Those mangoes look good, but I know where you can find ~~more big~~ bigger, ~~more ripe~~ riper mangoes than those."

fixed incorrect form of adjectives

Analyze

How did Marina check her draft for adjectives that compare? Why did Marina replace *most* and *more*? How did her changes affect her writing?

Write

Conventions

Edit your draft. Fix any incorrect form of an adjective.

For more practice in learning how to use adjectives that compare, use the exercises on the next two pages.

Adjectives

Know the Rule

An **adjective** describes, or tells about, a noun. Adjectives make sentences more interesting.

Examples:

A folktale is an **old** story that has been retold again and again.

Funny animals are often characters in folktales.

Practice the Rule

Number a sheet of paper 1–10. Read each sentence. Find the adjective in each sentence and write it on your paper.

1. A funny fable is about Rabbit and Turtle.
2. Rabbit wanted to prove that he was a fast runner.
3. Lazy Rabbit was fooled!
4. Rabbit stopped under a tall tree.
5. Under the tree, Rabbit took a long nap.
6. Rabbit had a loud snore!
7. Turtle was a slow racer, but he just kept moving.
8. Turtle kept a steady pace.
9. While Rabbit rested, the slow animal won the race!
10. Turtle won his first race.

Comparative and Superlative Adjectives

Know the Rule

Comparative Adjectives Add **-er** to most short adjectives to compare two things. For most longer adjectives, use the word **more** before the adjective.
Superlative Adjectives Add **-est** to short adjectives to compare more than two things. For most longer adjectives, use **most** before the adjective.

Adjective	Comparative	Superlative
tall	taller	tallest
quick	quicker	quickest
wonderful	more wonderful	most wonderful
important	more important	most important

Practice the Rule

Number a sheet of paper 1–10. Write each sentence using the correct form of the adjective.

1. Fables and folktales are some of the (older/oldest) stories around.
2. A fable is often (shorter/shortest) than a folktale.
3. In some stories, two animals argue over who is (smarter/smartest).
4. One of the (most funny/funniest) stories is about a rabbit and a turtle.
5. Everyone knows a rabbit can run (faster/fastest) than a turtle.
6. Rabbit wanted to prove that he was the (faster/fastest) animal of all.
7. Beating Turtle in a race would be the (easier/easiest) thing he had ever done.
8. However, Rabbit was also the (lazier/laziest) animal of all.
9. Turtle knew it was (more important/importanter) to keep moving.
10. As Rabbit rested, the (slower/slowest) animal won.

Publish +Presentation

Publishing Strategy Record your folktale for a class radio show.

Presentation Strategy Pictures support the text.

My folktale is finished! Now it's time to publish it. Everyone in class wanted to hear each other's folktales. We decided to put together a radio show so everyone could hear the tales.

First, I will practice reading my folktale aloud with feeling. I need to plan a short introduction to tell the title, the country it came from, and my name. I'll also introduce some pictures to go with the story. Then, my classmates and I will record our stories. Finally, we will work together to create a radio show or podcast of our folktales. Afterward, we will display our folktales and pictures in the classroom. I'll make sure that I've done everything on my final checklist.

My Final Checklist

Did I—

- ✔ use adjectives correctly?
- ✔ edit and proofread carefully?
- ✔ make a neat final copy to display with my pictures?

Write

Use the checklist for your folktale. Then make a final copy to record.

Smart and Smarter
by Marina

Long ago, in a faraway place, there were some happy monkeys and some unhappy crocodiles. The monkeys lived in the trees and ate mangoes all day. The crocodiles lived in the river. They were often hungry. One day, a young crocodile decided to catch a monkey and eat it for dinner.

The next day, Crocodile went up to one of the biggest, fattest, most cheerful monkeys. He said, "Those mangoes look good, but I know where you can find bigger, riper mangoes than those."

Monkey was interested right away. She asked where the mangoes were. Crocodile said they were on an island. He told Monkey that he could easily take her there. All she had to do was get on Crocodile's back, and he would swim across the river with her. When Monkey agreed to this plan, Crocodile thought to himself, "What a smart crocodile I am!"

Crocodile was almost at the island when he told Monkey that he was going to eat her for dinner. Monkey was surprised, but she was not so surprised that she couldn't think fast. She said in her most agreeable voice, "Oh, that's too bad. If I had known, I would have brought my heart. That's the most delicious part of me!"

Crocodile didn't want to miss such a tasty part of Monkey. He said in an even more agreeable voice, "That's really no problem, Monkey. I can take you back home. Then you can get your heart for me." So he turned around and swam down the river with Monkey still on his back.

When Crocodile reached Monkey's home, Monkey said, "My heart is up in that big, tall tree. Just give me a minute, and I'll climb the tree and get it." She leaped off Crocodile's back and ran quickly to the top of the tree.

When Monkey reached the highest branch, she laughed loudly. "Ha! You can't eat me now, Crocodile," she called. She thought to herself, "What a smart monkey I am!"

Analyze

Use the rubric to check whether Marina's story has all the traits of a good folktale. Then use the rubric to evaluate your folktale.

What's a Fable?

It's a story that teaches a lesson.

What's in a Fable?

Plot
The plot is what happens in the story. It has a beginning, middle, and end. The plot of a fable tells about a problem and how the problem is solved.

Setting
The setting is where and when the story takes place. A story with animal characters often takes place where animals live. The story events might happen in the present, past, or future.

Characters
In a fable, the characters are often animals. They talk, act, and think like people.

Dialogue
This is what the characters say. The dialogue helps tell the story of a fable.

Moral
What happens to the characters teaches a lesson. That lesson is called the moral of the story.

Why write a Fable?

There are many reasons to write a fable. Here are four reasons I can think of.

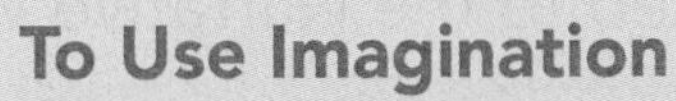

To Use Imagination
You can really use your imagination and creativity to make up a story about talking animals.

To Teach
Fables are simple, but they teach important lessons. The moral of a fable tells us how to act.

To Reflect
Writing a fable can help you think about a lesson you've learned and would like to teach others.

To Entertain
You can share your fable with others and talk about the lesson in it. You can discuss how that lesson applies to people in their daily lives.

Linking Narrative Writing Traits to a Fable

In this chapter, you will write a story that teaches a lesson. This type of narrative writing is called a fable. Marina will guide you through the stages of the writing process: Prewrite, Draft, Revise, Edit, and Publish. In each stage, Marina will show you important writing strategies that are linked to the Narrative Writing Traits below.

Narrative Writing Traits

- a topic that is just the right size, not too big or too small
- descriptive details that answer the reader's questions (such as *who, what, where, when*, and *why*)

- a logical sequence of events
- a strong beginning and a satisfying ending
- temporal words and phrases that signal the order of events

- a voice that is friendly and speaks directly to the audience
- dialogue that, if used, fits the characters

Word Choice

- exact words that tell the story

- a variety of sentence lengths that makes the story flow smoothly

- no or few errors in spelling, punctuation, and capitalization

Before you write, read Warren Palmer's fable on the next page. Then use the fable rubric on page 80 to decide how well he did. (You might want to look back at What's in a Fable? on page 76, too!)

The Ant and His Smile

by Warren Palmer

dialogue

characters

"Why does everyone smile at you?" Albie Ant asked his best friend Jojo. "No one ever smiles at me."

"Did you ever think to smile first?" Jojo suggested.

Albie scratched his chin. "Hmmm . . . you know I'm kind of shy, Jojo," he answered.

plot

setting

On the next day, Albie thought he'd try smiling first. While walking down the ant path, he saw another ant coming his way. Albie felt very nervous. "What if she doesn't smile back?" he asked himself. Still, Albie decided he'd be brave and overcome his fear and shyness. "What do I have to lose?" he thought.

So as the other ant approached closer, Albie looked straight at her and started smiling.

Albie couldn't believe it, but she smiled back! He was on cloud nine. He ran to tell Jojo.

"Good for you, Albie! How does that make you feel?"

"Great!" Albie answered.

From that day onward, and ever after, Albie gave a smile to everyone he saw, and everyone smiled back. And, if once in a very great while, he didn't get a smile back, that was all right, too. Albie understood that people can have their moods. But this didn't happen very often.

Fable Rubric

Use this rubric to analyze the model. Then use it to plan and score your own fable.

	6	5	4
Ideas	The events in the story and the dialogue lead to the moral that provides closure.	Most of the events and dialogue lead to the moral.	Some of the events and dialogue lead to the moral.
Organization	The fable has a strong beginning, middle, and ending. Temporal words and phrases signal the order of events.	The fable has a beginning, middle, and ending. Most temporal words and phrases signal the order of events.	The fable has a beginning, middle, and ending. Some temporal words and phrases signal the order of events.
Voice	The dialogue sounds natural and fits the characters.	Most of the dialogue sounds natural and fits the characters.	Some of the dialogue sounds natural and fits the characters.
Word Choice	Strong verbs move the story along.	Most verbs are strong and move the story along.	Several verbs are weak and slow the story.
Sentence Fluency	Different types of sentences make the dialogue flow smoothly.	Most sentences are different types. The dialogue flows smoothly.	Some sentences are different types. Most of the dialogue flows smoothly.
Conventions	The writing has no errors. Irregular verb forms are correct.	A few minor errors are present. Irregular verb forms are correct.	Several errors may confuse the reader. Irregular verb forms are correct.

+Presentation The fable is neat and legible.

3	2	1	
Too few events or too little dialogue leads to the moral.	Events or dialogue may not lead to the moral.	The moral is unclear or missing.	Ideas
The fable has a beginning, middle, and ending, but they are weak. Few temporal words and phrases signal the order of events.	The fable has no beginning or ending. It just starts and stops. Events are out of order, and temporal words and phrases are missing.	The writing is not organized.	Organization
Dialogue does not sound natural for all of the characters.	The dialogue does not fit the characters at all.	Dialogue is not provided.	Voice
Many verbs are weak and slow the story.	Many verbs are overused.	Verbs are very weak or incorrect.	Word Choice
Most sentences are the same type. Dialogue is choppy or awkward to read.	Sentence variety is lacking. Dialogue does not flow smoothly.	Sentences are incomplete. Dialogue is not present.	Sentence Fluency
Many errors confuse the reader. Some irregular verb forms may be incorrect.	Serious errors stop the reader. Irregular verb forms are incorrect.	The writing has not been edited.	Conventions

See Appendix B for 4-, 5-, and 6-point narrative rubrics.

Using the Fable Rubric to Analyze the Model

Did you notice that the model on page 79 points out some key elements of a fable? As he wrote "The Ant and His Smile," Warren used these elements to help him tell his story. He also used the 6-point rubric on pages 80–81 to plan, draft, revise, and edit the writing. A rubric is a great tool to evaluate writing during the writing process.

To get started, look at the top score for each trait as you study the model. Do you agree that Warren has earned a 6 for each trait?

- **The events in the story and the dialogue lead to the moral that provides closure.**

In Warren's fable, Albie and his best friend talk about smiling. Albie wonders why no one smiles at him, but everyone smiles at Jojo. Jojo tells Albie to try smiling first. Albie follows Jojo's advice, and we learn the moral of the story: *Sometimes you have to make the first move.*

> From that day onward, and ever after, Albie gave a smile to everyone he saw, and everyone smiled back.

- **The fable has a strong beginning, middle, and ending.**
- **Temporal words and phrases signal the order of events.**

At the beginning of Warren's fable, Jojo gives Albie some advice. In the middle of the story, Albie tries it. At the end, Albie has learned a lesson. Warren uses temporal words and phrases like *On the next day* and *While walking* to guide the reader through the story.

On the next day, Albie thought he'd try smiling first. While walking down the ant path, he saw another ant coming his way.

- **The dialogue sounds natural and fits the characters.**

The dialogue between Albie and Jojo really sounds like two best friends talking. Best friends can give advice to each other. They can be honest in what they say.

"Did you ever think to smile first?" Jojo suggested.

Albie scratched his chin. "Hmmm . . . you know I'm kind of shy, Jojo," he answered.

Using the Fable Rubric to Analyze the Model

- **Strong verbs move the story along.**

I could really tell what was going on in the story and what the characters were feeling. I like how Warren used the verb *overcome* to make it clear that Albie had to make a big effort to get over his fear and shyness.

> Still, Albie decided he'd be brave and overcome his fear and shyness. "What do I have to lose?" he thought.

- **Different types of sentences make the dialogue flow smoothly.**

When people talk, they use all kinds of sentences, including exclamations and questions. Sometimes they don't even use a complete sentence. For example, *Great!* is not a complete sentence, but it sounds very natural in dialogue.

> "Good for you, Albie! How does that make you feel?"
> "Great!" Albie answered.

- **The writing has no errors. Irregular verb forms are correct.**

Warren is careful to spell, punctuate, and capitalize correctly in his fable. He has made sure that he used the correct forms of irregular verbs. For example, the past form of *see* is *saw*.

While walking down the ant path, he saw another ant coming his way.

+Presentation The fable is neat and legible.

My Turn!

Now it's my turn to write a fable. I'll use the rubric and good writing strategies to help me. Follow along to see how I do it.

Prewrite

Focus on **Ideas**

The Rubric Says The events in the story and the dialogue lead to the moral that provides closure.

Writing Strategy Choose a moral. Make up a plot and characters to teach the moral.

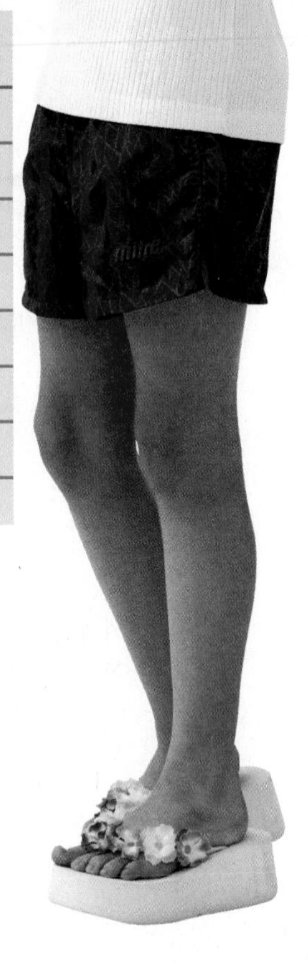

Our class has been reading fables. We've really enjoyed them. The lessons they teach make you think. Now our teacher wants each of us to write one. The fable can be modeled on one we've read in class. I just read a fable with a moral I want to remember. I can use it in my story. Here are my ideas.

My Bear and Monkey Fable

Moral: *Enjoying the journey shortens the trip.*

- ✔ Bear and Monkey climb a mountain to visit Goat
- ✔ Bear keeps complaining about the upward climb
- ✔ Monkey whistles and finds things to enjoy along the way
- ✔ Bear gets to top tired and grumpy
- ✔ Monkey gets to top in a good mood
- ✔ Bear learns a lesson

Write

Decide on a moral. Then list ideas for your fable.

Prewrite

Focus on **Organization**

The Rubric Says The fable has a strong beginning, middle, and ending.

Writing Strategy Use a Story Map to plan the fable.

I know that a fable is a special form of a story. It has the same parts as a story, so it makes sense to organize the events in a Story Map. Here is how my Story Map looks so far.

Writer's Term

Story Map

A **Story Map** helps to organize the events of a story into a beginning, a middle, and an ending.

Story Map

Beginning Characters: Bear, Monkey, Goat

Setting: A faraway mountain

Problem: Bear and Monkey have to climb a mountain to visit Goat.

Middle Bear keeps finding things to complain about. The walk is long. The sun is hot. They have so far to climb.

Monkey keeps finding things to be happy about. He sees unusual rocks and pretty birds. He likes being outside on a sunny day.

Ending Bear and Monkey reach the top. Bear is grumpy and complains about what a long journey it was. Monkey is happy and says the journey wasn't long at all. Goat asks why they feel differently about the same walk. Monkey tells the moral of the story: The trip is shorter if you enjoy the journey itself.

Analyze

Examine the Story Map. How will it help Marina write her fable?

Write

Look at your notes and use them to create a Story Map.

Draft

Focus on **Word Choice**

The Rubric Says Strong verbs move the story along.

Writing Strategy Choose strong, specific verbs.

Now I'm ready to write. The rubric says to use strong verbs. A fable is usually a very short story, so every word counts. Strong verbs will keep the action moving along. Verbs like *grumbled* or *ruffled* tell more about the action than *complained* or *touched*. If I can't think of the perfect verb while I'm writing, I can circle it and find a better one later.

As I draft my fable, I'll look out for mistakes in grammar and spelling, but I know I can fix those mistakes later. Here's my draft.

Writer's Term

Strong Verbs

Strong verbs tell what the subject is doing. They show action and move the narrative along.

Proofreading Marks

⊐ Indent	ℓ Take out something
≡ Make uppercase	⊙ Add a period
/ Make lowercase	¶ New paragraph
∧ Add something	(sp) Spelling error

[DRAFT]

Bear and Monkey's Journey

Bear and Monkey had to climb a mountain to visit their friend Goat. They started their walk. Bear has brown fur.

"It's such a long way up," Bear said, looking up. "How will we ever get to the top?"

"We'll get there one step at a time," Monkey told Bear. "Do you hibernate in winter?" Monkey wasn't looking up. He was whistling softly. He was admiring the things he saw along the way. He saw some interesting rocks.

strong verbs

"Who cares about old rocks," Bear said. They had a long way to go.

A breeze ruffled Monkey's fur. They continued their clime. He said he liked being outside in the sun.

"Oh, I wish you hadn't mentioned the sun to me right now," Bear said. "Walking in the sun always makes me so hot."

Monkey seen too humingbirds on some wildflowers. They had colorful feathers.

They had walked halfway up the mountain.

Monkey looked down. He told Bear to look at how far they had come.

Bear didn't look down. He looked up instead. "Monkey, you've got to be kidding. We're only halfway there," Bear said.

They made it to the top.

Goat greeted them. "May I ask how your walk was?" Goat asked.

"It was beautiful!" said Monkey. "And it didn't take long at all."

"It was tiring and long," answered Bear.

Analyze

Read the beginning of Marina's draft. Did she follow her Story Map?

Write

Use your Story Map to draft your own fable.

Revise

Focus on **Ideas**

The Rubric Says The events in the story and the dialogue lead to the moral that provides closure.

Writing Strategy Use details and dialogue that relate to the moral.

I finished my draft. Then I looked back at the rubric. It says that all the details have to relate to the fable and the moral. If there are details or dialogue that have nothing to do with the fable, the reader will be confused.

[DRAFT]

They started their walk. ~~Bear has brown fur.~~

"It's such a long way up," Bear said, looking up. "How will we ever get to the top?"

"We'll get there one step at a time," Monkey told Bear. ~~"Do you hibernate in winter?"~~

took out unrelated detail and dialogue

Write

Read your draft to yourself or a partner. Look for details and dialogue that have nothing to do with the lesson of the fable. Take them out.

Revise

Focus on **Organization**

The Rubric Says Temporal words and phrases signal the order of events.

Writing Strategy Use temporal words and phrases to guide the reader through the story.

In most stories, the events are told in the order in which they happened. This is true of fables, too. Temporal words and phrases like *first, next,* and *in the morning* tell the reader when events happen. I'm going to look at my draft to see if the events are in order.

I read my draft again and found three places that could use temporal words and phrases. What do you think of my changes?

Writer's Term

Temporal Words and Phrases

Here are some examples of **temporal words**: **soon, afterward, earlier, last, finally, later, before,** and **then**.

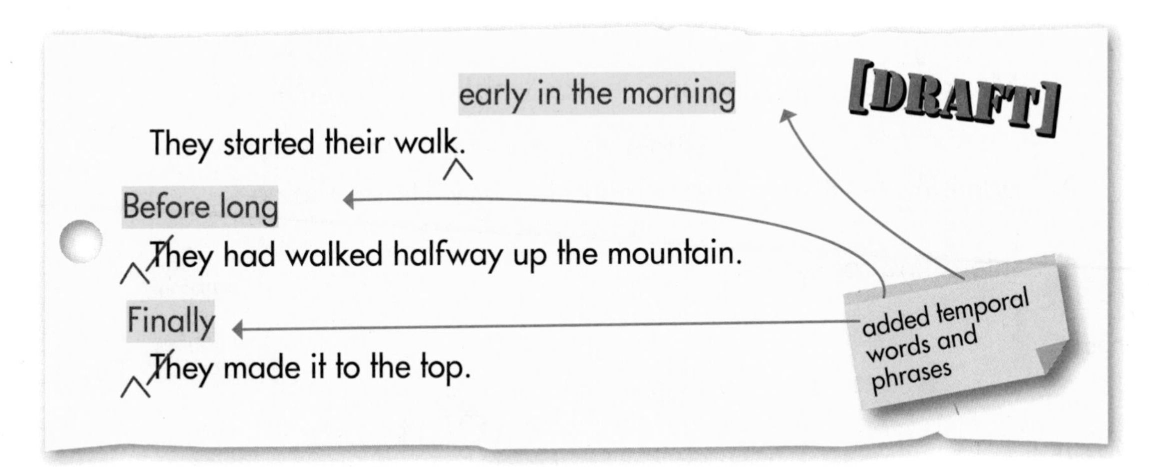

Analyze

Look at Marina's revisions. How do the temporal words and phrases guide the reader?

Write

Read your draft carefully. Revise your fable to add helpful temporal words and phrases.

Revise

Focus on **Sentence Fluency**

The Rubric Says Different types of sentences make the dialogue flow smoothly.

Writing Strategy Use different types of sentences.

The rubric reminds me to use different types of sentences. It also reminds me to make the dialogue flow smoothly. I found a place where I wrote four short sentences in a row. They sound choppy. I can combine the sentences that belong together. I can also write the last sentence as dialogue. I'll remember to use quotation marks around Monkey's words. Do you think my changes improve the flow of my draft?

[DRAFT]

and

Monkey wasn't looking up. He was whistling softly. ~~He was~~

"Those big rocks have interesting shapes," he noted.

admiring the things he saw along the way. ~~He saw some~~

~~interesting rocks.~~

wrote dialogue

combined two short sentences

Write

Read your draft aloud. Be sure your sentences flow smoothly. Combine short sentences that belong together. Write dialogue instead of descriptions where you can.

Edit

Focus on Conventions

The Rubric Says The writing has no errors. Irregular verb forms are correct.

Writing Strategy Check to make sure that all verb forms are correct.

The rubric reminds me to check my spelling, capitalization, and grammar. I also want to be sure that all my verbs are used correctly, especially irregular verbs.

Writer's Term

Irregular Verbs

Not all verbs use **-ed** to show past tense. These are called **irregular verbs**. For example, the verb **go** is irregular:

Present	Past	With *have, has,* or *had*
go	went	gone

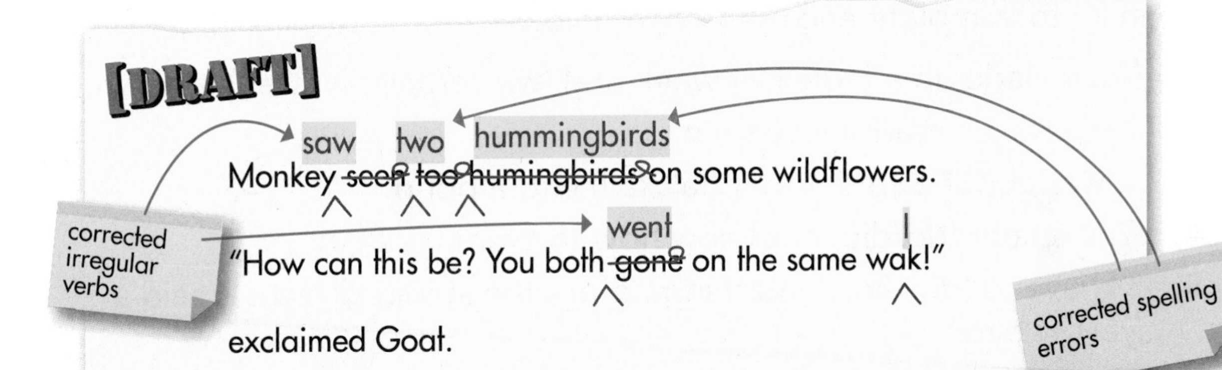

Analyze

Look at Marina's editing. Did she proofread her writing and fix any irregular verb tenses? How did Marina's changes make her writing clearer?

Write

Conventions

Edit your draft for spelling, punctuation, and capitalization. Fix any incorrect irregular verb tenses.

For more practice with irregular verb forms, use the exercises on the next two pages.

Irregular Verbs

Know the Rule

The past tense of regular verbs is formed by adding *-ed*. Other verbs form the past tense in different ways. These verbs are called **irregular verbs**.

Irregular Verbs

Present	Past	With *have, has,* or *had*
do(es)	did	done
fall(s)	fell	fallen
read(s)	read	read
write(s)	wrote	written

Practice the Rule

On a separate sheet of paper, write the correct form of the irregular verb in ( ) to complete each sentence below.

1. Josh made up a fable last week and (wrote/have written) it down.
2. Yesterday I (read/has read) it.
3. It was about a spider that (fall/fell) into a pond.
4. The spider (do/did) not know how to swim.
5. "I have to (do/did) something before the spider drowns," said a yellow bird.
6. The bird picked up a leaf that had (fell/fallen) on the ground.
7. The bird dropped the leaf on the water near the spider. The spider got onto the leaf and was saved. The spider was grateful for what the bird had (did/done).
8. "Thank you, bird," said the spider. "I hope I never (fall/fell) into the water again."
9. "Accidents happen," said the bird. "We all must (do/done) our best to look out for one another."
10. I like Josh's fable so much that I should (write/wrote) one, too.

Irregular Verbs

Know the Rule

Remember that some verbs do not form the past tense with *-ed*. These are **irregular verbs**.

Irregular Verbs

Present	Past	With *have, has,* or *had*
let(s)	let	let
say(s)	said	said
see(s)	saw	seen

Practice the Rule

On a separate sheet of paper, write the correct form of an irregular verb from the box to complete each unfinished sentence below.

1. Long ago, a lion _____ a little mouse and trapped it with its paw.
2. "Please _____ me go now, and I may do you a favor one day," pleaded the mouse.
3. "Just this once," _____ the lion to the mouse.
4. Then the lion _____ the mouse go.
5. The mouse and lion thought they had _____ the last of each other.
6. However, weeks later, the mouse _____ the lion in a trap.
7. "May I _____ that I am very happy to see you!" the lion told the mouse.
8. "Yes, I _____ that you are in trouble," the mouse replied.
9. "Now it's my turn to help you," _____ the mouse.
10. The mouse gnawed through the rope that held the lion and _____ it go free.

Publish +Presentation

Publishing Strategy Make a copy of the fable to read aloud.

Presentation Strategy Use your best handwriting or word processing.

I want to share my fable with my classmates by reading it aloud. In fact our teacher may help us do podcasts of our fables. I don't want to make mistakes when I read aloud, so I will be sure to make a very neat final copy. Before I share my fable, I'm going to check it one more time. My writing partner made quite a few suggestions. When I write my final copy, I will remember to make the dialogue in my fable sound natural. I will also look for places that I can use strong verbs and temporal words and phrases to make my fable more interesting. I want to make sure that the plot and dialogue of my story lead to the moral. Here is the final checklist I will use.

My Final Checklist

Did I—

- ✔ make sure there are no spelling, grammar, or punctuation errors?
- ✔ use the correct forms of irregular verbs?
- ✔ put the title of my fable and my name at the top of the paper?
- ✔ use my best handwriting or word processing?

Write

Use Marina's checklist to review your own fable one more time. Then make a final copy to share with your classmates.

Bear and Monkey's Journey
by Marina

Bear and Monkey had to climb a mountain to visit their friend Goat. They started their walk early in the morning.

"It's such a long way up," Bear grumbled, looking up. "How will we ever get to the top?"

"We'll get there one step at a time," Monkey reassured Bear. Monkey wasn't looking up, though. He was whistling softly and admiring the things he saw along the way. "Those big rocks have interesting shapes," he noted.

"Who cares about old rocks? See how far we still have to go?" Bear complained.

A breeze ruffled Monkey's fur as they continued their climb. "I really love being outdoors on a sunny day, don't you?" he remarked.

"Oh, I wish you hadn't mentioned the sun to me right now," Bear replied. "Walking in the sun always makes me so hot."

Just then Monkey saw two hummingbirds hovering over some wildflowers. "Look at the colorful feathers on those birds!"

Before long they had hiked halfway up the mountain.

Monkey looked down the mountainside. "See how far we've come already?" he said.

Bear didn't look down. He looked up instead. "Monkey, you've got to be kidding. We're only halfway there!" Bear exclaimed.

Finally they made it to the top.

Monkey whistled, but Bear only grunted.

Goat greeted them. "How was your walk?" he asked.

"Beautiful!" exclaimed Monkey. "And it didn't take long at all."

"Tiring and long," answered Bear.

"How can this be? You both went on the same walk!" exclaimed Goat.

"Well, it's like this, Goat," said Monkey. "I enjoy the journey itself and don't worry about reaching the end. Therefore the journey never seems long."

Analyze

Use the rubric to evaluate Marina's fable. Are all the traits of a good fable there? Then use the rubric to evaluate your own fable.

PART 1

Next Generation Narrative Assessment

When you take a narrative writing assessment, you use the skills you have learned when you write narratives. For this kind of assessment, you are asked to write a narrative that includes information from sources you have read. For example, you may be asked to write a personal narrative that includes facts and descriptive details about a historical event.

Now let's analyze each part of this test, so you can really see what the assessment looks like.

Part 1: Close Reading

Your Task
You will examine three sources about the American flag. Then you will answer three questions about what you have learned. Later, in Part 2, you will write a personal narrative about what the American flag means to you.

Steps to Follow
In order to plan and write your personal narrative, you will do all of the following:

1. Examine three sources.
2. Make notes about the information from the sources.
3. Answer three questions about the sources.

Directions for Beginning
You will have 55 minutes to complete Part 1. You will now examine three sources. Take notes because you may want to refer to your notes when you write your personal narrative. You can re-examine any of the sources as often as you like. Answer the questions in the spaces provided.

Your Task This section of the directions gives information about the whole test. You will have two parts to complete. In Part 1, you will read and answer questions. In Part 2, you will write a personal narrative.

Steps to Follow This section reviews the task as a list. It tells how many sources you will examine. You also find out how many questions you have to answer. In this assessment, you will have to examine three sources and answer three questions.

Directions for Beginning This section gives information about Part 1 only—the reading part. You'll need to decide how you want to take notes. Will you write them on a piece of paper or use a note tool online? The directions in this section also tell you that you have 55 minutes to complete your task. Since there are three sources, you will have about 15 minutes to spend on each source plus a little extra time for checking your responses.

TEST TIP

I like to preview the text by reading the title and the first paragraph. That helps me know what I'll be reading about. Then I read the question before I start reading the entire text. You can do this too. It will help you know what to focus on as you read.

Source 1: Text

"The Promise of America" from *Ellis Island*
by Dana Townsend

Imagine leaving the only home you've ever known. After packing your bags, you board a ship. You are going to America, a place you've never even seen. You know that you'll have to learn a new language, new customs, and new way of life. You'll have to make new friends. You have no idea whether you'll fit in.

You know it won't be easy. You'll miss your family and friends. You'll miss simple things, like your favorite foods and special toys.

Why would you decide to make such a difficult journey? You have heard that life in America is wonderful. You can go to a free school and get a good job. If you work hard, you might even get rich. Like many people, you are traveling to America to follow your dreams.

To people all over the world, America is a land of hope and opportunity. And for hundreds of years, immigrants have been coming to America to find a better life.

In the 1800s, millions of immigrants flocked to America. Poverty, war, famine, and disease were reasons that people were willing to leave their homelands for an unknown land. They were ready to begin a new phase in their lives, hoping to find freedom and happiness in a new land.

Immigrants traveled to America by steamship. It cost about $10 for a ticket in 1910. That isn't a lot of money today. But it often took months or even years to save enough money for a ticket. Many families sold almost everything they owned to be able to afford the journey.

Passengers could take only what they could carry. They packed suitcases, trunks, sacks, and bundles. Since there was no bedding on the ship, people had to take heavy feather quilts, mattresses, and pillows for the long ocean voyage. Many immigrants wore all their clothes at once, so they had less to carry.

Most immigrants could only afford the cheapest ticket. They had to stay in the dark, dirty basement of the ship. It was overcrowded, smelly, and noisy.

People slept in bunks stacked three high. Sometimes there wasn't enough room to sit up in bed. There was no place to take a bath. Many people got lice. Hundreds of passengers had to share just a few toilets. When a storm hit, the ship rocked violently, and people became seasick.

Finally, the morning would come for all of the weary immigrants when someone would shout, "America!" Everyone crowded on deck to get a glimpse of Lady Liberty. Children jumped up and down. Men and women cried tears of joy, happy they had finally arrived.

Why did immigrants think it was worth the risk to come to America? Identify three details from the text to support your answer.

To answer this question I need to identify details. I have some good ideas, but I will read the text again and pause to write down the details I find.

My Response

The immigrants heard that it is wonderful to live in America. There are free schools and lots of jobs. Also, they hoped that they would get rich if they worked hard.

Analyze

How well did Marina identify details from the text to support her answer? Are there other details she could have included?

Source 2: Text

from *Our American Flag*
by Mary Firestone

I'm Mary Pickersgill. I sewed one of the most famous flags in the history of the United States. . . .

Countries around the world use flags as symbols. The U.S. flag is a symbol of freedom and patriotism. It is also a symbol of the country's land and people.

During the Revolutionary War (1775–1783), soldiers from the American colonies carried all kinds of flags into battle. They didn't have one official flag. Because of that, soldiers often didn't know who was a friend and who was an enemy.

In 1775, Benjamin Franklin suggested that the American colonies use one common flag. Soon they all agreed to fly the Grand Union flag. This flag had 13 red and white stripes. Each stripe stood for one of the 13 colonies. The flag also had a small British Union flag in the canton. A canton is the upper-left section of a flag.

In 1777, Congress wanted the flag to look more American. They removed the British Union flag from the canton and put 13 stars in its place. Like the stripes, each star stood for one of the 13 colonies.

This flag became the official flag of the United States on June 14, 1777. But people wondered: How many points should the stars have? Should they be put in a circle or in rows? The country had all kinds of different flags again!

Each time a new state was added to the United States, a stripe and a star were added to the flag. By 1794, the flag had 15 stars and 15 stripes.

About 20 years later, they asked me, Mary Pickersgill, to sew a flag—a big one that could be seen easily from far away. They wanted to fly it over Fort McHenry during the War of 1812. Each stripe and star on the finished flag was 2 feet (60 centimeters) wide!

The British bombed Fort McHenry for 25 hours. When the smoke cleared, my beautiful flag was still flying.

A lawyer named Francis Scott Key saw the flag and wrote a poem about 

it. The poem was later set to music, and the song became the national anthem of the United States.

In 1818, five new states joined the country. Congress members knew that if they kept adding stripes and stars for each new state, the flag would grow too big. So, they went back to 13 stripes, which stood for the original 13 colonies. Only a star would be added for each new state. But people still lined up the stars in different ways.

In 1912, President William Howard Taft put the flag's stars in official order. The country then had 48 states, so the flag had six rows of stars, with eight stars in each row. Each star had one point facing up.

More changes to the flag came in 1959 and 1960. Two stars were added as Alaska and Hawaii became states.

Today, the U.S. flag has 50 stars for 50 states.

Why did the writer use both first- and third-person point of view? Use two examples from the text to explain your answer.

I see the first-person pronouns *I* and *my* in the text. But I also see third-person pronouns such as *he* and *they*. I'm not sure why this is, so I'll reread the text to figure it out.

My Response

Mary, the narrator, uses first-person point of view to explain that she sewed a famous U.S. flag. She shows that she is proud when she says "my beautiful flag." In the rest of the text, Mary uses third-person point of view to give facts about the history of the flag and how it has changed.

Analyze

How well did Marina identify the different points of view in the text? What examples would you give?

Source 3: Text

"Symbolism of the American Flag"
by Ariel Mondave

The American flag is a familiar symbol. We see it flying from buildings and homes. People proudly wear flag pins and badges. No matter where it is seen in the world, our flag represents the United States of America. It stands for our country, but not only as a place. It also stands for our values of freedom and democracy. It has carried the message of liberty to many parts of the world.

Stars and Stripes

Our flag did not always look exactly as it looks today. It began with the same 13 red and white stripes. Each stripe represented one of the 13 original colonies. But, there weren't stars in the corner as there are today. In that spot was a British flag!

On June 14, 1777, Congress passed the Flag Act to make the design of the flag a law. Thirteen white stars on a blue field replaced the British flag. Today, the 13 stripes on the flag still stand for the 13 original colonies. The white stars stand for the number of states. The flag will always have 13 stripes. There are 50 states in the United States today. So, there are 50 stars on the flag. If more states are added, more stars will be added.

The stripes on the flag represent rays of light coming from the sun. The stars have two meanings. When the first flag was designed, the United States was a brand new country. The stars represented "a new constellation." A constellation is a group of stars that forms a pattern in the sky that looks like a picture. The stars are also a symbol of the high goals people reach for.

Red, White, and Blue

Red, white, and blue are the official colors of the United States. Red is the symbol of valor and bravery. America needed to be fearless and brave to stand up against Britain. White symbolized the purity and innocence of a new nation. Blue stood for perseverance, vigilance, and justice.

Sometimes a flag may have gold fringe. The fringe doesn't mean anything special. It is used to dress up the flags for ceremonies and special events. It isn't an official part of the flag.

On Flag Day in 1917, President Wilson said that the flag is "the emblem of our unity, our power, our thought and purpose as a nation." The American flag is full of meaning. It is flown at half-staff as a sign of mourning. In times of disaster, the flag flies as a symbol of American spirit. It says that we will pick up the pieces and carry on. We will not be defeated. We will not give up.

How are the symbols on the flag connected to the history of the United States? Use three symbols as examples in your answer.

The question asks me to describe the connections between the symbols on the flag and the history of the United States. I've got some good ideas, but I'll look in the text again to make sure I know exactly what the symbols stand for.

My Response

The 13 stripes are for the original colonies. The 50 stars, one for each state, show how the country has grown since then. The colors on the flag stand for the traits of the American people when they were fighting for independence from Britain.

Analyze

How well did Marina describe connections between the flag symbols and U.S. history? What are some other connections you can make?

PART 2

Next Generation Narrative Assessment

Now that Part 1 is complete, it's time to write the personal narrative. Usually you will complete Part 1 on one day and Part 2 on the next day. The directions for Part 2 are longer than for Part 1 and continue on a second page. So remember to read the directions carefully and ask questions if you don't understand.

Part 2: Writing to Multiple Sources

Setup

You will now have 70 minutes to review your notes and sources, plan, draft, and revise a personal narrative. You may use your notes and refer to the sources. You may also look at the answers you wrote to questions in Part 1, but you cannot change those answers. Now read your assignment and the information about how your personal narrative will be scored. Then begin your work.

Your Assignment

You have probably seen the American flag in many places, such as outside homes, schools, and office buildings. People show the flag because it means something important to them. What does it mean to you? Your assignment is to write a personal narrative telling a story that shows what the flag means to you. Support your personal narrative with concrete details and examples from each of the sources you have examined. The audience for your narrative will be the people in your community.

Setup This section lets you know how much time you have to complete Part 2. You can divide the time into the different parts of the writing proess. Here's an example of what Marina plans to do.

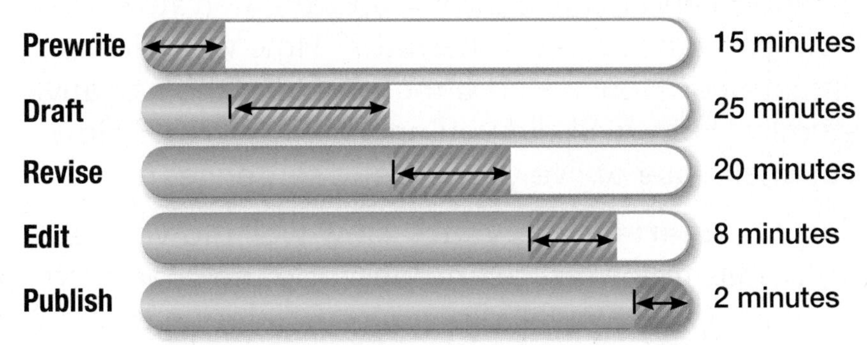

The directions also tell you that you can go back and examine the sources for Part 1, but answers can't be changed.

Your Assignment This part explains your writing assignment. The topic of your assignment usually appears in the first few sentences in this section. In this case, it's the first four sentences. Finally, you are given a clue about the kind of voice you should use in your narrative. Your audience is the people in your community, so you should use a voice that sounds respectful and knowledgeable.

Scoring Guide

Your personal narrative will be scored on the following criteria:

1. **Focus and organization** How well did you grab the reader's attention and keep it throughout the narrative? How well did you introduce the narrator? How well did you describe situations? How well did the events in the narrative unfold naturally? How well did you end the narrative? How well did you make use of lively, energetic sentences?
2. **Elaboration of experiences/events** How well did you use descriptive details to introduce and describe the characters, setting, and events? How well did you use dialogue to bring the characters to life? How well did you use words such as precise nouns and strong verbs to help your reader "see" your narrative?
3. **Conventions** How well did you follow the rules of grammar? Did you check your punctuation, capitalization, and spelling?

Now begin work on your personal narrative. Manage your time carefully so that you can:

- plan your narrative.
- write your narrative.
- revise and edit for a final draft.

Spell check is available to use.

Type your response on the following page. Write as much as you need to. Remember what your task is. Check the scoring guide to make sure you cover all the traits.

Writing Traits in the Scoring Guide

The second page of the directions tells you how your personal narrative will be scored. This scoring guide includes all of the writing traits. You can use what you have learned about the writing traits to help you write an effective personal narrative.

1 Focus and organization

- How well did you make use of lively, energetic sentences?

- How well did you grab the reader's attention and keep it throughout the narrative?

2 Elaboration of experiences/events

- How well did you use descriptive details to introduce and describe the characters, setting, and events?

- How well did you use dialogue to bring the characters to life?

- How well did you use words such as precise nouns and strong verbs to help your reader "see" your narrative?

3 Conventions

- How well did you follow the rules of grammar, punctuation, capitalization, and spelling?

Before you start Part 2, review your plan for how you will divide your time. Remember there is no word limit, but don't feel you have to fill the entire space with your thoughts. Now it's time for Marina to start writing her personal narrative.

Prewrite

Focus on **Ideas**

Writing Strategy Respond to the assignment.

Prewrite 15 minutes

The first step in successful test writing is making sure you know what the assignment asks for. Gather information from the directions. Reread the assignment. It tells what your topic should be and who your audience is.

From my assignment, I know I'm supposed to write a personal narrative, and I know what the topic is.

> You have probably seen the American flag in many places, such as outside homes, schools, and office buildings. People show the flag because it means something important to them. What does it mean to you? Your assignment is to write a personal narrative telling a story that shows what the flag means to you. Support your personal narrative with concrete details and examples from each of the sources you have examined.

topic

genre

First, I'm going to write a sentence stating my topic. Then, I'll think about how the sources support my topic. I can't remember all the details about the sources, but I want to see what I can remember.

My Topic:
What does the American flag mean to me?

Sources That Support My Topic:
What the flag meant to Mary Pickersgill
What America meant to immigrants
What the symbols on the flag stand for

Prewrite

Focus on Organization

Writing Strategy Choose a graphic organizer.

Prewrite 15 minutes

I need to start organizing my ideas. A good graphic organizer for a narrative is a Story Map. It will help me organize my thoughts and ideas for the narrative I am going to write.

Beginning

Character: Uncle Eduardo
Topic: Uncle Eduardo loves the American flag.

↓

Middle

He came from Cuba.
He got a janitor job at the school.
He raised and lowered the flag at school.
The flag got torn during a hurricane.
By the next day he had mended it.

↓

End

Uncle Eduardo explains why the flag means so much to him.

Analyze

Does Marina's graphic organizer include enough events and experiences to support her topic? Is there anything she left out?

Draft

Focus on **Ideas**

Writing Strategy Describe the characters, setting, and events.

Draft | 25 minutes

I know that every narrative should contain details about the characters, setting, and events. I'll follow my Story Map to make sure I include all the details that explain who and what my narrative is about and where and when it takes place.

main character

Uncle Eduardo came here from Cuba a few years ago. He did not speak much English, and he was worried about learning a new way of life, but he knew how to fix things. He got a job as the janitor's helper at my school.

setting

One of uncle Eduardos tasks was to raise the flag in the morning and lower it at the end of the day.

"This is my favoret part of my job he told me. I laughed. "Why?"

"Someday maybe you understand," he shrugged.

One day my uncle asked me, "What do the stars and stripes mean?" I told him what I'd learned in school: 13 stripes for the 13 original colonies and one star for each state today. He thought about it and nodded.

event

Last year, a big storm was coming. Uncle Eduardo and his boss, the janitor, protected the windows and turned off the water and the electricity. The wind was starting to blow.

Uncle Eduardo began raising the flag.

"There's no time for that," his boss scolded.

During the storm, the flag got torn. That evening, Uncle Eduardo lowered the flag and took it home. The next morning, the flag was flying. It was in one piece. Uncle Eduardo had mended it. He said he had mended it because it was his country's flag.

Now when I think of the flag, I think of my uncle. The red color on the flag stands for bravery. I think Uncle Eduardo was brave to start a new life here. And I understand that to my uncle, the flag means everything in his new life of freedom. Because of that, it means everything to me too.

Analyze

How does Marina introduce the setting of her personal narrative? How does she make her events clear?

Revise

Focus on **Organization**

Writing Strategy Grab the reader's attention at the beginning and keep it throughout the narrative.

Revise 20 minutes

Now it's time to check my draft against the scoring guide. I want to be sure I've included all the points that will be scored.

The scoring guide reminds me to grab the reader's attention and keep it throughout my narrative. I should write an interesting beginning. Then I should look for places to add exciting details. This might make the reader curious and want to read more.

grabbed reader's attention

I never thought much about the American flag until I saw how Uncle Eduardo felt about it. Uncle Eduardo came here from Cuba a few years ago.

During the storm, a metal strip flew off a store sign across the street and into the flag. Our ~~the~~ flag got torn.

kept reader's attention

Analyze

Did Marina's new sentences grab and keep your attention more than the original sentences? Why or why not?

Revise

Focus on **Voice**

Writing Strategy Use dialogue to bring the characters to life.

Revise 20 minutes

I want my readers to be able to picture and understand Uncle Eduardo the way I do. One way to do this is to let him speak for himself, using his own words in a way that sounds just right for him. I see a place where I can add dialogue. I'll remember to add quotation marks to show where his words begin and end.

The next morning, the flag was flying. It was in one piece. Uncle Eduardo had mended it. ~~He said he had mended it because it was his country's flag.~~

"This is my country's flag," Uncle Eduardo said proudly, with happy tears in his eyes. "It is a symbol of a better life. It means everything."

added dialogue

Analyze

How does adding dialogue make Uncle Eduardo seem more real? Are there other places where Marina might use dialogue?

Revise

Focus on **Word Choice**

Writing Strategy Use descriptive words that help the reader "see" your narrative.

Revise 20 minutes

The scoring guide reminds me to use descriptive language to help my reader "see" what I'm describing. I need to use specific nouns and stronger verbs. I'll reread my draft and add words that describe.

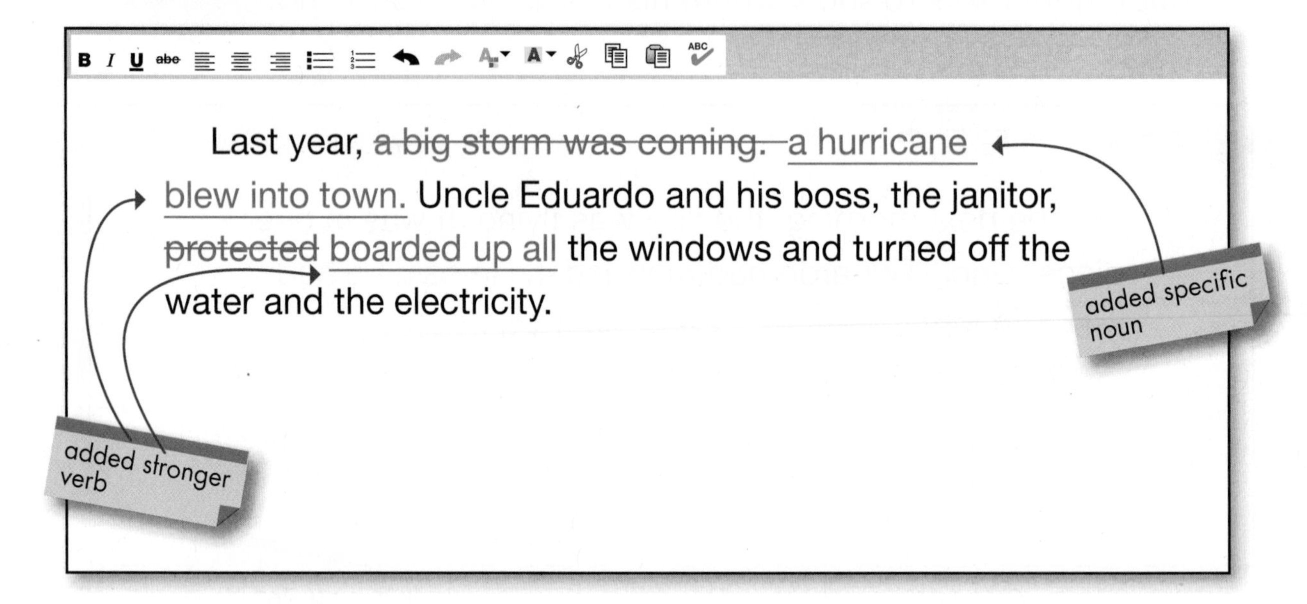

Analyze

In what ways are the added words stronger than the original words? Where else in the narrative can Marina improve her word choices?

Edit

Writing Strategy Check grammar, spelling, capitalization, and punctuation.

Edit — 8 minutes

The scoring guide reminds me to use correct grammar, spelling, capitalization, and punctuation. I made sure to leave time to correct those errors. I will use the spell-check feature to save some time, but I will think about each word before I accept the computer's spelling.

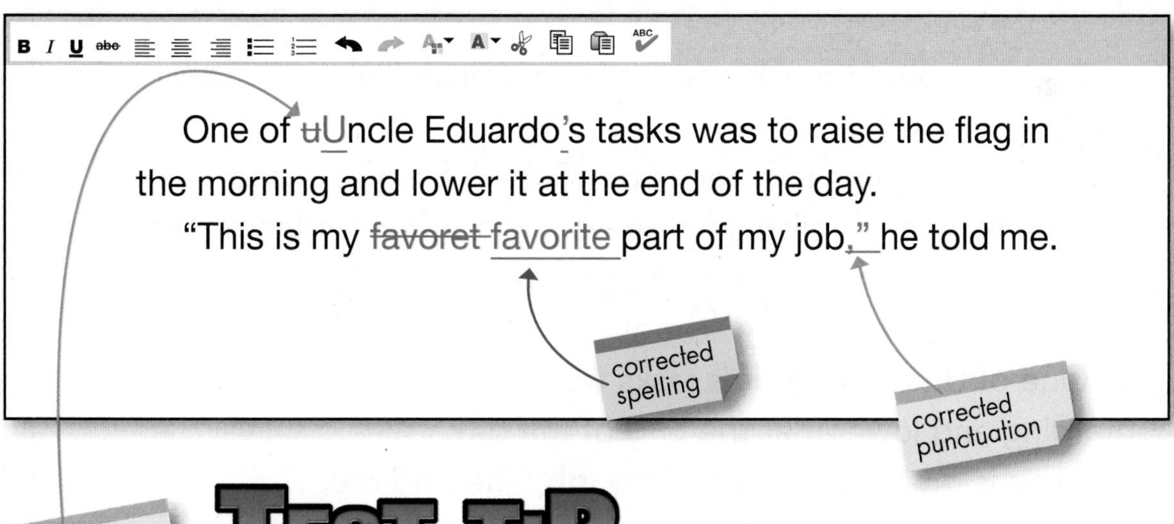

TEST TIP

Take a few minutes to edit your writing. Check for spelling and punctuation mistakes and fix them. Remember: If the people who score your test see poor spelling or missing punctuation, they might not notice how interesting your personal narrative is!

Publish

Writing Strategy Submit the final draft of your personal narrative.

Publish 2 minutes

I'm almost done with my assessment. I used information in the scoring guide and the writing traits to complete my narrative. Now I am going to use the spell-check feature one more time to make sure I didn't miss any spelling errors. Then I will submit my final draft.

I never thought much about the American flag until I saw how Uncle Eduardo felt about it.

Uncle Eduardo came here from Cuba a few years ago. He did not speak much English, and he was worried about learning a new way of life, but he knew how to fix things. He got a job as the janitor's helper at my school.

One of Uncle Eduardo's tasks was to raise the flag in the morning and lower it at the end of the day.

"This is my favorite part of my job," he told me.

I laughed. "Why?"

"Someday maybe you understand," he shrugged.

One day my uncle asked me, "What do the stars and stripes mean?" I told him what I'd learned in school: 13 stripes for the 13 original colonies and one star for each state today. He thought about it and nodded.

Last year, a hurricane blew into town. Uncle Eduardo and his boss, the janitor, boarded up all the windows and turned off the water and the electricity. The wind was starting to blow. Uncle

Eduardo began raising the flag. He pulled hard at the rope as the wind blew more fiercely.

"There's no time for that," his boss scolded.

"This is the most important thing," Uncle Eduardo shouted above the wind.

During the storm, a metal strip flew off a store sign across the street and into the flag. Our flag got torn. That evening, with the storm howling, Uncle Eduardo lowered the flag and took it home.

The next day, the sky was clear. As I hopped off the bus in front of the school, I saw the flag flying. It was in one piece. Uncle Eduardo had mended it.

"This is my country's flag," Uncle Eduardo said proudly, with happy tears in his eyes. "It is a symbol of a better life. It means everything."

Now when I think of the flag, I think of my uncle. The red color on the flag stands for bravery. I think Uncle Eduardo was brave to start a new life here. And I understand that to my uncle, the flag means everything in his new life of freedom. Because of that, it means everything to me too.

Now It's Your Turn

Don't forget all the advice Marina gave you during her assessment. Now, it's your turn to practice taking a narrative assessment.

Informative/ Explanatory writing

tells about a topic or explains a process.

Hi, my name is Emma. I'm learning all about informative/explanatory writing. I'm very excited about it. There are a lot of things that I am interested in. As I learn strategies for writing essays and reports, I can share information about the kinds of things I love to do!

IN THIS UNIT

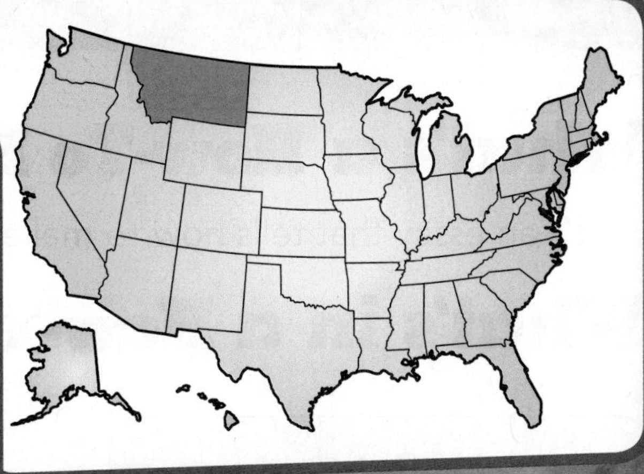

Name:	Emma
Home:	Montana
Favorite Activities:	horseback riding and camping
Favorite Animals:	horses and dogs
Favorite Subjects in School:	science and computers
Favorite Book:	*The Kids' Horse Book* by Sylvia Funston
Favorite Food:	buffalo burgers

What's a How-To Essay?

It's an essay that tells how to make or do something.

What's in a How-To Essay?

Materials
These are what I need to do my project. If I want to explain how to grow bread mold, I'll tell my readers they will need bread, water, and plastic wrap.

Steps
Steps are the actions I do to complete the project. I will have to put them in order and write them clearly.

Temporal Words
These are words like *first, next, after, then,* and *last.* Temporal words help readers understand the order of steps.

Why write a How-To Essay?

There are many reasons to write a how-to essay. Here are two reasons I can think of for writing about how to do something.

To Inform

If I know how to do something that others would like to know how to do, I could show each person how to do it. Or I could write a how-to essay and post it in the library or on a bulletin board.

People write how-to essays to explain things such as how to draw a horse, build a model car, or create a math puzzle. You can find essays like these in books and on the Internet.

To Inspire

I can write a how-to essay to inspire others to do something that they may think is difficult. If I share my excitement and write steps that are easy to follow, readers may decide to try the project themselves!

Linking Informative/Explanatory Writing Traits to a How-To Essay

In this chapter, you will explain how to do something. This type of informative/explanatory writing is called a how-to essay. Emma will guide you through the stages of the writing process: Prewrite, Draft, Revise, Edit, and Publish. In each stage, Emma will show you important writing strategies that are linked to the Informative/Explanatory Writing Traits below.

Informative/Explanatory Writing Traits

Ideas	• a clear, focused topic • supporting details that are complete and accurate
Organization	• related information that is grouped in paragraphs • a strong introduction, body, and conclusion • temporal words and phrases that connect ideas
Voice	• a voice that connects directly to the reader
Word Choice	• exact words that are appropriate for the reader • definitions for words that the reader may not know
Sentence Fluency	• clear, direct sentences • different sentence types to make the writing flow
Conventions	• no or few errors in spelling, punctuation, and capitalization

Before you write, read Oscar Cooper's how-to essay on the next page. Then use the how-to essay rubric on pages 128–129 to decide how well he did. (You might want to look back at What's in a How-To Essay? on page 124, too!)

The Perfect Sandwich

by Oscar Cooper

Does your stomach ever scream, "I'm hungry"? Then you'll want to learn how to make the best peanut butter sandwich ever. Not only does it taste great, but it's good for you, too!

First, gather all the ingredients. You'll need two slices of bread, a big glob of peanut butter, a banana, several raisins, strawberry jam, and some granola. Put them on your kitchen counter.

Next, spread the peanut butter on one side of a slice of bread. Be sure that the peanut butter covers the whole surface of the bread evenly. There shouldn't be any lumps.

Now, use the banana, raisins, jam, and granola to make a face on the peanut butter. Cut three round banana slices. Use two for the eyes and one for the nose. Place the raisins side by side in a curve to form a smiling mouth. Then drop a dab of strawberry jam on either side of the nose to make rosy cheeks. Add some crunchy freckles by sprinkling a little granola over the face.

Finally, it's time to enjoy your creation! Take a minute to admire the smiling face. Smile back as you think about how happy your stomach is going to be. Put the second piece of bread on top of the first. You're about to taste the best sandwich ever made!

materials

steps

temporal words

How-To Essay Rubric

Use this rubric to analyze the model. Then use it to plan and score your own how-to essay.

	6	5	4
Ideas	The writer focuses on one process. All necessary facts and details are included.	The writer focuses on one process. Most necessary facts and details are included.	The writer's focus may not be clear enough. A few necessary facts or details may be missing.
Organization	The process is organized into paragraphs. Temporal words and phrases make the steps clear.	The process is organized into paragraphs. A few more temporal words and phrases are needed.	The process is organized into paragraphs. Few temporal words and phrases are present.
Voice	The writer uses a natural voice to speak directly to the reader.	The writer's voice speaks directly to the reader most of the time.	The writer does not use a natural voice and speaks directly to the reader only occasionally.
Word Choice	Strong, specific verbs help the reader know exactly what to do.	Verbs are strong and striking most of the time.	Most of the verbs are specific and helpful to the reader.
Sentence Fluency	A variety of sentence patterns makes the writing flow. Short sentences are combined.	The writing is smooth and easy to read. Most of the time, sentence variety is used.	There is a variety of sentence patterns. A few short sentences should be combined.
Conventions	The essay has been edited carefully. Spelling, punctuation, and capitalization are correct. Homophones are used correctly.	Most of the essay has been edited carefully. One homophone may be used incorrectly.	Most of the essay has been edited. Several homophones may be used incorrectly.

+Presentation Helpful illustrations are provided.

	3	2	1
Ideas	The writer's focus may not be clear. Some facts or details may be unrelated.	The writer's focus is not clear. Some facts or details may confuse the reader.	The writer's focus is not clear. Facts and details are not provided.
Organization	One paragraph may be out of order. More temporal words and phrases are needed.	Several paragraphs are not in order. Temporal words and phrases are confusing or not used.	The writing is not organized. Temporal words and phrases are not used.
Voice	The writer uses a generic voice that seldom speaks directly to the reader.	The voice is not consistent or does not speak to or connect with the reader.	The essay lacks a writer's voice.
Word Choice	Many verbs are too general to help the reader.	The verbs are weak or used too many times.	Verb choice feels random or accidental.
Sentence Fluency	More variety of sentence patterns would improve the flow. Short sentences make it choppy.	The sentences are all the same or incomplete. The writing is difficult to read.	The piece lacks fluency due to repeated short, choppy sentences and no variety.
Conventions	Errors in spelling, punctuation, or capitalization are present. Homophone errors confuse the reader.	Too many errors make the writing very difficult to read.	Serious, frequent errors make the writing too difficult to read.

See Appendix B for 4-, 5-, and 6-point informative/explanatory rubrics.

Using the How-To Essay Rubric to Analyze the Model

Did you notice that the model on page 127 points out some key elements of a how-to essay? As he wrote "The Perfect Sandwich," Oscar Cooper used these elements to help him explain how to make his sandwich. He also used the 6-point rubric on pages 128–129 to plan, draft, revise, and edit the writing. A rubric is a great tool to evaluate writing during the writing process.

To get started, look at the top score for each trait as you study the model. Do you agree that Oscar has earned a 6 for each trait?

- **The writer focuses on one process.**
- **All necessary facts and details are included.**

Oscar explains how to make a sandwich. He remembers to include every step, and he gives complete information for each one. This helps me to understand the steps.

Now, use the banana, raisins, jam, and granola to make a face on the peanut butter. Cut three round banana slices. Use two for the eyes and one for the nose. Place the raisins side by side in a curve to form a smiling mouth.

- **The process is organized into paragraphs.**
- **Temporal words and phrases make the steps clear.**

Oscar uses paragraphs to explain each step in the process. Temporal words, such as *first, next, now,* and *finally,* lead me from one step to the next.

First, gather all the ingredients.

Next, spread the peanut butter on one side of a slice of bread.

- **The writer uses a natural voice to speak directly to the reader.**

My stomach often screams, "I'm hungry," so I understand exactly what Oscar means. I feel like he is talking to me. I'm looking forward to finding out more about his sandwich.

Does your stomach ever scream, "I'm hungry"? Then you'll want to learn how to make the best peanut butter sandwich ever. Not only does it taste great, but it's good for you, too!

Using the How-To Essay Rubric to Analyze the Model

- **Strong, specific verbs help the reader know exactly what to do.**

Instead of using a general word like *put* when describing how to make the "cheeks," Oscar uses a strong, specific verb, *drop*. This helps me know exactly what to do.

Then drop a dab of strawberry jam on either side of the nose to make rosy cheeks.

- **A variety of sentence patterns makes the writing flow.**
- **Short sentences are combined.**

Oscar uses different sentence patterns. He uses both long and short sentences. He begins the sentences in different ways, too. This variety makes the writing flow smoothly.

Finally, it's time to enjoy your creation! Take a minute to admire the smiling face. Smile back as you think about how happy your stomach is going to be.

- **The essay has been edited carefully. Spelling, punctuation, and capitalization are correct.**
- **Homophones are used correctly.**

Oscar is careful to use homophones correctly, such as *its/it's* and *your/you're.* These words sound the same, but they have different spellings and different meanings. Look at the paragraph below. In the first sentence, the writer chose *it's,* the contraction for *it is.* Whenever I write *it's,* I read it as two words. Then I usually get it right!

Finally, it's time to enjoy your creation! Take a minute to admire the smiling face. Smile back as you think about how happy your stomach is going to be. Put the second piece of bread on top of the first. You're about to taste the best sandwich ever made!

+Presentation Helpful illustrations are provided.

My Turn!

Now I'm going to write my own how-to essay. I'll use good writing strategies and the rubric to help me. Follow along to see how I do it.

Prewrite

Focus on **Ideas**

The Rubric Says The writer focuses on one process. All necessary facts and details are included.

Writing Strategy Make a list of the steps and the materials needed to do a task.

My teacher says we are all experts at something. What do I know a lot about that I can explain in a how-to essay?

I thought about how much I like to go camping. I've set up a tent many times. I know exactly how to do it. I decided it would make a great how-to essay. Others could learn how to do it, too! First I'll make a list of all the steps and materials someone would need to do this project.

Steps and Materials for Setting Up a Tent

1. put a sheet of plastic on the ground
2. put the tent up
3. put tent poles together
4. drive tent stakes in the ground
5. use a hammer or a rock for pounding

Write

Now think of something you know how to do. Begin by making a list of steps and materials that you need to do it.

Prewrite

Focus on **Organization**

The Rubric Says The process is organized into paragraphs.

Writing Strategy Make a Sequence Chain to organize the steps.

I know from the rubric that I need to organize my essay into paragraphs. My paragraphs will explain step-by-step how to set up a tent. The steps need to be in order, or else my readers will get confused! I'll use a Sequence Chain to organize the list of steps and materials I just made. It will help me know how to plan my paragraphs.

Writer's Term

Sequence Chain

A **Sequence Chain** shows steps in the order in which they should happen.

Sequence Chain

Topic: Setting Up a Tent

Step 1 Decide where to put the tent and get ground ready.

Step 2 Lay plastic sheet and tent on the ground.

Step 3 Attach poles and raise the tent.

Step 4 Fold in edges of the plastic sheet.

Step 5 Pound in stakes to keep the tent from moving.

Analyze

Look at Emma's list of steps and her Sequence Chain. Are all the steps included? Are they in order?

Write

Now it's your turn. Look at the steps you listed. Make a Sequence Chain to organize the steps and help plan your paragraphs.

Draft

Focus on **Ideas**

The Rubric Says The writer focuses on one process. All necessary facts and details are included.

Writing Strategy Introduce and explain the process.

Now it's time to begin writing my draft. I have to explain how to set up a tent very clearly so my readers will know what to do. Each of my paragraphs should stick to one main idea. I can use my Sequence Chain to help me.

My beginning paragraph should introduce the process I will explain. Then I'll write the how-to steps. I need to remember to include the materials, too. I will write one paragraph for each main step I listed in my Sequence Chain.

As I write, I'll do my best with grammar and spelling, but I won't worry about mistakes. I'll fix them later. Here's the first part of my draft.

Writer's Term

Paragraph

A **paragraph** is a group of sentences that have the same topic or purpose. The sentences focus on a single main idea or thought. The first sentence of a paragraph starts on a new line and is indented.

Proofreading Marks

]	Indent	ℓ	Take out something
≡	Make uppercase	⊙	Add a period
/	Make lowercase	¶	New paragraph
∧	Add something	(sp)	Spelling error

[DRAFT]

Building My Tent in the Woods

If you like being outdoors and camping, then you will want to learn to set up a tent. It's easy to do!

introduces the process

First, you need to find a good spot for your tent. Choose a place where the ground is levul. It should not be hilly or rocky.

presents one main idea in each paragraph

Put down a sheet of plastic. Smooth it out with you're hands so that their are no rinkles. Spread out the tent on top of the plastic.

Now it's time to put in the poles. First, take them out of they're bag. Next, slide each pole into it's sleeve on the tent. The ends of the poles will stick out. To raise the tent, lift each pole and place the end into a metal ring on the floor of the tent. Oh, before you slide the poles into the sleeves, you have to take out each one, and put the ends of the sections into place.

Next, fold in the edges of the plastic. Don't let the plastic hang out. It could let rainwater run under the tent!

Analyze

Read Emma's draft. Is there one main idea in each paragraph? What, if any, facts and details are missing from the paragraphs?

Write

Use your Sequence Chain to write a draft of a how-to essay. Remember to stick to one main idea in each paragraph.

Revise

Focus on Organization

The Rubric Says Temporal words and phrases make the steps clear.

Writing Strategy Use temporal words and phrases to help the reader follow the steps in order.

I can tell from the rubric that temporal words are important in a how-to essay. I'll read my draft again. I'll look for places where I can add temporal words. My essay will be easier to follow. It will also help my readers follow the steps in order.

Writer's Term

Temporal Words

Temporal words are signal words that tell the order in which steps or events happen.

Temporal words include:

first	**next**	**today**
second	**then**	**yesterday**
third	**last**	**tomorrow**

[DRAFT]

Second, ~~P~~put down a sheet of plastic. Smooth it out with you're hands so that their are no rinkles. Then ~~S~~spread out the tent on top of the plastic.

added temporal words

Write

Read your draft again. Revise your how-to essay to add temporal words and phrases that make your essay easier to follow.

Revise

Focus on **Voice**

The Rubric Says The writer uses a natural voice to speak directly to the reader.

Writing Strategy Use a friendly, personal voice to connect with the reader.

The rubric says that I should use natural language in my essay. That means I can be a little informal and write the way I would talk to people in my family or my friends. If I use the word *you*, my readers will feel like I am speaking directly to them.

Writer's Term

Natural Language

Natural language is the language you use when you speak with family members and friends. Contractions and casual language are part of using a natural-sounding voice.

[DRAFT]

If you like being outdoors and camping, then ~~you will~~ you'll want to learn to set up really a tent. Don't worry! It's easy to do!

added natural language

Analyze

Look at Emma's revisions. How do they make her language sound more natural? How does Emma speak directly to her readers?

Write

Read your draft again. See if you can add any contractions and informal words. Speak directly to the reader by using *you*.

Revise

Focus on Word Choice

The Rubric Says Strong, specific verbs help the reader know exactly what to do.

Writing Strategy Use strong verbs.

The rubric tells me to use strong, specific verbs. Using specific verbs helps my readers know exactly what to do. I see that I've used the verb *put* too many times. I can replace it with better, more exact verbs. I'll look for other places where I can use more specific verbs, too.

[DRAFT]

Now it's time to ~~put in~~ attach the poles.

used strong verbs

used strong verbs

~~Oh, before you slide the poles into the sleeves, you have to take~~ Unfold ~~out~~ each one, and ~~put~~ snap the ends of the sections into place.

Write

Read your draft. Replace overused or weak verbs with strong verbs.

Edit

Focus on **Conventions**

The Rubric Says The essay has been edited carefully. Spelling, punctuation, and capitalization are correct. Homophones are used correctly.

Writing Strategy Check that each homophone fits its meaning.

Next I will check my spelling, punctuation, and capitalization. The rubric reminds me to pay attention to homophones. I'll make sure I've used every homophone correctly.

Writer's Term

Homophones

Homophones are words that sound the same but have different spellings and meanings.

Word	Meaning	Example
its	belonging to it	I love **its** smoky flavor.
it's	it is	Now **it's** my turn to cook.
their	belonging to them	We used **their** tent.
there	at or in that place	Put the logs over **there**.
they're	they are	**They're** hiking today.

[DRAFT]

Second, put down a sheet of plastic. Smooth it out with ~~you're~~ your hands so that ~~their~~ there are no ~~rinkles~~ wrinkles.

used correct homophones

corrected spelling error

Analyze

Look at Emma's edits. Did she homophones correctly? What could happen if you use the wrong homophone in a sentence?

Write

Conventions

Edit your draft for spelling, punctuation, and capitalization. Fix any incorrect homophones.

For more practice fixing errors with homophones, use the exercises on the next two pages.

Conventions **Grammar, Usage & Mechanics**

Homophones

Know the Rule

Some words sound the same but are spelled differently and have different meanings. These words are called **homophones**.

Your means "belonging to you." **You're** is a contraction that means "you are."

Their means "belonging to them." **They're** is a contraction that means "they are." **There** means "at or in that place."

Its means "belonging to it." **It's** is a contraction that means "it is" or "it has."

Practice the Rule

Number a sheet of paper 1–12. Then write the word in ( ) that correctly completes each sentence.

1. If _____ going camping, bring a flashlight. (your/you're)
2. Don't forget _____ batteries. (its/it's)
3. Is _____ a campground nearby? (their/they're/there)
4. The counselor said _____ planning to leave early. (their/they're/there)
5. I know _____ going to enjoy this trip. (your/you're)
6. How will we know when _____ time to leave? (its/it's)
7. I think _____ about to call us. (their/they're/there)
8. You will need _____ blanket to stay warm. (your/you're)
9. It is colder _____ than you think. (their/they're/there)
10. Hikers who forgot to bring _____ water will be sorry. (their/they're/there)
11. _____ a long hike to the campground. (Its/It's)
12. Find a nice, clear place to put up _____ tent. (your/you're)

More Homophones

Know the Rule

The words below are **homophones**. It is important to tell them apart because electronic spell checkers will not catch errors in their use.

Hair means "the soft strands that grow on your head or body or on the body of an animal." **Hare** means "an animal like a rabbit."

Here means "at or in this place." **Hear** means "to listen with your ears."

Hole means "a hollow place." **Whole** means "all of something."

Two means "the numeral 2." **Too** means "also" or "very."

Practice the Rule

Number a sheet of paper 1–10. Then write the word in ( ) that correctly completes each sentence.

1. Sahil only has to collect _____ more titles to complete the book series. (two/too)
2. My little sister got gum in her _____ so she has to have it cut. (hair/hare)
3. Did you _____ the loud thunder last night? (here/hear)
4. Apples taste great, and they are good for you, _____ ! (two/too)
5. Marco ate the _____ pizza all by himself. (hole/whole)
6. The Arctic _____ has white fur to blend into the snow. (hair/hare)
7. Mei tore a _____ in her pants when she fell on the sidewalk. (hole/whole)
8. If I wear a sweater, I'll be _____ hot. (two/too)
9. You can put that pile of books right _____ on the table. (hear/here)
10. The snake disappeared down the _____ next to the driveway. (hole/whole)

Publish + Presentation

Publishing Strategy Publish my essay in a class book of how-to essays.

Presentation Strategy Include helpful illustrations.

My classmates wrote about many interesting things. Now we are going to publish our work in a class book of how-to essays. To organize the information and make the temporal words stand out, I'll indent each paragraph. Before publishing my essay, I will read through it one last time. Then I'll draw pictures of the steps. Finally I'll make sure that I've done everything on my final checklist.

My Final Checklist

Did I—

- ✔ use homophones correctly?
- ✔ indent each paragraph?
- ✔ use neat handwriting or word processing?
- ✔ put my name on my paper?
- ✔ add helpful illustrations?

Check your own how-to essay against the checklist. Then make a final copy of your how-to essay to put into a class book. Be sure to illustrate key steps in your process.

Building My Tent in the Woods
by Emma

If you like being outdoors and camping, then you'll want to learn to set up a tent. Don't worry! It's really easy to do!

First, you need to find a good spot for your tent. Choose a place where the ground is level. It should not be hilly or rocky. Then pick up everything that might make lumps under your tent, like stones or twigs.

Second, put down a sheet of plastic. Smooth it out with your hands so that there are no wrinkles. Then spread out the tent on top of the plastic.

Now it's time to attach the poles. First, take them out of their bag. Unfold each one, and snap the ends of the sections into place. Next, slide each pole into its sleeve on the tent. The ends of the poles will stick out. To raise the tent, lift each pole and place the end into a metal ring on the floor of the tent.

Next, fold in the edges of the plastic. If the plastic hangs out, it could let rainwater run under the tent!

Finally, pull out the big loops at the bottom edges of the tent. Put a tent stake through each loop. Use a hammer or a rock to pound the stakes into the ground. Now your tent won't move, and you're ready to spend a great night in the woods!

Use the rubric to analyze Emma's essay. Did she include all the traits of a good how-to essay? Use the rubric to judge your how-to essay.

What's a Research Report?

A research report gives information that is real, not made up. It gives facts about a topic.

What's in a Research Report?

Topic
This is what I'm writing about. I can write about anything that I can find information about. I may write about a sport like fishing or an animal like the wild horse.

Introduction
This is my first paragraph. In my introduction I will tell about the topic and get my readers interested.

Body
The body of my research report will be two paragraphs. In these paragraphs I will give interesting facts about the topic.

Conclusion
This is the last paragraph. In it I will tie my main ideas together.

Why write a Research Report?

There are many reasons people write a research report. Here are some reasons I can think of for writing one.

To Inform
I might write a research report about a topic I'm interested in because I want to share the information with others.

Scientists sometimes write research reports about studies they are conducting to keep others informed about their progress.

Journalists write research reports about events that are happening around the world. They publish their reports in newspapers and magazines.

To Advertise
Marketing groups write research reports about products. People who read advertisements can learn facts about products and services.

To Entertain
Many people enjoy reading research reports for fun. Magazines publish research reports about people, events, and products from all around the world.

Linking Informative/Explanatory Writing Traits to a Research Report

In this chapter, you will research a topic and write about it. This type of informative/explanatory writing is called a research report. Emma will guide you through the stages of the writing process: Prewrite, Draft, Revise, Edit, and Publish. In each stage, Emma will show you important writing strategies that are linked to the Informative/Explanatory Writing Traits below.

Informative/Explanatory Writing Traits

 Ideas	• a clear, focused topic • supporting details that are complete and accurate
 Organization	• related information that is grouped in paragraphs • a strong introduction, body, and conclusion • linking words and phrases that connect ideas
 Voice	• a voice that connects directly to the reader
 Word Choice	• exact words that are appropriate for the reader • definitions for words that the reader may not know
 Sentence Fluency	• clear, direct sentences • different sentence types to make the writing flow
 Conventions	• no or few errors in spelling, punctuation, and capitalization

Before you write, read Sally Loz's research report on the next page. Then use the research report rubric on pages 150–151 to decide how well she did. (You might want to look back at What's in a Research Report? on page 146, too!)

Game Time

by Sally Loz

introduction

topic

You might be eight or nine years old, but chances are you've played a game that has been around for thousands of years. What is that game? It's checkers. The game of checkers has a long and surprising history.

body

It isn't clear exactly where and when checkers was first played. However, a board game similar to checkers was discovered in the ruins of an ancient city in Iraq. That game is about 5,000 years old! Another early form of checkers was played in Egypt more than 3,000 years ago. Game boards have been found carved into the stone of ancient Egyptian temples. You might still be able to see one today. The ancient games used smaller boards with different markings.

How did checkers spread to other parts of the world? About 1,300 years ago, some people from Africa invaded Spain. They brought their form of checkers with them. The game changed a little when someone in France decided to play it on a chessboard and use more pieces. The rules changed a few times over the years until the game became our modern game of checkers.

conclusion

Today checkers is played all over the world. It has many different names. If you were in England, you would play draughts (pronounced *drafts*). In Italy you would play darma. Almost anywhere you go, you can play this popular game with its very long history.

Sources:

"board game." *Compton's by Britannica. Britannica Online for Kids.* Encyclopædia Britannica, Inc., 2013. Web. 8 Oct. 20__.

Wulffson, Don. *Toys! Amazing Stories Behind Some Great Inventions.* New York City: Henry Holt and Company, 2000.

Research Report Rubric

Use this rubric to analyze the model. Then use it to plan and score your own research report.

	6	5	4
Ideas	The report answers at least two questions about the topic. Factual examples support the main points.	The report answers one question about the topic. At least one factual example is provided.	The report attempts to answer a question. Example(s) may not be helpful.
Organization	The report is well organized. The beginning is strong, and the conclusion ties everything together.	The report is fairly well organized with a strong beginning and a satisfying conclusion.	The report is somewhat organized. The beginning and conclusion are present.
Voice	The voice sounds knowledgeable and enthusiastic. It comes through to the audience.	The voice sounds knowledgeable and enthusiastic most of the time.	The writer occasionally uses a knowledgeable voice that connects with the audience.
Word Choice	The vocabulary is right for the topic. The words fit the purpose and audience.	Most of the time the vocabulary fits the topic, purpose, and audience.	Sometimes the vocabulary fits the topic. A few words seem too informal or vague.
Sentence Fluency	Well-written sentences are informative and clear. The report is easy to read and understand.	In general, sentences are informative and clear. The report can be read and understood easily.	Most of the report is easy to read and understand. A few sentences are not clear and direct.
Conventions	Verb tenses are correct. The writer's message is clear.	Most verb tenses are correct. The writer's message is clear.	A few verb tenses are incorrect, but they do not confuse the meaning.

+Presentation The text is placed neatly on the page.

	3	2	1	
	The topic is clear. Example(s) may not be factual.	The topic may not be clear. Examples may be unrelated.	The writer does not focus on one topic. Examples are not provided.	Ideas
	Some parts of the report are not well organized. The beginning and conclusion are weak.	The writing is not organized logically. It is difficult to follow.	The text is a collection of random thoughts. The reader cannot follow the message.	Organization
	The voice is weak in parts of the report. The writer needs to connect with the audience more.	The voice of the writer is faint, too formal, or fails to connect with the audience.	Little or no voice is present. The writer does not connect with the audience.	Voice
	More words related to the topic would improve the report.	The words do not fit the writer's purpose or audience.	Word choice feels random, and the writer's purpose is not clear to the audience.	Word Choice
	Some sentences are too long. They may include unnecessary or unfamiliar words.	Most sentences are long and rambling. They confuse the reader.	Run-on, choppy, and incomplete sentences confuse the reader.	Sentence Fluency
	Many verb tenses are incorrect and confuse the reader.	The writing contains many errors. It is very difficult to read.	Serious, frequent errors make the piece very difficult to read and understand.	Conventions

See Appendix B for 4-, 5-, and 6-point informative/explanatory rubrics.

Using the Research Report Rubric to Analyze the Model

Did you notice that the model on page 149 points out some key elements of a research report? As she wrote "Game Time," Sally Loz used these elements to help her write her report. She also used the 6-point rubric on pages 150–151 to plan, draft, revise, and edit the writing. A rubric is a great tool to evaluate writing during the writing process.

To get started, look at the top score for each trait as you study the model. Do you agree that Sally has earned a 6 for each trait?

- **The report answers at least two questions about the topic.**
- **Factual examples support the main points.**

Sally's report answers two questions about the game of checkers. The second paragraph tells how long people have been playing checkers. The third paragraph tells how the game spread around the world.

The writer doesn't just tell us that games like checkers have been around for a long time. She supports this idea by giving factual examples of early forms of the game.

However, a board game similar to checkers was discovered in the ruins of an ancient city in Iraq. That game is about 5,000 years old! Another early form of checkers was played in Egypt more than 3,000 years ago.

- The report is well organized.
- The beginning is strong, and the conclusion ties everything together.

The report is very well organized. It includes an introduction, a body, and a conclusion. Sally's beginning is strong. It made me curious to find out what game she was talking about. Her conclusion refers back to a statement in her introduction.

You might be eight or nine years old, but chances are you've played a game that has been around for thousands of years.

Almost anywhere you go, you can play this popular game with its very long history.

- The voice sounds knowledgeable and enthusiastic.
- It comes through to the audience.

Sally connects with her reader by using a confident, enthusiastic voice all the way through her essay. I can tell that she knows and cares about her topic. I can also tell that she wants to share her topic with me.

How did checkers spread to other parts of the world? About 1,300 years ago, some people from Africa invaded Spain. They brought their form of checkers with them. The game changed a little when someone in France decided to play it on a chessboard and use more pieces.

Using the Research Report Rubric to Analyze the Model

- The vocabulary is right for the topic.
- The words fit the purpose and audience.

The writer does not joke around or talk as if she is telling friends about checkers. She is writing a report to teach people about the history of the game, so she is serious and factual. This helps readers have confidence that what she says is true.

Another early form of checkers was played in Egypt more than 3,000 years ago. Game boards have been found carved into the stone of ancient Egyptian temples. You might still be able to see one today.

- Well-written sentences are informative and clear.
- The report is easy to read and understand.

I really learned a lot about checkers by reading Sally's report. It is well written and interesting, and it is easy to read and understand! In this example, Sally tells about the names checkers has in different parts of the world.

Today checkers is played all over the world. It has many different names. If you were in England, you would play draughts (pronounced *drafts*). In Italy you would play darma. Almost anywhere you go, you can play this popular game with its very long history.

- **Verb tenses are correct.**
- **The writer's message is clear.**

All verb tenses are formed correctly in Sally's report. This makes her message clear and easy to read. In these two sentences, the writer uses the correct past-tense forms of the verbs *bring*, *change*, and *decide*.

They brought their form of checkers with them. The game changed a little when someone in France decided to play it on a chessboard and use more pieces.

+Presentation The text is placed neatly on the page.

My Turn!

Now I'm going to write my own research report. I will use the rubric and good writing strategies to help me. Read along to see how I do it.

Prewrite

Focus on **Ideas**

The Rubric Says The report answers at least two questions about the topic.

Writing Strategy Choose a topic and write two research questions.

My assignment is to write a research report on a topic that I want to learn more about. I really like snowshoeing. My mom told me that Native Americans used snowshoes hundreds of years ago. I want to know more about the history of snowshoes. First, I'll write two questions that I have about them. Then, I'll do research using books and websites to find the answers. I'll be sure to take notes and cite my sources as I gather my information.

My Topic: History of Snowshoes

Question 1: Where and when were snowshoes first used?

Question 2: Have snowshoes changed over the years?

My Notes:

- early snowshoes—made of wood and leather
- snowshoes—came to America over land bridge from Asia
- new snowshoes—made of metal and cloth

My Sources:

Van Vleet, Carmella. *Amazing Arctic & Antarctic Projects You Can Build Yourself.* White River Junction: Nomad, 2008.

"winter sports." *Britannica Online for Kids.* Encyclopædia Britannica, Inc., 2013. Web. May 1, 20__.

Write

Choose a topic to research. Write two questions about that topic. Take notes and cite your sources.

Prewrite

Focus on **Organization**

The Rubric Says The report is well organized.

Writing Strategy Use a Network Tree to organize the notes.

I know from the rubric that my report should be well organized. A Network Tree will help me plan my report. First I'll write down my questions. Then I'll write the facts I found that answer the questions.

Writer's Term

Network Tree

A **Network Tree** organizes information. For a research report, the topic goes at the top of the tree, questions go on the next level, and facts that answer the questions go on the bottom level.

Network Tree

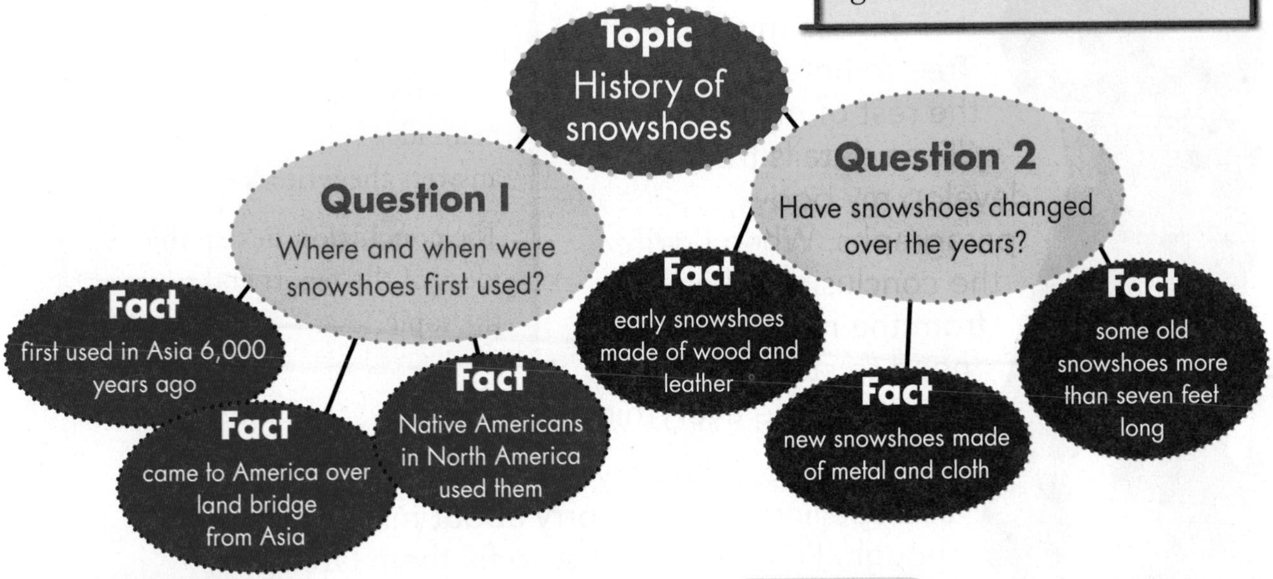

Topic
History of snowshoes

Question 1
Where and when were snowshoes first used?

Fact
first used in Asia 6,000 years ago

Fact
came to America over land bridge from Asia

Fact
Native Americans in North America used them

Question 2
Have snowshoes changed over the years?

Fact
early snowshoes made of wood and leather

Fact
new snowshoes made of metal and cloth

Fact
some old snowshoes more than seven feet long

Analyze

Look at Emma's notes and Network Tree. How will they help Emma write a good research report?

Write

Think about the topic and questions you decided to focus on. Use a Network Tree to organize facts that answer your questions.

Draft

Focus on **Organization**

The Rubric Says The beginning is strong, and the conclusion ties everything together.

Writing Strategy Write an introduction that will capture the reader's interest.

I'm ready to write my draft. I will start by writing an interesting introduction so my readers will want to find out more about my topic.

I'll use my Network Tree to help me write the rest of my report. I will use details from it to develop my body paragraphs. When I write the conclusion, I know from the rubric that I will need to state the topic again and tie everything together.

As I write, I'll do my best with grammar and spelling. I won't worry about mistakes, though. I'll have a chance to fix them later.

Writer's Term

Parts of a Report

The **introduction** is the first paragraph of a report. It states the topic and should catch the audience's attention.

The **body** is the main part of the report. It comes between the introduction and the conclusion. The body gives the main ideas of the report and answers the writer's questions.

The **conclusion** ties up the ideas of the report and restates the topic.

Proofreading Marks

⊐ Indent	ℓ Take out something
≡ Make uppercase	⊙ Add a period
/ Make lowercase	¶ New paragraph
∧ Add something	(sp) Spelling error

Walking on Snow

Have you ever tried walking in deep snow? If you have ever tried walking in deep snow, you know that your feet sink in the deep snow, and it is hard to move. Long ago, people found a solution to this problum–snowshoes!

introduction captures readers' attention

Many scientists think that snowshoes were first used about 6,000 years ago in asia. Some scientists believe that people first bring them two America by crossing over a land bridge That bridge join Asia and Alaska. Native Americans start wearing snowshoes. They made many different kinds of snowshoes for different types of snow.

Snowshoes have change over the years. The old ones had wood frames and leather webbing. Some were more than seven feet long. Modern snowshoes are usually made of metal and cloth. Most kids who use them want to have a blast in the snow!

Analyze

Read the beginning of Emma's draft. How does her introduction make you want to keep reading?

Write

Use your Network Tree to write your draft. Craft your introduction to capture your readers' attention.

Revise

Focus on **Voice**

The Rubric Says The voice sounds knowledgeable and enthusiastic. It comes through to the audience.

Writing Strategy Think about the audience and the purpose for writing.

The rubric reminds me that my writing voice should come through to my audience. I think I've done a good job of sharing what I learned about the history of snowshoes. But I also want to hold my reader's interest. I found a place in my draft where I can speak to the reader and show enthusiasm. Do you think my voice comes through better now?

[DRAFT]

Snowshoes have change over the years. The old ones had wood frames and leather webbing. You may be surprised to learn that ~~S~~some were more than seven feet long~~.~~!

improved voice

Write

Read your draft aloud. Be sure your voice sounds knowledgeable and enthusiastic all the way through your report.

Revise

Focus on **Word Choice**

The Rubric Says The vocabulary is right for the topic.

Writing Strategy Use words that fit the topic and the purpose for writing.

The rubric reminds me that all my words should fit my topic. I also want my readers to take my report seriously. As I reread my draft, I found one place where I used casual words that don't belong in a research report. I'll replace them with words that fit my topic and purpose for writing.

Writer's Term

Vocabulary

Vocabulary is the choice of words a writer uses. It should fit the topic and the type of writing.

[DRAFT]

snowshoes are usually made of metal and cloth. Most ~~kids~~ people who use them want to have ~~a blast~~ fun in the snow!

replaced casual words

Analyze

How do Emma's new word choices improve her report?

Write

Read your report again and think about the vocabulary. Does it fit the topic and audience? If not, revise your report so that it does.

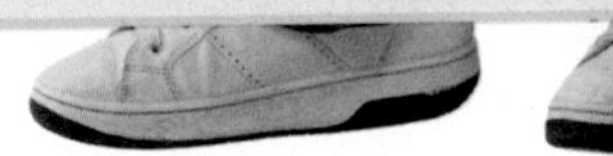

Revise

Focus on Sentence Fluency

The Rubric Says Well-written sentences are informative and clear. The report is easy to read and understand.

Writing Strategy Take out unnecessary or repeated words.

The rubric says that my sentences need to be well written, informative, and clear. My friend Joy listened as I read my report. Even though my introduction grabbed her attention, my second sentence really confused her! She helped me realize that I repeated some words. I'll take out those words so that my meaning will be clear.

[DRAFT]

Have you ever tried walking in deep snow? If you have ~~ever tried walking in deep snow?~~, you know that your feet sink in ~~the deep snow,~~ and it is hard to move.

took out repeated words

Write

Reread your draft. As you revise, take out any unnecessary or repeated words to make your writing clear and easy to understand.

Edit

Focus on **Conventions**

The Rubric Says Verb tenses are correct. The writer's message is clear.

Writing Strategy Use correct verb tense.

The rubric reminds me that I should pay special attention to verb tenses. When I reread my draft, I see places where I didn't use past-tense verbs correctly. I also notice that I wrote *two* instead of *to* and forgot to end a sentence with a period. I'll fix those mistakes now.

Writer's Term

Past-Tense Verbs

Past-tense verbs show that action happened in the past. Many end in **-ed**.

printed **started** **talked** **washed**

Some verbs don't add **-ed** to make the past tense. These are called **irregular verbs**.

brought **did** **ran** **went**

[DRAFT]

6,000 years ago in Asia. Some scientists believe that people first ~~bring~~ brought them ~~two~~ to America by crossing over a land bridge. That bridge join(ed) Asia and Alaska.

corrected past-tense verbs

Analyze

Look at Emma's edits. Are the corrections necessary and clear? How do Emma's changes make her writing more understandable?

Write

Conventions

Reread your draft. Fix any errors in verb tenses. Check to make sure that capitalization, punctuation, and spelling are correct.

For more practice with past-tense verbs, use the exercises on the next two pages.

Conventions **Grammar, Usage & Mechanics**

Past-Tense Verbs

Know the Rule

Past-tense verbs show that the action happened in the past. Many past-tense verbs end in *-ed*.

Some verbs do not add *-ed* to form the past tense. Here are the past-tense forms of some of these irregular verbs.

Present Tense	Past Tense	With *have, has,* or *had*
take(s)	took	taken
sleep(s)	slept	slept
go(es)	went	gone
eat(s)	ate	eaten

Examples:
I **go** to the mountains. I **went** to the mountains. I **have gone** to the mountains.

Practice the Rule

Number a sheet of paper 1–10. Read each sentence. Write the word in ( ) that correctly completes the sentence.

1. Last year my sister and I _____ a trip to the mountains. (took/taked)
2. We both _____ to learn to ski. (wanted/wants)
3. I had not _____ well because I was so excited. (sleeped/slept)
4. I _____ someone to teach me to ski. (wants/wanted)
5. I soon _____ how to put on my skis. (learn/learned)
6. Later in the morning, we _____ a ride on the ski lift. (taked/took)
7. At the top of the mountain, everyone _____ off the lift. (jump/jumped)
8. I had _____ my eyes, and I forgot where I was. (closed/closes)
9. Suddenly my chair _____, and I was going down the mountain. (turn/turned)
10. While others _____ down the mountain, I rode down. (skis/skied)

Verbs and Time

Know the Rule

The tense of a verb shows when an action takes place. A **present-tense verb** shows that the action happens in the present.

Example:
Both my sister and I **ski** in the winter.

A **past-tense verb** shows that the action happened in the past.

Example:
Yesterday we **skied** for six hours.

Practice the Rule

Number a sheet of paper 1–10. Decide whether the underlined verb is a past-tense verb or a present-tense verb. Write **past tense** or **present tense** after the number.

1. I love the winter.
2. My sister and I take skiing lessons every Thursday.
3. We go up the mountain on a chair lift.
4. We went down on our skis.
5. My brother flew down the mountain on his snowboard.
6. Uncle Larry stays in the lodge by the fireplace.
7. At lunchtime we all ate the delicious sandwiches Dad made.
8. In the afternoon, the ski patrol brought an injured skier down the mountain on a special toboggan.
9. We sleep well after a whole day of skiing.
10. I want to go skiing again next week!

Publish

+Presentation

Publishing Strategy Read the report to a small group of classmates.

Presentation Strategy Balance the amount of white space and text.

My research report is finished! Now it's time to publish it. We will present our reports in class soon, so I want to make sure it's ready. I also want my report to be easy for me to read aloud. I'll make sure that my writing isn't crowded on the page. I'll use good margins and extra space between lines so that I won't lose my place while I'm reading. I'll read through the report one more time. Here's my final checklist.

My Final Checklist

Did I—

- ✔ use verb tenses correctly?
- ✔ properly cite all my sources?
- ✔ balance the amount of white space and text?
- ✔ use neat handwriting or word processing?
- ✔ put my name on my paper?

Write

Make a checklist for your research report. Then make a final copy to read aloud to classmates. Be prepared to answer any questions they may have.

Walking on Snow
by Emma

Have you ever tried walking in deep snow? If you have, you know that your feet sink in, and it is hard to move. Long ago, people found a solution to this problem—snowshoes!

Many scientists think that snowshoes were first used about 6,000 years ago in Asia. Some scientists believe that people first brought them to America by crossing over a land bridge. That bridge joined Asia and Alaska. Native Americans started wearing snowshoes so they could hunt, trap, and move around more easily in winter. They made many different kinds of snowshoes for different types of snow.

Snowshoes have changed over the years. The old ones had wood frames and leather webbing. You may be surprised to learn that some were more than seven feet long! Modern snowshoes are usually made of metal and cloth. Most people who use them want to have fun in the snow!

Snowshoeing is very popular today. Modern snowshoes are simple to use. You don't need to learn any fancy footwork. Just strap them on your feet, and do something people did thousands of years ago!

Sources:

Van Vleet, Carmella. *Amazing Arctic & Antarctic Projects You Can Build Yourself.* White River Junction: Nomad, 2008.

"winter sports." *Compton's by Britannica. Britannica Online for Kids.* Encyclopædia Britannica, Inc., 2013. Web. 1 May 20__.

Analyze

Use the rubric to score Emma's finished report. Are all the traits of a good report included? Use the rubric to score your report, too.

What's a Problem-Solution Essay?

It's an essay that tells about a problem and different ways to solve it.

What's in a Problem-Solution Essay?

A Problem
A problem is something that I think needs to be solved. For example, I might write to explain my ideas for getting students involved in recycling projects.

Multiple Paragraphs
A problem-solution essay needs at least four paragraphs. The introduction presents the problem in detail, the second and third paragraphs present possible solutions, and the conclusion ties the main ideas together.

Solutions
These are some of the ways the problem could be solved. I'll think of some ideas first. Then I may talk to my friends to see if they have any other ideas.

Why write a Problem-Solution Essay?

There are many reasons to write a problem-solution essay. Here is a reason that I can think of for writing one.

To Explain

I can write a problem-solution essay when I see a problem and want to bring about a change in order to solve it.

In education, a principal might write a problem-solution essay about ways to improve students' test scores.

In business, a sales manager might write a problem-solution essay about ways to increase sales.

In science, a zoologist might write a problem-solution essay about ways to protect and save endangered animals.

Linking Informative/Explanatory Writing Traits to a Problem-Solution Essay

In this chapter, you will write a solution to a problem. This type of informative/explanatory writing is called a problem-solution essay. Emma will guide you through the stages of the writing process: Prewrite, Draft, Revise, Edit, and Publish. In each stage, Emma will show you important writing strategies that are linked to the Informative/Explanatory Writing Traits below.

Informative/Explanatory Writing Traits

Ideas	• a clear, focused topic • supporting details that are complete and accurate
Organization	• related information that is grouped in paragraphs • a strong introduction, body, and conclusion • linking words and phrases that connect ideas
Voice	• a voice that connects directly to the reader
Word Choice	• exact words that are appropriate for the reader • definitions for words that the reader may not know
Sentence Fluency	• clear, direct sentences • different sentence types to make the writing flow
Conventions	• no or few errors in spelling, punctuation, and capitalization

Before you write, read Enrique Aguilar's problem-solution essay on the next page. Then use the problem-solution essay rubric on pages 172–173 to decide how well he did. (You might want to look back at What's in a Problem-Solution Essay? on page 168, too!)

Clearing the Roads at Rush Hour

by Enrique Aguilar

"Rush hour" is a busy time on the roads here in Springfield. It happens in the early morning and late afternoon. Everyone is trying to get somewhere. Workers are going to their jobs. Students are headed toward their schools.

During rush hour, traffic jams fill the roads. Cars, buses, and trucks come to a complete stop. Traffic jams cause many problems. First of all, they make people late for work. Second, where there is more traffic, there are more traffic accidents.
And finally, cars waste gasoline while they are stuck in traffic.

the problem

Yes, rush hour congestion and traffic jams are big problems. It's time to find solutions.

multiple paragraphs

What can we do to ease congestion? One way is to change the way we build roads. If the roads were wider, they could handle more cars. People could also take trains and buses instead of driving their cars. One bus could take the place of 40 cars. Hundreds of people can ride a train at the same time. Or, if people have to drive for some reason, they could form a carpool with their neighbors.

possible solution

What if more people could work or study at home? They wouldn't have to travel to their offices and schools at all. Computers make it possible to do this.

possible solution

There is one more way to help clear the roads at rush hour. You can have a home close to where you work. People who live in cities and large towns such as Springfield often walk or ride a bicycle to work. Many of them don't need a car at all.

possible solution

There are ways to fix the rush hour problem. Better roads can improve traffic flow. Using other transportation or working from home can clear the roads. Let's find a way to say, "Problem solved!"

conclusion

Sources:

Gray, Leon. *Transportation.* New York City: DK Publishing, 2012.
"Public Transportation Benefits." *Apta: American Public Transportation Association.* American Public Transportation Association, 2013. Web. 15 Oct. 20__.

Problem-Solution Essay Rubric

Use this rubric to analyze the model. Then use it to plan and score your own problem-solution essay.

	6	5	4
Ideas	The essay states the problem and presents several possible solutions clearly.	The essay presents the problem and at least two possible solutions.	The essay presents the problem and only one solution.
Organization	The beginning is strong. The conclusion ties everything together. Linking words and phrases connect ideas and guide the reader.	The beginning is strong. The conclusion ties everything together. Most linking words and phrases connect ideas and guide the reader.	The beginning is weak. The conclusion ties most of the ideas together. More linking words and phrases are needed to connect ideas.
Voice	The writer's voice is serious and informative. It is clear that the writer cares about the topic.	The writer's voice is serious and informative most of the time.	The voice sounds serious and informative in the beginning but fades.
Word Choice	Exact words hold the reader's interest. No vague words have been used.	Most of the time the author uses the exact words needed to hold the reader's interest.	A few vague words could be replaced with more descriptive ones to hold the reader's interest.
Sentence Fluency	A variety of sentence types makes the essay flow smoothly.	Sentence variety is inconsistently used but the essay still flows smoothly.	A few more sentences of different types would make the essay flow better.
Conventions	Nouns and pronouns are used correctly. The writing is clear.	Most nouns and pronouns are used correctly. The writing is easy to understand.	A few nouns and pronouns are used incorrectly, but they do not confuse the meaning.

+Presentation The essay is neat and legible.

	3	2	1
Ideas	The essay presents a problem without possible solutions.	The essay does not clearly state the problem and offers weak or no solutions.	The essay does not have the organization of a problem-solution essay.
Organization	The beginning and conclusion are weak. Few linking words and phrases connect ideas.	The beginning and conclusion are very weak or missing. Linking words and phrases are missing.	The writing is not organized into paragraphs. It is impossible to follow the writer's ideas.
Voice	The voice may not match the writer's purpose in places. It is not clear how much the writer knows about the topic.	The voice is weak or inappropriate. The reader cannot tell whether the writer cares about the topic.	The writer's voice does not come through at all.
Word Choice	The words show limited knowledge of the topic or are too general to be meaningful.	The writer's words are dull and ordinary. The reader must make the connections.	Many incorrectly used words cause the reader to lose interest.
Sentence Fluency	Too many simple sentences make the writing seem unfinished and choppy.	Many sentences are incorrect or incomplete, which makes the piece hard to understand.	This piece is challenging to read aloud due to repeated sentence beginnings and lack of variety.
Conventions	Many nouns and pronouns are incorrect and confuse the reader.	The writing contains many errors. Since it is very difficult to read, the reader must read slowly.	Serious, frequent errors make understanding the writing challenging, if not impossible.

See Appendix B for 4-, 5-, and 6-point informative/explanatory rubrics.

Problem-Solution Essay Using the Rubric to Analyze the Model

Did you notice that the model on page 171 points out some key elements of a problem-solution essay? As he wrote "Clearing the Roads at Rush Hour," Enrique Aguilar used these elements to help him describe a problem and possible solutions. He also used the 6-point rubric on pages 172–173 to plan, draft, revise, and edit the writing. A rubric is a great tool to evaluate writing during the writing process.

To get started, look at the top score for each trait as you study the model. Do you agree that Enrique has earned a 6 for each trait?

- **The essay states the problem and presents several possible solutions clearly.**

Enrique tells exactly what he is worried about. He explains the problem in detail in the first two paragraphs. In the third paragraph he clearly states the problem again.

Enrique also gives clear ideas about how the problem can be solved. Here is one example.

> What if more people could work or study at home? They wouldn't have to travel to their offices and schools at all.

- **The beginning is strong.**
- **The conclusion ties everything together.**
- **Linking words and phrases connect ideas and guide the reader.**

Enrique presents the problem right away. He gets the reader's attention by writing about something familiar to most people. In the second paragraph, he uses linking words and phrases (*First of all, Second, And finally*) to guide the reader. His conclusion ties the solutions together.

Traffic jams cause many problems. First of all, they make people late for work. Second, where there is more traffic, there are more traffic accidents. And finally, cars waste gasoline while they are stuck in traffic.

There are ways to fix the rush hour problem. Better roads can improve traffic flow. Using other transportation or working from home can clear the roads. Let's find a way to say, "Problem solved!"

- **The writer's voice is serious and informative.**
- **It is clear that the writer cares about the topic.**

Enrique writes about a serious problem and offers serious solutions. He knows and cares about his topic. He tells us in the first sentence that this is his own town he is writing about.

"Rush hour" is a busy time on the roads here in Springfield.

Using the Problem-Solution Essay Rubric to Analyze the Model

- Exact words hold the reader's interest.
- No vague words have been used.

The writer is specific in telling how to solve the traffic problem. He doesn't just say that people could use other vehicles instead of driving cars. He tells which vehicles. He doesn't just say that buses can take the place of lots of cars. He tells how many cars.

People could also take trains and buses instead of driving their cars. One bus could take the place of 40 cars. Hundreds of people can ride a train at the same time.

- A variety of sentence types makes the essay flow smoothly.

The sentences in the essay are not all the same type. They are not all simple or compound or complex. In this passage, Enrique wrote one simple sentence and two complex sentences. This variety makes the essay flow smoothly.

What can we do to ease congestion? One way is to change the way we build roads. If the roads were wider, they could handle more cars.

- Nouns and pronouns are used correctly.
- The writing is clear.

I reread Enrique's essay. The writing is easy to read and understand. He has used nouns and pronouns correctly.

Hundreds of people can ride a train at the same time. Or, if people have to drive for some reason, they could form a carpool with their neighbors.

Presentation The essay is neat and legible.

My Turn!

Now I'm going to write a problem-solution essay. I'll use the rubric and good writing strategies to help me. Follow along to see how I do it.

Prewrite

Focus on **Ideas**

The Rubric Says The essay states the problem and presents possible solutions clearly.

Writing Strategy Decide on a problem. Write notes about possible solutions.

My teacher asked us to think about a problem that interests us. He wants us to write a problem-solution essay telling ways to solve the problem.

I'll write about a problem I've heard my parents talk about. Here in Montana there are a lot of rural areas. Some people live so far from cities that it is hard for them to get to the doctor's office. I've read about some interesting ways people use technology to help with this problem. I'll write down possible solutions that will interest my classmates.

Technology and Health Care

- ✔ e-mail
- ✔ websites
- ✔ photographs
- ✔ robots
- ✔ videoconferences
- ✔ scanners

My Sources

"High blood pressure." Mayo Foundation for Medical Education and Research, 2013. Web. February 21, 20__.

"Robot doctors get thumbs-up from students." *NBC News*, 2013. Web. February 22, 20__.

Write

Choose a problem that interests you. List possible solutions. Then choose two or three solutions to write about in a problem-solution essay. Be sure to list your sources.

Prewrite

Focus on **Organization**

The Rubric Says The beginning is strong.

Writing Strategy Make a Problem-Solutions Chart to help summarize the problem and organize the notes.

I've used different kinds of graphic organizers. I think a Problem-Solutions Chart will best help me organize my ideas. The rubric reminds me that my first paragraph needs to grab the reader's attention. A Problem-Solutions Chart can help me decide what goes into my introduction and what kind of linking words to use.

Problem-Solutions Chart

Problem

What is the problem?

health care for people in rural areas

Why is it a problem?

distance from a doctor's office

Solutions

computers robots

Conclusion

people get the health care they need

Writer's Term

Problem-Solutions Chart

A **Problem-Solutions Chart** organizes information. It tells about a problem and solutions.

Analyze

Look at Emma's Problem-Solutions Chart. How will it help her write a good problem-solution essay?

Write

Think about the problem you want to write about. Organize your ideas in a Problem-Solutions Chart.

Draft

Focus on **Voice**

The Rubric Says The writer's voice is serious and informative. It is clear that the writer cares about the topic.

Writing Strategy Sound like an expert on the topic.

Now I'm ready to write my draft. I know from the rubric that I need to sound serious about my topic. My audience will trust what I say if I sound well-informed and support my ideas with factual details.

I'll use the ideas for solutions from my Problem-Solutions Chart to write my essay. As I write, I'll do my best with grammar and spelling, but I won't worry too much about mistakes.
I can fix any errors later.

Writer's Term

Audience

The **audience** is the person or people who will read or hear what you write. You should keep your audience in mind all the way through the writing process.

[DRAFT]

Proofreading Marks

Indent	Take out something
Make uppercase	Add a period
Make lowercase	New paragraph
Add something	Spelling error

High-Tech Health

For some people with problems, getting to the doctor's office is difficult. They might live a long distance away. They do not drive cars or use buses or trains. What should they do? Today modern technology helps people get the health care they need through the use of machines.

Doctors have store patients' medical stuff on computers. Computers also help doctors share stuff with their patients. Patients can describe there problems in an e-mail. Doctors can tell patients what to do in order to feel better. Patients can even send photographs to help the doctor understand the problem.

Their are several medical tests patients can do on their own, such as checking their blood pressure. This information can be sent to the doctor's office.

facts make the writer sound like an expert

Analyze

Read the beginning of Emma's draft. In what ways does Emma sound like an expert?

Write

Refer to your Problem-Solutions Chart as you write your own draft. Remember to use facts to help you sound like an expert.

Revise

Focus on **Ideas**

The Rubric Says The essay states the problem and presents several possible solutions clearly.

Writing Strategy Check the information to be sure it is correct.

I have finished my draft. My next step is to improve it. I think I've done a good job of sounding like an expert. Now I have to make sure my facts are correct. If my facts are not correct, then my solutions won't work. Also, my readers won't trust what I have to say.

Writer's Term

Fact-Checking

Fact-checking is the process of reading through a piece of writing and checking each fact for accuracy.

I see a sentence in my very first paragraph that may not actually be true. I need to fix that.

[DRAFT]

They ~~do~~ might not drive cars or use buses or trains.

corrected information

Write

Fact-check your draft. If you are unsure of a piece of information, check your sources again. Then revise any information that is incorrect.

Revise

Focus on **Word Choice**

The Rubric Says Exact words hold the reader's interest. No vague words have been used.

Writing Strategy Replace any vague words with exact words.

The rubric tells me to choose exact words, not vague ones. The words I use should help the reader picture the problem or solution. I noticed that I used the word *machines.* That's pretty vague. There are many kinds of machines. I should say what kinds of machines I mean.

Writer's Term

Vague Word

A **vague word** is a word that is unclear. A vague word may be too general.

should they do? Today modern technology helps people get the health care they need through the use of ~~machines~~ computers and robots.

replaced vague words with exact words

Analyze

Look at Emma's revisions. Do her exact words hold your interest? How do they make the essay clearer?

Write

Read your draft again. Look for any vague words. Replace them with exact words to make your writing clearer.

Revise

Focus on Sentence Fluency

The Rubric Says A variety of sentence types makes the essay flow smoothly.

Writing Strategy Use a variety of sentence types.

The rubric reminds me that I need to have a variety of sentence types. I reread my draft and saw that I wrote a lot of simple sentences. I found two sentences that I can combine into a compound sentence. That will help my essay flow. I will also check to see if all my verb tenses are formed correctly.

Writer's Term

Sentence Types

Simple sentences have a subject and a predicate.

Compound sentences have two independent clauses, which are connected with a punctuation mark and a conjunction.

[DRAFT]

Patients can describe their problems in an e-mail, and doctors can tell them what do do in order to feel better. Patients can even send photographs to help the doctor understand the problem.

Write

Check your draft to see if you have too many sentences of the same type. Revise your writing to add sentence variety.

Edit

Focus on **Conventions**

The Rubric Says Nouns and pronouns are used correctly. The writing is clear.

Writing Strategy Make sure nouns and pronouns are used correctly.

I always check my spelling, punctuation, and capitalization whenever I write something. The rubric reminds me to be sure I have used nouns and pronouns correctly. I'll check to make sure that I formed plural nouns the right way.

I noticed mistakes in my conclusion. I'll fix them now.

Writer's Term

A **singular noun** identifies one person, place, or thing. *(violin, class)* Add **-s** or **-es** to most singular nouns to form a **plural noun**. *(violins, classes)* **Irregular plural nouns** are formed in different ways and must be memorized. *(foot/feet; child/children; person/people; leaf/leaves)*

[DRAFT]

corrected a spelling error

Everyone needs to visit a doctors now and then. Today computer s and robots are helping more people get the helth a care they need.

corrected errors in singular and plural nouns

Analyze

Look at Emma's edits. Has she proofread carefully and corrected the errors in the conclusion? How have her edits clarified her writing?

Write — Conventions

Edit your draft for spelling, capitalization, and punctuation. Fix any errors in singular nouns, plural nouns, and pronouns.

For more practice with singular nouns, plural nouns, and pronouns, use the exercises on the next two pages.

Singular and Plural Nouns

Know the Rule

A **singular noun** shows "one." (*girl*)
A **plural noun** shows "more than one." (*girls*)

- To make most nouns plural, add *-s* to the singular noun. (*robot/robots*)
- If the noun ends in **s, ch, sh, x,** or **z,** add *-es.* (*brush/brushes*)
- For most nouns that end in **y,** change the **y** to **i** and add *-es.* (*family/families*)
- For nouns that end in a vowel plus **y,** just add *-s.* (*boy/boys*)

Irregular plural nouns are formed in different ways and must be memorized. Some nouns do not change at all. (*tooth/teeth; man/men; mouse/mice; wolf/wolves; fish/fish; deer/deer*)

Practice the Rule

Number a sheet of paper 1–10. Read each sentence. Write the sentences, adding the word in ( ) to the blank. Make the word plural if you need to.

(robot) **1.** In movies, we see _____ that look like humans.
(machine) **2.** A robot, however, is a _____.
(job) **3.** Robots can do many _____ that humans cannot.
(robot) **4.** One kind of _____ is called the Tentacle Arm.
(octopus) **5.** Tentacle Arms got their name because they move like _____.
(factory) **6.** Robots in _____ do jobs such as putting wrappers on ice cream bars.
(laboratory) **7.** Other robots are used in _____.
(person) **8.** Robots can do tasks that would be too dangerous for _____ to do.
(name) **9.** The _____ of robots tell you what they do.
(material) **10.** A robot called HazBot explores hazardous _____.

Pronouns for Things

Know the Rule

The pronouns **this** and **these** refer to a thing or things close by.
The pronouns **that** and **those** refer to a thing or things far away.

Practice the Rule

Number a sheet of paper 1–10. Decide whether the thing or things being referred to are close by or far away. Write the correct pronoun.

1. Take _____ bag of clothes right here to the clothing drive. (that/this)
2. I'm wearing my sweatshirt, so _____ must be yours over there. (that/this)
3. Are _____ your shoes upstairs in the hall? (these/those)
4. _____ is his father's car over there. (That/This)
5. The dishes I'm holding are clean, but _____ over there are dirty. (these/those)
6. _____ are my best friends sitting next to me. (These/Those)
7. "What is _____?" asked Mom as she pulled a ball of paper out of my backpack. (that/this)
8. "Look over there. Did you see _____?" shouted Eli. (that/this)
9. "Are _____ the batteries you want?" I said as I held out my hand. (these/those)
10. "No, I need _____," Mike said, pointing up at the shelf. (these/those)

Publish + Presentation

Publishing Strategy Display your essay on family night.

Presentation Strategy Use neat handwriting or word processing.

I've finished my problem-solution essay! It's time to publish it. Students in my class wrote about many important problems in our community and world. We wanted to share our ideas for solutions, so we are planning a family night. All the essays will be put on display. Family members and friends will be able to read about topics that interest them.

I want to be sure to write neatly or use word processing. People won't be able to read or understand my essay if it is messy! If I decide to use a computer to write my final draft, I'll use the spell-check feature. I still have to proofread my essay, though. The computer doesn't catch every mistake!

My Final Checklist

Did I—

- ✔ use singular nouns, plural nouns, and pronouns correctly?
- ✔ use neat handwriting or word processing?
- ✔ put my name on my paper?
- ✔ include my sources?

Write

Make a checklist for your own problem-solution essay. Then make a final copy. Help your teacher create a display of the essays, and plan a family night so others may read your work.

High-Tech Health

by Emma

For some people, getting to the doctor's office is difficult. They might live a long distance away. They might not drive cars or use buses or trains. What should they do? Today modern technology helps people get the health care they need through the use of computers and robots.

For many years, doctors have stored patients' medical histories on computers. Now computers also help doctors share information with their patients. Patients can describe their problems in an e-mail, and doctors can tell them what to do in order to feel better. Patients can even send photographs to help the doctor understand the problem.

There are several medical tests patients can do on their own, such as checking their blood pressure. This information can be sent to the doctor's office.

Some remote hospitals have robotic doctors. Human doctors use a control called a "joystick" to move the robot around the room, so they can "look" at the patient. Doctors and patients can see each other on video screens built into the robot. The robot can also act as a telephone that lets the doctor and patient talk to each other.

Everyone needs to visit a doctor now and then. Today computers and robots are helping more people get the health care they need.

Sources

"High blood pressure." *Mayo Clinic.* Mayo Foundation for Medical Education and Research, 2013. Web. 21 Feb. 20__.

"Robot doctors get thumbs-up from students." *NBC News*, 2013. Web. 22 Feb. 20__.

Analyze

Use the rubric to analyze Emma's essay and your own.

What's a Business Letter?

It's a letter to a place of business, such as a store or a manufacturer.

What's in a Business Letter?

Greeting
The greeting usually starts with *Dear* and the person's name, followed by a colon (:).

Organization
The beginning of the letter tells your purpose for writing. The middle of the letter includes details and facts. The end of the letter restates the purpose.

Heading and Inside Address
The heading is your address and the date. The inside address shows to whom you are writing and the address of the business.

Body
This is where the message is. The body gives details about the reason for writing the letter.

Closing and Signature
The closing is often *Sincerely* followed by a comma (,) and your full name. Your full name should be signed. Below your signature, print or type your name.

Why write a Business Letter?

The main purpose for writing a business letter is to make a request or to give information.

To Ask

In a business letter you can ask for

- information. For example, you can request information about a product.
- something to be done. For example, you might ask a business to replace something you bought that does not work properly.

To Tell or Inform

You can explain something. For example, you might want to tell a business how much you like a product you bought there or praise someone who helped you. You can also tell a business how much your school group is charging for items you are making for a fundraising activity.

Linking Informative/Explanatory Writing Traits to a Business Letter

In this chapter, you will write a letter to a business. This type of informative/explanatory writing is called a business letter. Emma will guide you through the stages of the writing process: Prewrite, Draft, Revise, Edit, and Publish. In each stage, Emma will show you important writing strategies that are linked to the Informative/Explanatory Writing Traits below.

Informative/Explanatory Writing Traits

Ideas	• a clear, focused topic • supporting details that are complete and accurate
Organization	• related information that is grouped in paragraphs • a strong introduction, body, and conclusion • linking words and phrases that connect ideas
Voice	• a voice that connects directly to the reader
Word Choice	• exact words that are appropriate for the reader • definitions for words that the reader may not know
Sentence Fluency	• clear, direct sentences • different sentence types to make the writing flow
Conventions	• no or few errors in spelling, punctuation, and capitalization

Before you write, read Ping Yu's business letter on the next page. Then use the business letter rubric on pages 194–195 to decide how well he did. (You might want to look back at What's in a Business Letter? on page 190, too!)

342 High Crest Avenue
Victorville, CA 92395
August 28, 20__

Go Fly a Kite Company
298 Linwood Road
Cincinnati, OH 45208

Dear Go Fly a Kite Company:

I am writing to ask you for a refund of $7.00. On August 21, I ordered four dragon kites from you. I received the kites a couple of days ago. However, when I opened the box, there were only three kites. Inside the box there was also a letter. It said that you were out of dragon kites right now, and that you would send me another kite as soon as you got more.

I don't want to wait for another kite. I would rather just get the money back for the kite you did not send.

Each kite was $7.00. I paid $28.00 for four. Would you please refund me the $7.00 for the kite I did not get?

Sincerely,

Ping Yu

Ping Yu

Business Letter Rubric

Use this rubric to analyze the model. Then use it to plan and score your own business letter.

	6	5	4
Ideas	The topic is clear. Strong facts and details develop the topic.	The topic is clear. Most facts and details are strong and develop the topic.	The topic is clear. One fact or detail may not develop the topic.
Organization	Information is organized and follows proper business letter format. Helpful linking words and phrases connect the writer's ideas.	Most information is organized and follows business letter format. Linking words and phrases connect ideas.	Information is organized and follows business letter format. Some linking words and phrases are needed to connect similar ideas.
Voice	The writer uses a polite and formal voice all the way through.	The writer uses a polite and formal voice most of the time.	The writer uses a polite voice sometimes. It may be too informal or casual in parts.
Word Choice	The writing has just the right number of words to give the information.	The writing has some words that are not necessary for meaning.	The writing has too many words that are not necessary for meaning.
Sentence Fluency	Sentences are different lengths and flow smoothly.	Sentences are mostly different lengths and flow smoothly.	A few sentences in a row are the same length, interrupting the flow.
Conventions	The letter is error free and punctuated correctly. Prepositional phrases are correct.	The letter contains occasional errors. Prepositional phrases are correct.	A few minor errors are present, but they do not confuse the reader. Prepositional phrases are correct.

+Presentation The letter has all six parts. The letter is neat and legible.

	3	2	1
Ideas	The topic is stated. The facts or details are weak.	A topic is stated. Facts or details may not belong to the topic.	No topic is stated. The details may not belong together.
Organization	Some information may be out of order or hard to follow. Linking words and phrases may be repeated or used incorrectly.	Parts of the business letter are out of order or missing. Linking words and phrases are confusing or missing.	Information is not organized. Linking words and phrases are not used.
Voice	The writer's voice is not consistent throughout the letter.	The writer uses a voice that is not appropriate for the purpose of the letter.	The voice is very weak or absent.
Word Choice	The writing contains many extra words that confuse the reader and are not necessary for meaning.	The writing is wordy and confusing, making it difficult to read.	The writing is wordy, and the meaning is lost in the extra words.
Sentence Fluency	Many sentences are the same length and distract the reader.	Most sentences are not clear or complete.	Sentences are incomplete or written incorrectly.
Conventions	Many errors confuse the reader. Some prepositions are incorrect.	Many errors make the text difficult to read. The reader must fill in the gaps to understand the text.	The letter has not been edited.

See Appendix B for 4-, 5-, and 6-point informative/explanatory rubrics.

Using the Business Letter Rubric to Analyze the Model

Did you notice that the model on page 193 points out some key elements of a business letter? As he wrote to the Go Fly a Kite Company, Ping used these elements to help him write a business letter. He also used the 6-point rubric on pages 194–195 to plan, draft, revise, and edit the writing. A rubric is a great tool to evaluate writing during the writing process.

To get started, look at the top score for each trait as you study the model. Do you agree that Ping has earned a 6 for each trait?

- **The topic is clear.**
- **Strong facts and details develop the topic.**

Ping tells the purpose of his letter in the first sentence. I can understand why it is important to be clear from the beginning, since you are writing to someone you don't know. The person who reads the letter probably has many letters to read and needs to understand right away why this one was sent. The rest of Ping's letter contains facts and details that support his refund request.

I am writing to ask you for a refund of $7.00.

- **Information is organized and follows proper business letter format.**
- **Helpful linking words and phrases connect the writer's ideas.**

Ping organizes the information in the letter carefully and includes all the parts of a business letter. He begins by telling the reader why he is writing and what happened to his order. I noticed that Ping uses the linking word *However* to tie important ideas together. It tells the reader the difference between what he expected and what he actually received.

On August 21, I ordered four dragon kites from you. I received the kites a couple of days ago. However, when I opened the box, there were only three kites.

- **The writer uses a polite and formal voice all the way through.**

A business letter sounds different from a friendly letter. Ping's voice sounds formal, not like he's talking to a friend. I also notice that he speaks directly to the reader to request the refund. He uses the word *please,* which sounds polite and direct.

Would you please refund me the $7.00 for the kite I did not get?

Using the Business Letter Rubric to Analyze the Model

- **The writing has just the right number of words to give the information.**

Everything in Ping's letter is important information. He asks for a refund, and then he explains why he wants the refund. He doesn't add unnecessary words.

> I don't want to wait for another kite. I would rather just get the money back for the kite you did not send.

- **Sentences are different lengths and flow smoothly.**

Ping uses a variety of sentences in his letter. Some sentences are long; some are short. This makes his writing flow smoothly. I noticed that he puts the facts about his purchase in shorter sentences so they are easy to find and stand out for the reader.

> It said that you were out of dragon kites right now, and that you would send me another kite as soon as you got more.

> Each kite was $7.00. I paid $28.00 for four.

- **The letter is error free and punctuated correctly.**
- **Prepositional phrases are correct.**

Ping is careful to spell, punctuate, and capitalize correctly in his letter. He makes sure that he uses prepositional phrases correctly. Here are three examples of prepositional phrases Ping uses. Can you find them?

On August 21, I ordered four dragon kites from you.

Inside the box there was also a letter.

Presentation The letter has all six parts. The letter is neat and legible.

My Turn!

Now I'm going to write a business letter. I'll use the rubric and good writing strategies to help me. Follow along to see how I do it.

Prewrite

Focus on **Ideas**

The Rubric Says The topic is clear.

Writing Strategy State the message clearly.

Our math teacher wants us to do some writing to show what we know about math. He said we could write anything as long as it showed that we understand what we have learned. I decided to write a business letter.

I have a really good reason to write a business letter. Our class is doing a fundraiser for a special field trip. We are making greeting cards with painted flowers on them to sell. A local craft store wants to order 100 cards from us. They want to know how much that will cost. The store also wants to know how long it will take for us to make the cards. I will write to the store to answer their questions.

The body of my letter needs to have a clear message. I'll make some notes about what I want to say.

My Notes

- ✔ The order will cost $70.00.
- ✔ There are 10 cards in a box. Each box costs $8.00.
- ✔ Need 10 boxes to get 100 cards.
- ✔ 10 boxes times $8.00 a box equals $80.00.
- ✔ $10 discount on large orders like this.
- ✔ We need two weeks to make 100 cards.

Write

Think about a reason to write a business letter. Make notes about your message.

Prewrite

Focus on **Organization**

The Rubric Says Information is organized and follows proper business letter format.

Writing Strategy Use a Business Letter Organizer to organize the information.

A Business Letter Organizer will help me put the information I need, like the addresses, in the correct order. It will also help me organize the body of my letter.

Writer's Term

Business Letter Organizer

A **Business Letter Organizer** helps to put the information needed for a business letter in a logical order.

Business Letter Organizer

Heading and Date

[street] 567 Fox Lane

[city, state, zip code] Billings, MT 59106

[today's date] February 7, 20__

Inside Address

[name] Handmade Delights

[street] 421 Grand Avenue

[city, state, zip code] Billings, MT 59106

Greeting

Dear Handmade Delights:

Body

There are 10 cards in a box. Each box costs $8.00. To get 100 cards, you need 10 boxes. Ten times $8.00 is $80.00. Subtract $10.00 discount for large order. The store can get the cards two weeks after order.

Closing and Signature

Sincerely,

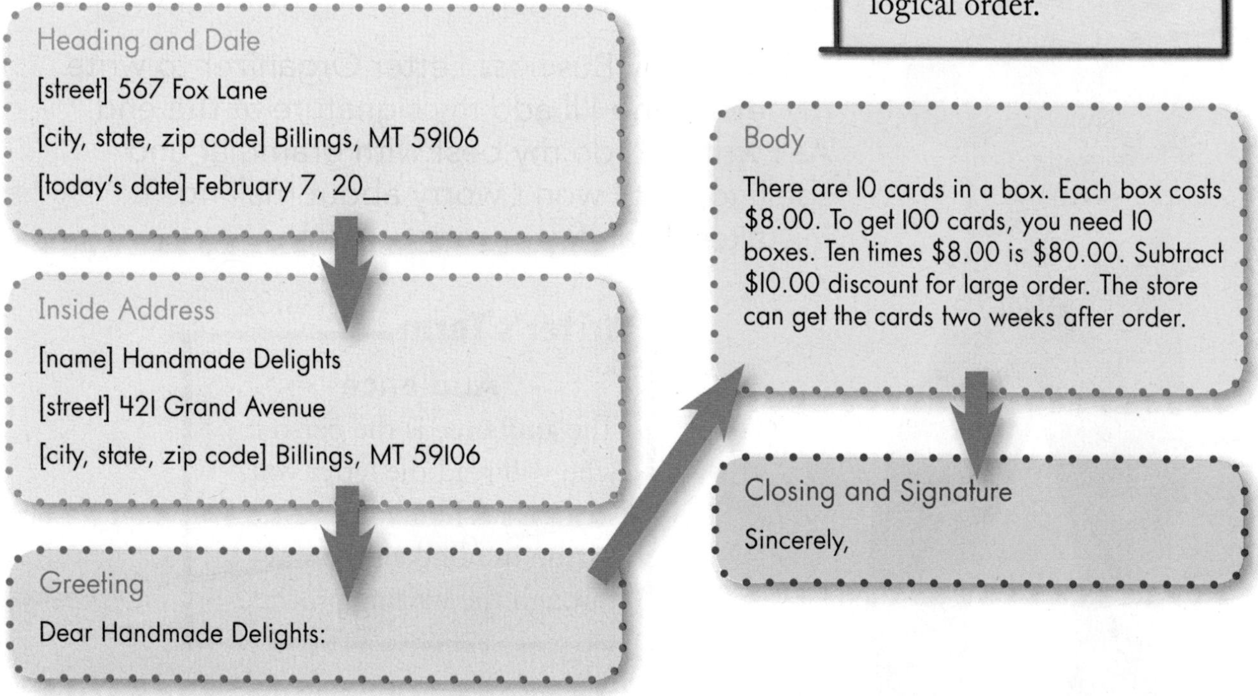

Analyze

How will the organizer help Emma write her letter?

Write

Use a Business Letter Organizer to organize your notes.

Draft

Focus on Word Choice

The Rubric Says The writing has just the right number of words to give the information.

Writing Strategy Avoid using unnecessary words and phrases.

Now I'm ready to write my draft. I want to choose words that get my meaning across to my reader. I will also remember that using polite language doesn't mean using more words than are necessary. Long sentences and repetitions would cloud the meaning and possibly confuse the reader. So I'll stick to my message.

I'll use my Business Letter Organizer to write my letter, and I'll add my signature at the end. As I write, I'll do my best with grammar and spelling, but I won't worry about making mistakes. I can fix any errors later.

Writer's Term

Audience

The **audience** is the person who will read the letter you write. You should keep that person in mind all the way through the writing process.

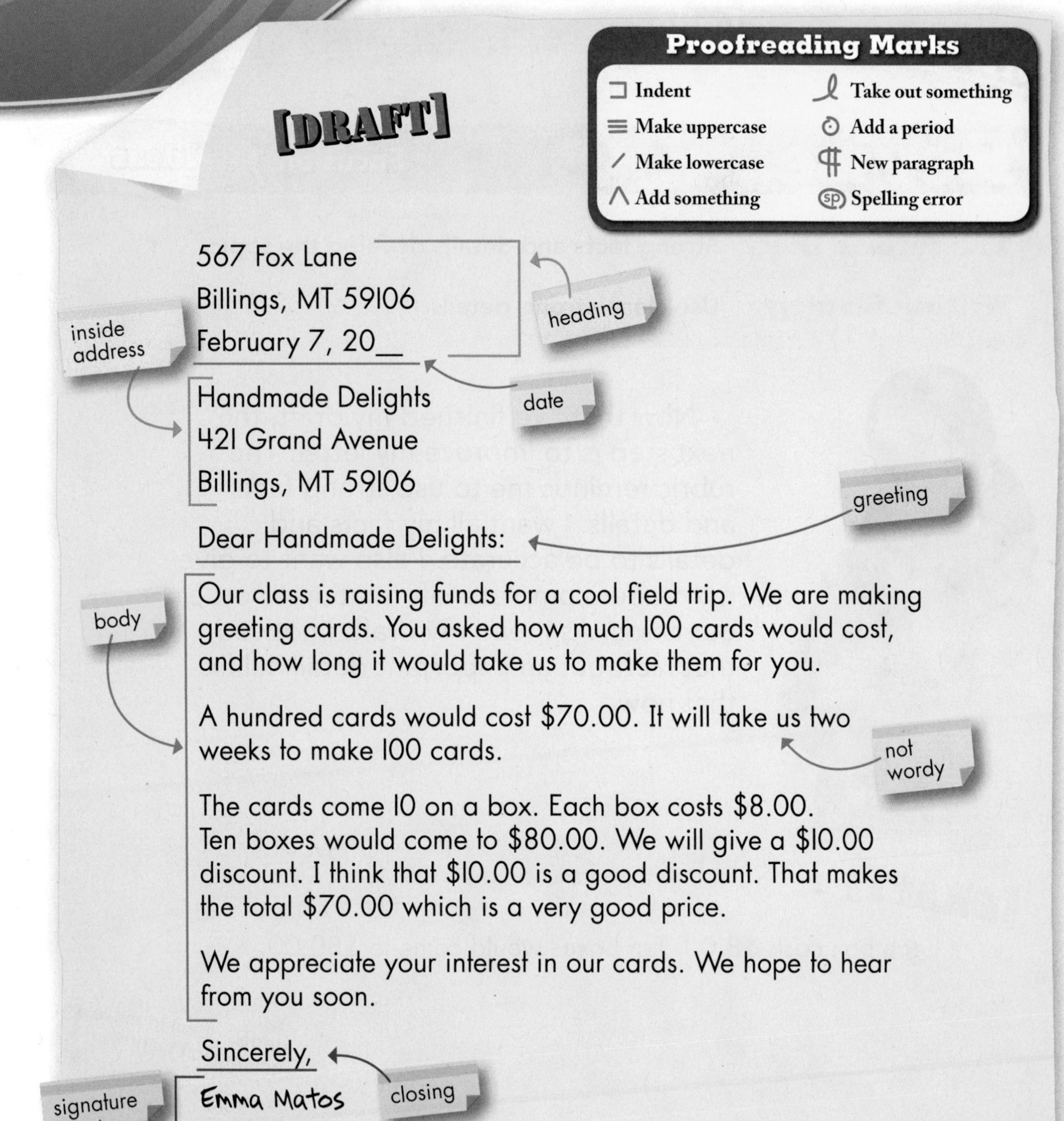

Proofreading Marks

Indent	Take out something
Make uppercase	Add a period
Make lowercase	New paragraph
Add something	Spelling error

[DRAFT]

567 Fox Lane
Billings, MT 59106
February 7, 20__

Handmade Delights
421 Grand Avenue
Billings, MT 59106

Dear Handmade Delights:

Our class is raising funds for a cool field trip. We are making greeting cards. You asked how much 100 cards would cost, and how long it would take us to make them for you.

A hundred cards would cost $70.00. It will take us two weeks to make 100 cards.

The cards come 10 on a box. Each box costs $8.00. Ten boxes would come to $80.00. We will give a $10.00 discount. I think that $10.00 is a good discount. That makes the total $70.00 which is a very good price.

We appreciate your interest in our cards. We hope to hear from you soon.

Sincerely,

Emma Matos

Emma Matos

Analyze

What do you think of Emma's choice of words? Which words help clarify her message?

Write

Use your Business Letter Organizer to write your draft. Choose words that convey your message clearly.

Revise

Focus on **Ideas**

The Rubric Says Strong facts and details develop the topic.

Writing Strategy Use clear, strong details.

Now that I've finished my draft, the next step is to improve my letter. The rubric reminds me to use strong facts and details. I want all my facts and details to be accurate. I also want to give my reader complete information to order our cards. As I read my draft, I noticed that I left out an important detail. I'll fix that now.

[DRAFT]

Each box costs $8.00. ^ You will need 10 boxes to get 100 cards. Ten boxes would come to $80.00.

added detail to make information clearer

Write

Read your draft. Find places where you can clarify and strengthen details in your letter.

Revise

Focus on **Organization**

The Rubric Says Helpful linking words and phrases connect the writer's ideas.

Writing Strategy Use linking words and phrases that tell how ideas are connected.

The rubric reminds me to use linking words, such as *and*, to connect similar ideas. It also reminds me to use the word *but* to connect different ideas. It's important to use helpful linking words to get my meaning across. I found two places where I need linking words to connect my ideas. Do you think my changes improve this part of my letter?

Writer's Term

Linking Words and Phases

Use the **linking words and, or,** and **in addition** to connect similar ideas. Use the linking words **but, although,** and **however** to connect different ideas.

[DRAFT]

connected different ideas

, but

Ten boxes would come to $80.00. We will give a $10.00 discount.

, and

We appreciate your interest in our cards. We hope to hear from you soon.

connected similar ideas

Analyze

Look at Emma's revisions so far. How have they improved her letter?

Write

Read your draft again. Revise your letter to add linking words and phrases to connect ideas in your letter.

Revise

Focus on **Sentence Fluency**

The Rubric Says Sentences are different lengths and flow smoothly.

Writing Strategy Add prepositional phrases to sentences.

The rubric reminds me that a variety of sentence lengths can make my writing flow more smoothly. One thing a writer can do to make some sentences longer is to add information in the form of a prepositional phrase. Prepositional phrases often tell *how*, *when*, or *where*. They help give sentences a smooth flow, which makes reading easier. They also make the sentences more informative. I reread my draft and found a place where I can combine two sentences by using prepositional phrases. See what I did below!

[DRAFT]

Our class is raising funds for a cool field trip ~~. We are~~ to the Art Museum by making greeting cards.

combined sentences with prepositions

Write

Check your draft to see if there are places where you can add prepositional phrases.

Edit

Focus on **Conventions**

The Rubric Says The letter is error free and punctuated correctly. Prepositional phrases are correct.

Writing Strategy Check punctuation. Be sure that prepositional phrases make sense.

I'm ready to check my draft for spelling, capitalization, and punctuation. The rubric reminds me to make sure that my prepositional phrases are correct, too.

Writer's Term

Prepositional Phrase

A **prepositional phrase** is a group of words that begins with a **preposition.** The words **at, by, in, on,** and **to** are examples of prepositions. The phrases can add more meaning to a sentence.

The cards come 10 ~~on~~ in a box.

corrected the preposition

Analyze

Look at Emma's edit. Do you agree with her correction? What else, if anything, should she correct in her draft?

Write

Conventions

Edit your draft for spelling, capitalization, and punctuation. Fix any incorrect prepositions.

For practice with prepositional phrases and punctuation, use the exercises on the next two pages.

Prepositional Phrases

Know the Rule

A **prepositional phrase** begins with a preposition. *Under, at, after, from, in, by, to,* and *into* are prepositions. Prepositional phrases often tell more about what happens in a sentence. They usually tell *where, how,* or *when.*

Examples:
Ellie saw some items she wanted **in a catalog**. (*where*)
She wanted to tell the company **by writing a letter**. (*how*)
She sent her letter **at noon**. (*when*)

Practice the Rule

Number a sheet of paper 1–10. Read each sentence carefully. Write the prepositional phrase in each one. Some sentences might have more than one prepositional phrase.

1. Jake ordered a butterfly book on June 9.
2. Every day he looked into his mailbox.
3. After two weeks, he started to worry.
4. Jake wondered if the book had gotten lost in the mail.
5. Jake wrote a letter to the book company.
6. He got the idea from his mom.
7. Jake walked to the post office.
8. He gave his letter to the postal worker.
9. A few days later, Jake saw a mail truck stopping in front of his house.
10. His butterfly book came to him by special delivery.

Punctuate a Letter

Know the Rule

A business letter has six parts. Each part has special punctuation.

- In the **heading** and **inside address,** use a comma to separate the city and the state. Use another comma to separate the day and the year.
- Begin the **greeting** with an uppercase letter and end with a colon.
- Punctuate the sentences in the **body** correctly.
- Start the **closing** with an uppercase letter and end with a comma.
- Start your **signature** with an uppercase letter.

Practice the Rule

Copy the letter below on a separate sheet of paper. Label each part. Correct four punctuation or capitalization errors.

43 Gilman Street
Madison WI 53703
April 5, 20__

Nature Book Company
9257 President Street
Brooklyn, NY 11215

dear Nature Book Company,

Thank you for sending my butterfly book to me by special delivery. It was definitely worth the wait. I understand now that I had to wait because you did not have the book in stock yet.

sincerely,

Jake Pine

Jake Pine

Publish

+Presentation

Publishing Strategy	Send the letter.
Presentation Strategy	Make sure the letter has all the parts and is neat.

I've finished my letter! It's time to send it. A messy letter will make a bad impression or be unreadable, so it has to be neat. It's best to type it on the computer and then print it out. Before I send my letter, I'll read it one more time. Here's my final checklist.

My Final Checklist

Did I—

- ✔ put the parts of a business letter in the correct places?
- ✔ make sure prepositions are used correctly?
- ✔ check my spelling, punctuation, and capitalization?
- ✔ sign my letter?

Write

Use this checklist for your own business letter. Then write a final copy and send it!

567 Fox Lane
Billings, MT 59106
February 7, 20__

Handmade Delights
421 Grand Avenue
Billings, MT 59106

Dear Handmade Delights:

Our class is raising funds for a special field trip to the Art Museum by making greeting cards. You asked how much 100 cards would cost and how long it would take us to make them.

A hundred cards would cost $70.00. It will take us two weeks to make 100 cards.

The cards come 10 in a box. Each box costs $8.00. You will need 10 boxes to get 100 cards. Ten boxes would come to $80.00, but we will give a $10.00 discount. That makes the total $70.00.

We appreciate your interest in our cards, and we hope to hear from you soon.

Sincerely,

Emma Matos

Emma Matos

Analyze

Use the rubric to analyze Emma's business letter. Evaluate your own business letter in the same way.

PART 1

Next Generation Informative/Explanatory Assessment

When you take a writing assessment, you might be asked to read, too. In the reading part, you will read texts or watch video clips and answer questions about them. After reading or viewing the texts or video clips, you will need to use the information you learned to help you write an informative/explanatory piece, such as a report.

Let's analyze each part of this test to see what the assessment looks like.

Part 1: Close Reading

Your Task

You will examine three sources about the Underground Railroad. Then you will answer three questions about what you have learned. Later, in Part 2, you will write a report about a woman named Harriet Tubman and the part she played in the Underground Railroad.

Steps to Follow

In order to plan and write your report, you will do all of the following:

1. Examine three sources.
2. Make notes about the information from the sources.
3. Answer three questions about the sources.

Directions for Beginning

You will have 55 minutes to complete Part 1. You will now examine three sources. Take notes because you may want to refer to your notes while writing your report. You can re-examine any of the sources as often as you like. Answer the questions in the spaces provided.

Your Task This section of the directions gives information about the whole test. You will have two parts to complete. In Part 1, you will read and answer questions. In Part 2, you will write a report.

Steps to Follow This section reviews the task as a list. It tells how many sources you will examine. You also find out how many questions you have to answer. In this assessment, you will have to examine three sources and answer three questions.

Directions for Beginning This section gives information about Part 1 only—the reading part. You'll need to decide how you want to take notes. Will you write them on a piece of paper or use a note tool online? This section also tells how long you'll have to complete your task. These directions tell you that you have 55 minutes. Since there are three sources, you'll have about 15 minutes to spend on each source, plus a few minutes to check your answers.

TEST TIP

Sometimes I skim the text before I read it. I do this by reading the title, any headings, and the first few sentences. This helps me understand a little about the main idea before I begin reading the whole text.

Source 1: Text

From *The Underground Railroad: People and Places*
by Ellen Wettersten

Harriet Tubman

The Underground Railroad was a network of people who helped slaves in the American South escape to freedom in the North or Canada. It was started by a group of people called abolitionists who believed slavery was wrong. They had a common purpose: to end slavery in the United States.

Both black people and white people provided places where fleeing slaves could stop and rest. Some helpers gave money and supplies. Others led slaves north by helping them move from one stop to the next. These people were called *conductors*, a word that came from the real railroads. Harriet Tubman was a conductor on the Underground Railroad.

Harriet Tubman was born a slave. In 1849, she ran away from a plantation in Maryland. Wanting to be free, Harriet made her way to Philadelphia. There she became free and got a job as a cook. She could have stayed there safely, but she didn't. Harriet went south again to bring her family to be near her. Then she returned again and again to lead others to freedom.

Harriet Tubman was a small woman, but she was strong from years of hard work. She also had enormous courage. She could not read and write, so she kept no record of her journeys. We know about her from interviews and from the stories of others.

We know that she liked to make the trip in winter and at night. The long winter nights meant more hours to travel. During the day, Tubman and her followers rested and tried to stay hidden.

People said she was a great actress. She often changed the way she looked. She might pretend to be an elderly woman, or even a man. Sometimes she wore a big hat to cover her face.

Anyone who started out with her had to finish the trip. She told her followers that a slave who went back might be forced to tell about hiding places, meaning her work would end. Once, a group had to spend the night in a swamp. One man wanted to go home. She is supposed to have said, "Move or die." The slaves knew she was in command.

Harriet Tubman led her parents to freedom. She bought a farm in New York just before the Civil War and lived there with them. During the Civil War, she was a scout and spy for the Union Army. She also served as a nurse and a guide.

After the Civil War, she took in orphans and elderly people. Her farm became the Harriet Tubman Home for the Aged. She lived there until she died.

What is the main idea the author wants you to know about Harriet Tubman? Use evidence from the text in your answer.

To find the main idea, I will reread the paragraphs about Harriet Tubman. Most of the them give details about her life and how she helped people on the Underground Railroad. The author wants me to know how important Harriet Tubman was.

My Response

Harriet Tubman helped many slaves escape to freedom on the Underground Railroad. She had a lot of courage and made many journeys as a conductor. She also had to be tough in order to protect her followers. When a man wanted to quit, she told him, "Move or die."

Analyze

How well did Emma identify the main idea in the text? Is there any other evidence she could have used in her answer?

Source 2: Text

From *The Underground Railroad for Kids*
by Mary Kay Carson

When Alfred Thornton first saw two men walking toward him one day in 1858, he wondered what they wanted. As they got nearer, Thornton recognized them as a local "constable," or lawman, and a slave trader. Now he was nervous. Alfred Thornton was a slave who'd lived on the Shinn plantation in Virginia all his 21 years. He knew that a slave trader coming for him meant only one thing—and it was about the worst thing that could happen to a slave. Thornton's master had sold him. That slave trader was coming to take young Thornton away, and the constable was there to make sure Thornton went without a fight.

Dread began to fill Thornton. Being sold meant he'd never see his mother, father, and friends again. He'd be moved to a new plantation far away. Thornton knew that the slave trader would take him into the Deep South. Everyone had heard how slaves were quickly worked to death on huge cotton plantations down there. The two men were getting closer.

In an instant before the lawman and the slave trader grabbed Thornton, the young slave took off . . . Thornton ran toward the pond. He jumped in and hid underwater. "I kept my head just above [water] and hid the rest part of my body for more than two hours." While hiding, Thornton thought about his next move . . . Thornton spent night after night walking and wandering. He frequently lost his way, rested a little, and ate even less.

But Alfred Thornton kept going. He finally managed to travel nearly 200 miles to the free state of Pennsylvania. Once in Philadelphia, he was helped by a group of people that secretly helped slaves escape. Thornton got on the Underground Railroad. It wasn't a real railroad, and it didn't run underground. But the name fit. Like anything underground, the Underground Railroad was mysterious and often difficult to find. Like a railroad, it quickly took people where they wanted to go. The Underground Railroad was a secret way that slaves used to escape. It was a loose network of people, pathways, and places that helped slaves reach freedom.

To help keep its people and places secret, travelers and workers along the Underground Railroad often spoke or wrote using code words copied from real train travel. Fugitive slaves were called "passengers," "travelers," "baggage," or "cargo." Underground Railroad "conductors" (like the famous Harriet Tubman) were people who worked in the Underground Railroad to guide runaways to freedom. People who mapped out "routes," "arranged passage," and made sure the way was safe were called Underground Railroad "agents." Safe houses, where runaways were sheltered, were called "stations." A person who ran a safe house was called a "stationmaster." "Brakemen" helped fugitives start new lives after they came to their final stops in free states or in Canada. The Underground Railroad helped thousands of runaway slaves like Alred Thornton escape slavery. It was a one-way ticket to freedom. All aboard!

Compare and contrast the Underground Railroad with real train travel. Use three examples from the text in your answer.

I think it's interesting that the Underground Railroad wasn't a real railroad at all! I'll re-examine the text and note some ways the two railroads were similar and ways they were different.

My Response

Both railroads used words like "baggage" and "stations." Both took people where they wanted to go. But one traveled on real tracks and the other did not.

Analyze

How well did Emma compare and contrast the two topics? What other examples could she use?

Source 3: Text

From *The North Star*
by Susan L. Rogers

The sweetest star in the sky is the North Star. I know. I was a slave down in Maryland. I was born a slave, and my momma was a slave.

I remember my momma showing me when I was just a little girl. She pointed to the stars in the sky that they call the Big Dipper. My momma said, "Follow those two stars up with your eyes, Betsy, and you'll find the North Star. Keep it in front of you, and you'll always be going north."

When I was 16, my momma died. I didn't have any reason to stay anymore. The master had sold the rest of my family. I knew I was going to run away and find freedom, or die trying!

I heard about a woman, Harriet Tubman, who used to be a slave in Maryland, too. She ran away, and then she came back! She helped other slaves escape.

I heard that Harriet was coming back again, and I made sure that she knew I wanted to come with her. It was scary just getting the message to her. I didn't know if I could trust the man I was talking to, or if he would just tell my master what I was planning. I got an answer to my message: She'd take me!

I left that night. The message said that Harriet was coming to get some people who lived about 20 miles away. I had to get there to meet them on my own, but the message had directions for me. All I had to do was follow them. Then we would all go on together.

I ran through the woods until I hit a stream, and then followed the stream down until I could see a big barn on top of a hill off to my right. Then I looked up and followed the North Star until I came to a little house in the woods. The message said that if there was a lantern hanging outside, it was safe to go in. If there was no lantern, I had to hide in the woods and wait.

There was a lantern hanging up by the door, so I knocked on the door. A man let me in. He was a white man, and I was nervous about that. But he spoke kindly and gave me some food to eat and a blanket.

Late that night, Harriet Tubman came in with five other runaways. The next night, we set out again, following the North Star. It was hard traveling at night. There were always people out looking for runaway slaves. People helped us along the way, but we had to be careful, too. If the station-masters were found out, they could be sent to jail, and we would be shipped back south. We stayed in secret hiding places in their homes. I remember one family had a secret room under their house where we stayed. In another house we hid in a room that was built behind some cupboards.

Harriet left us in New York, but she gave us directions to follow so that we could continue north. We traveled from station to station on the Underground Railroad. Finally, we made it all the way to Canada. Now, I look up at the North Star and know that there isn't a sweeter star in the whole sky.

Why do you think Harriet left Betsy and the other slaves in New York? What evidence supports your answer?

I wondered about this when I read the story. Why would she leave them before they got to a safe place? I'll reread the text and look for an answer to this question.

My Response

I don't see an answer in the text, but Betsy says that Harriet helped other slaves escape. So, I think Harriet left to go and help other people on the Underground Railroad.

Analyze

Did Emma use evidence from the text in her answer? Do you agree with her answer?

PART 2

Next Generation Informative/Explanatory Assessment

Now that Part 1 is complete, it's time to write the report. Usually you will complete Part 1 on one day and Part 2 on the next day. The directions for Part 2 are longer than Part 1 and continue on a second page. So remember to read the directions carefully and ask questions if you don't understand.

PART 2: Writing to Multiple Sources

Setup

You will now have 70 minutes to review your notes and sources, plan, draft, and revise a report. You may use your notes and refer to the sources. You may also refer to the answers you wrote to questions in Part 1, but you cannot change those answers. Now read your assignment and the information about how your report will be scored. Then begin your work.

Your Assignment

Your class is making a book for the school library about important events in American history. Your assignment is to write a report informing your classmates about the Underground Railroad and explaining the part Harriet Tubman played in its success. Support your topic with concrete details and examples from each of the sources you have examined. The audience for your report will be students in your school.

Setup This section lets you know how much time you have to complete Part 2. You can divide the time into the different parts of the writing process. Here's an example of what Emma plans to do.

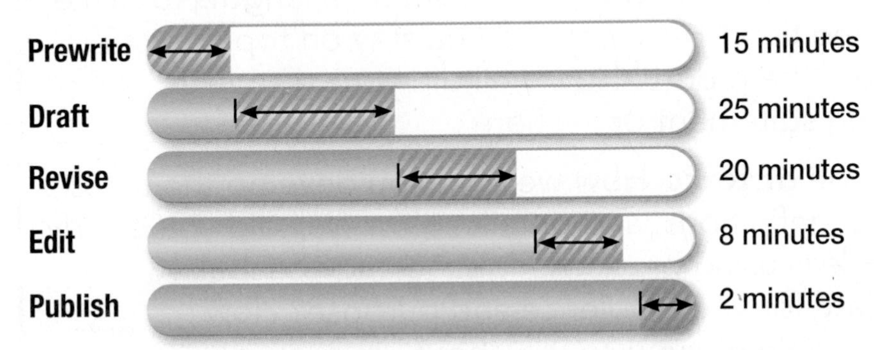

The directions also tell you that you can go back and examine the sources from Part 1, but the answers for that part can't be changed.

Your Assignment This part explains your writing assignment. The topic of your assignment usually appears in the first few sentences in this section. In this case, it's the first two sentences. Finally, you are given a clue to what kind of voice you should use in your report. Because your audience is other students who will read your report to learn facts about American history, you should use a serious and knowledgeable voice.

Scoring Guide

Your report will be scored on the following criteria:

1. **Focus and organization** How well did you introduce your topic? How well did you group related information together? How well did you vary sentence lengths to make your writing flow? How well did you stay on topic throughout the report? How well did you provide a concluding statement or section?
2. **Elaboration of topic** How well did you develop the topic with facts, definitions, and details? How well did you clearly express ideas using precise language and vocabulary appropriate for your audience and purpose? How knowledgeable did you sound about your topic?
3. **Conventions** How well did you check your grammar, punctuation, capitalization, and spelling?

Now begin work on your report. Manage your time carefully so that you can:

- plan your report.
- write your report.
- revise and edit a final draft.

Spell check is available to use.

Type your response in the space provided on the next page. Write as much as you need to in order to complete the task.

Writing Traits in the Scoring Guide

The second page of the directions tells you how your report will be scored. This scoring guide includes all of the writing traits. You can use what you have learned about the writing traits to help you write an effective report.

1 Focus and organization

- How well did you vary sentence lengths to make your writing flow?

- How well did you provide a concluding statement or section?

2 Elaboration of topic

- How well did you develop the topic with facts, definitions, and details?

- How knowledgeable did you sound about your topic?

- How well did you clearly express ideas using precise language and vocabulary appropriate for your audience and purpose?

3 Conventions

- How well did you follow the rules of grammar, punctuation, capitalization, and spelling?

Before you start Part 2, review your plan for how you will divide your time. Remember, there is no word limit, but don't feel you have to fill the entire space with your thoughts. Now it's time for Emma to start writing her report.

Prewrite

Focus on **Ideas**

Writing Strategy Respond to the assignment.

Prewrite ⟷ 15 minutes

Writers gather information before they begin to write. This is also important when writing for an assessment. You can learn a lot from the directions. Take another look at the assignment in the directions. The assignment explains what you need to write.

From my assignment, I know I'm supposed to write a report. I also know the topic.

> Your class is making a book for the school library about important events in American History. Your assignment is to write a report informing your classmates about the Underground Railroad and explaining the part Harriet Tubman played in its success.
>
> topic
>
> genre

First I'm going to write a sentence stating my topic sentence. Then, I'll think about which of the sources will support my topic sentence. I can't remember all the details about the sources, but I just want to see what I remember.

My Topic:

Many slaves escaped to freedom because of Harriet Tubman and the Underground Railroad.

Sources That Support My Topic:

The story about Harriet Tubman's life and work
The article explaining how the Underground Railroad worked
The article describing one slave's escape to freedom

Prewrite

Focus on Organization

Writing Strategy Choose a graphic organizer.

Prewrite ⟷ 15 minutes

I need to start organizing my ideas. A good graphic organizer for a report is a Network Tree. It will help me identify evidence from the sources in Part 1 to support my topic. I may want to go back now and examine the sources again so I can get even more specific.

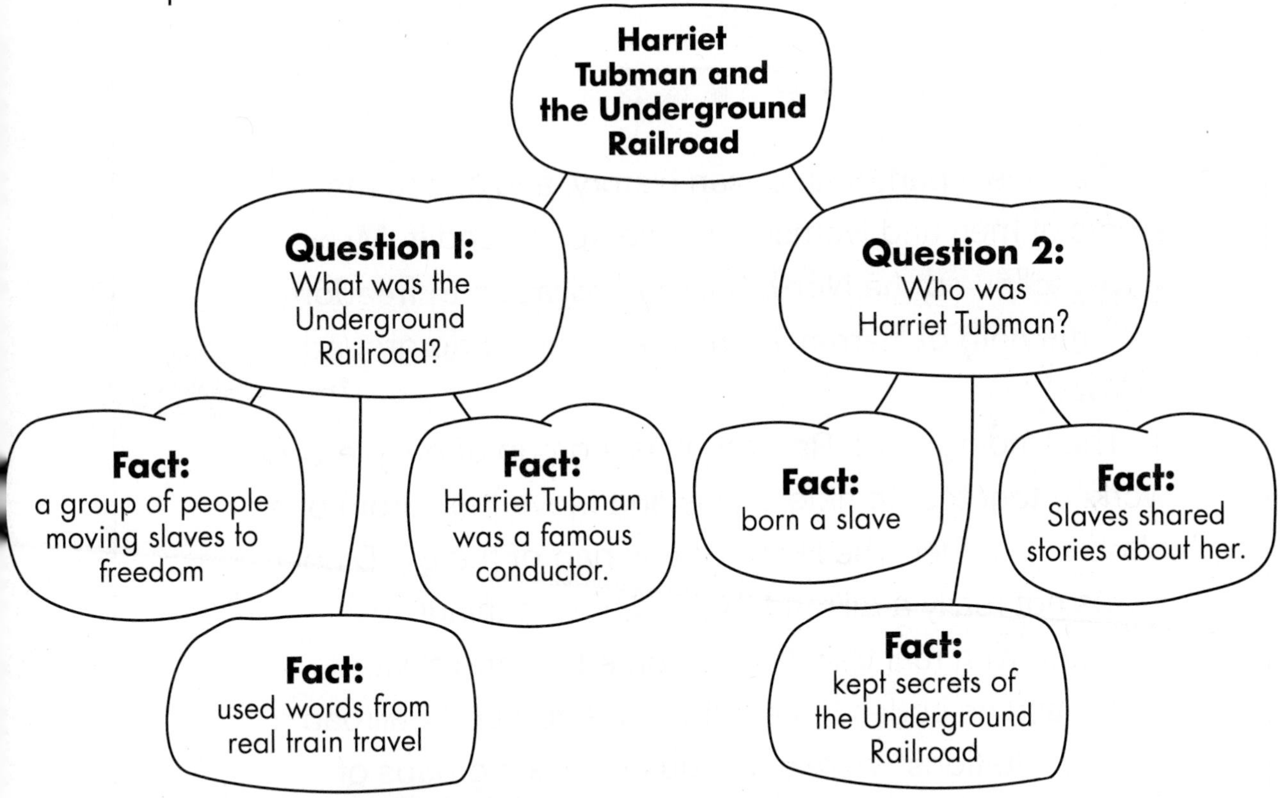

Harriet Tubman and the Underground Railroad

Question 1: What was the Underground Railroad?

- **Fact:** a group of people moving slaves to freedom
- **Fact:** used words from real train travel
- **Fact:** Harriet Tubman was a famous conductor.

Question 2: Who was Harriet Tubman?

- **Fact:** born a slave
- **Fact:** kept secrets of the Underground Railroad
- **Fact:** Slaves shared stories about her.

Analyze

Does the graphic organizer include evidence that supports Emma's topic? What other evidence could she add?

Draft

Focus on **Ideas**

Writing Strategy State your topic in the first paragraph. Make sure each paragraph has a main idea and facts related to it.

Draft 25 minutes

I'll begin my report by introducing my topic right away. Next I'll use my Network Tree as a guide for writing the body of my report. I'll make sure each paragraph has one main idea and several facts that relate to it.

Slavry is a part of american history, and so are the storys of men and women who worked to end it. Many slaves followed the North Star and escaped to freedom with the help of Harriet Tubman and the Underground railroad.

my topic sentence

The Underground Railroad was a group of people who worked together to hide slaves and move them from one place to another. The North Star is part of the Big Dipper. It was not really a railroad, but it did have things in common with real train travel. Some train travel words were used as codes to keep the Underground Railroad a secret. "Stations" were safe houses where groups of traveling slaves stayed. Slaves were called "passengers," "travelers," "baggage," and "cargo." Workers who guided slaves were called "conductors." Harriet Tubman was one of the most famous conductors.

Harriet was born a slave. She was able to run away and escape to freedom, but she wanted to free her family, too. She secretly went back south and led them north to safety. Soon she was working with the Underground Railroad to help free others. Tons of slaves began telling awesome stories of what Harriet did. They told how she wore all kinds of crazy costumes to hide herself and traveled mostly in winter at night. Slaves knew Harriet would keep them safe. She was tough. Those who went with her could not go back. She needed to keep the secrets of the Underground Railroad.

Analyze

Does each paragraph in Emma's draft have a main idea? Are the facts in each paragraph related to the main idea?

Revise

Focus on Organization

Writing Strategy Make sure you provide a concluding statement that is related to the information presented.

Revise  20 minutes

Now, it's time to check my draft against the scoring guide. I want to be sure I've included all the points that will be scored.

The scoring guide reminds me to provide a concluding statement or section that is related to the information that I presented. I noticed that I didn't include a concluding section. I just ended with my last piece of information. I'll add a couple of sentences at the end and make sure they relate to the information I presented in my report.

Slaves knew Harriet would keep them safe. She was tough. Those who went with her could not go back. She needed to keep the secrets of the Underground Railroad.

Harriet Tubman and others working on the Underground Railroad helped free thousands of slaves. They made life better for many people. We still tell their stories today.

concluding section

Analyze

Do you think Emma's concluding section makes sense with the rest of her report? Is there anything else she could do to improve her conclusion?

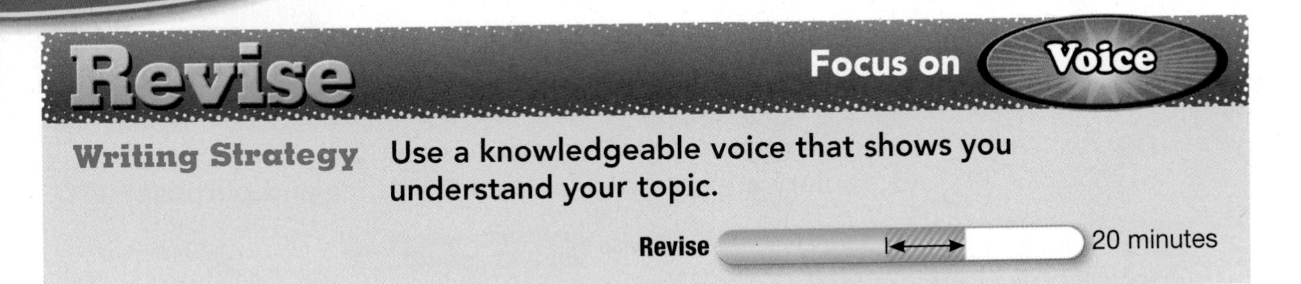

Revise

Focus on **Voice**

Writing Strategy Use a knowledgeable voice that shows you understand your topic.

Revise 20 minutes

Since the purpose of my report will be to inform readers who check out our class book from the library, I need to sound knowledgeable. When I read my draft again, I found two sentences where I sound too casual, as if I'm talking to my friends.

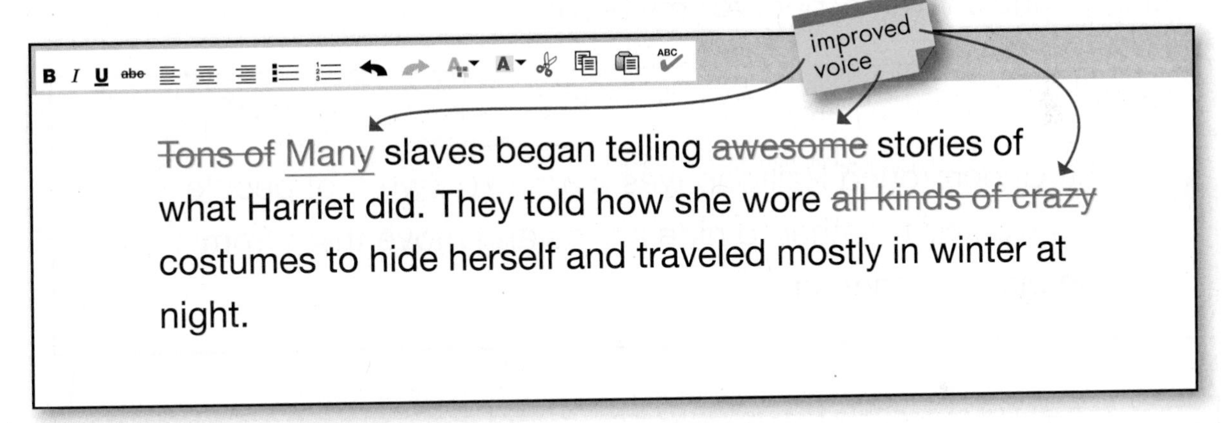

Analyze

How do the changes add a more serious tone to Emma's writing? Do the changes make her sound more knowledgeable?

Revise

Focus on **Word Choice**

Writing Strategy Clearly express ideas using precise language and vocabulary appropriate for your audience and purpose.

Revise 20 minutes

The scoring guide reminds me to use precise words to clearly express my ideas. I need to keep my audience in mind when I choose words. I notice a few places where I can replace vague words with more precise ones. Using more precise words makes my meaning clearer and shows respect for my reader.

The Underground Railroad was a ~~group~~ network of people who worked together to hide slaves and move them from one place to another.

Those who went with her could not go back. She needed to ~~keep~~ protect the secrets of the Underground Railroad.

used precise words

Analyze

Do you think the precise words Emma added make her ideas clearer? Are there any other places where she could use more precise words?

Edit

Focus on **Conventions**

Writing Strategy Check the grammar, spelling, capitalization, and punctuation.

Edit 8 minutes

The scoring guide reminds me to check for correct spelling and grammar in my report. I can use the spell-check feature to save time. I also need to make sure I've used capitalization and punctuation correctly. Planning my time was a good idea. Now I have time to check my writing for errors.

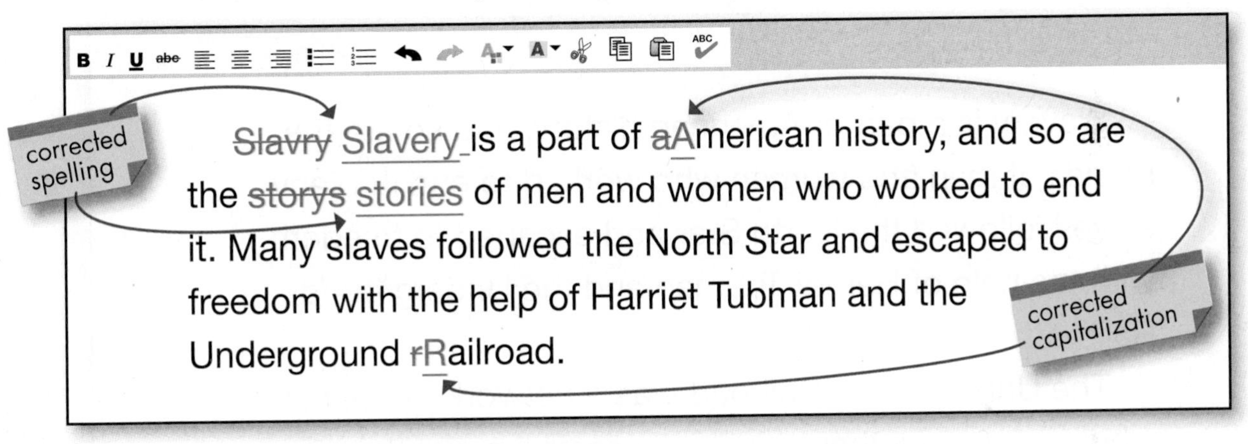

TEST TIP

Review your writing and make sure you capitalized all proper nouns. You should also reread your writing after you use the spell-check feature.

Publish

Publishing Strategy Submit the final draft of your report.

Publish 2 minutes

I am almost done with my assessment. I used information in the scoring guide and the writing traits to complete my report. Now, I will use the spell-check feature one more time to make sure I didn't miss any spelling errors. Then I will submit my final draft.

Slavery is a part of American history, and so are the stories of men and women who worked to end it. Many slaves followed the North Star and escaped to freedom with the help of Harriet Tubman and the Underground Railroad.

The Underground Railroad was a network of people who worked together to hide slaves and move them from one place to another. It was not really a railroad, but it did have things in common with real train travel. Some train travel words were used as codes to keep the Underground Railroad a secret. "Stations" were safe houses where groups of traveling slaves stayed. Slaves were called "passengers," "travelers," "baggage," and "cargo." Workers who guided slaves were called "conductors." Harriet Tubman was one of the most famous conductors.

Harriet was born a slave. She was able to run away and escape to freedom, but she wanted to free her family, too. She secretly went back south and led them north to safety. Soon she was working with the Underground Railroad to help free others. Many slaves began telling stories of what Harriet did. They told how she wore costumes to hide herself and traveled mostly in winter at night. Slaves knew Harriet would keep them safe since she was so tough. Those who went with her could not go back because she needed to protect the secrets of the Underground Railroad.

Harriet Tubman and others working on the Underground Railroad helped free thousands of slaves. They made life better for many people. We still tell their stories today.

Now It's Your Turn

Don't forget all the advice Emma gave you during her assessment. Now, it's your turn to practice taking an informative/explanatory assessment.

Opinion writing

states an opinion and supports it with reasons and examples.

Hi, my name is Marcus. I'm learning about opinion writing. I love telling people what I think about all sorts of things! Which is more fun—fishing or running? I've got my own opinions about things like these. Now I'm going to learn strategies for writing my opinions and convincing people to agree with me.

IN THIS UNIT

- Opinion Paragraph
- Opinion Essay
- Response to Literature
- SOCIAL STUDIES CONNECTION ▶ Brochure
- Next Generation Opinion Assessment

Name: Marcus

Home: Texas

Favorite Book: *Baseball Saved Us* by Ken Mochizuki

Favorite Activities: playing the guitar and riding horses with my family

Favorite Sports: baseball and running

Favorite Subjects in School: math and physical education

What's an Opinion Paragraph?

It's a short piece of writing that tells readers the writer's opinion.

What's in an Opinion Paragraph?

My Opinion
That's what I think about something. There are many topics I have strong opinions about. For example, I think math is the most interesting subject I study in school. I love numbers!

Supporting Reasons
When I explain my opinion, I try to keep my audience in mind and give reasons they will understand. If my sister asked me why I love math, I'd tell her about all the fun math games we play in class.

A Convincing Tone
My tone is how I say what I say. I want to be direct and show confidence in my opinion and my reasons, so I'll use strong, convincing words. Of course, I always show respect for my reader.

Why write an Opinion Paragraph?

People like to share their opinions on many topics. Here are some good reasons to write an opinion paragraph.

To Convince
I might write an opinion paragraph to convince my town library to buy more books for kids.

A music teacher might write an opinion paragraph for the school newspaper to encourage students to form a school band.

A parent might write an opinion paragraph to the editor of a newspaper about a recent concert or sports event.

To Debate
A social studies teacher might write an opinion paragraph for her class. She might state an opinion she knows many students will disagree with. She might want them to think about the issue, discuss it, and give reasons for their opinions.

To Sell
The makers of a product might write an opinion paragraph to urge people to buy their product.

Linking Opinion Writing Traits to an Opinion Paragraph

In this chapter, you will state your opinion in a short piece of writing. This type of writing is called an opinion paragraph. Marcus will guide you through the stages of the writing process: Prewrite, Draft, Revise, Edit, and Publish. In each stage, Marcus will show you important writing strategies that are linked to the Opinion Writing Traits below.

Opinion Writing Traits

Trait	
	• a clearly stated opinion • reasons that are supported by examples and details
	• a strong introduction, body, and conclusion • organized paragraphs that stick to one main idea • linking words and phrases that show how ideas are related
	• a voice and tone that are perfect for the piece of writing
	• strong words that convince the reader • no unnecessary words
	• varied sentences that flow
	• no or few errors in spelling, punctuation, and capitalization

Before you write, read Eva Sanchez's opinion paragraph on the next page. Then use the opinion paragraph rubric on pages 240–241 to decide how well she did. (You might want to look back at What's in an Opinion Paragraph? on page 236, too!)

Learning About the Past

by Eva Sanchez

If you are interested in learning about the past, talk to your grandparents or other older people. You will learn about things that are not in history books. For example, you can find out about the everyday problems they faced. They can tell about things they didn't have in their daily lives, like computers and cell phones. They can describe what they ate, how they lived, and what they did for fun. Grandparents can tell us a lot about history, too. Do your grandparents remember the first walk on the moon in 1969? Did they celebrate in 1976? The United States had a big birthday party that year. It turned two hundred! Your grandparents might remember those times. They can tell you what they did and how they felt. Another reason to ask about the past is to get closer to older people. You will feel closer to them because you know more about them. Grandparents or older relatives might tell you about your own family's past. Maybe your family came from another country or state. Older people might be able to describe the place. They might have photos to show you and letters to share. You will probably hear some good stories. If you want to learn about the past, visit some older folks!

opinion

supporting reason

strong, convincing tone

supporting reason

Opinion Paragraph Rubric

Use this rubric to analyze the model. Then use it to plan and score your own opinion paragraph.

	6	5	4
Ideas	The opinion is clear. It is supported by strong reasons and facts.	The opinion is clear. One or two supporting details are weak.	The opinion is somewhat unclear with few facts and supporting details.
Organization	The paragraph has a main idea sentence and supporting detail sentences. Useful linking words and phrases guide the reader from one idea to the next.	The paragraph has a main idea and supporting detail sentences. Most linking words and phrases are useful.	The paragraph has a main idea sentence and detail sentences. Some linking words and phrases are useful.
Voice	The writer uses a sincere voice to convince the audience.	The writer uses a sincere voice to convince the audience most of the time.	The writer has a sincere voice that convinces the audience some of the time.
Word Choice	Strong, convincing words support the writer's opinion.	Word choice is generally strong and supports the writer's opinion.	Most of the words support the writer's opinion.
Sentence Fluency	Strong, clear sentences support the purpose for writing.	Most of the sentences are strong and clear and support the writer's purpose.	Only a few of the sentences are strong and clear, which makes the writer's purpose less clear.
Conventions	Proper nouns begin with an uppercase letter. Pronouns are used correctly.	Most proper nouns begin with an uppercase letter and most pronouns are used correctly.	There are a few errors with proper nouns and pronouns, but they do not affect the meaning.

+Presentation The paragraph is legible and placed neatly on the page.

3	2	1	
The writer has an opinion, but the supporting details are vague or unrelated.	The opinion is unclear, and it is not supported with reasons or facts.	The writer's opinion is not clear.	Ideas
The paragraph has a main idea but few supporting details. Linking words and phrases are weak or not used.	Too few details support the main idea. Linking words and phrases are confusing.	The main idea is not stated. Details are not supportive. Linking words and phrases are not used.	Organization
The writer occasionally shows sincerity but is not particularly convincing.	Voice is minimal and does not convince the audience.	Voice, if present, does not suit the purpose of the writing.	Voice
Some strong words support the writer's opinion. Many words are too general.	General words or a very limited vocabulary fails to convince the reader.	Some words are used incorrectly and confuse the reader.	Word Choice
Many of the sentences are weak and rambling.	Most sentences are weak and rambling, and the writer's purpose is unclear.	The sentences are long and rambling and may confuse the reader.	Sentence Fluency
There are many errors with proper nouns and pronouns, and the writing is difficult to follow.	Numerous errors with proper nouns and pronouns confuse the reader.	There are so many errors with proper nouns and pronouns that the reader cannot follow the writing.	Conventions

See Appendix B for 4-, 5-, and 6-point opinion rubrics.

Using the Opinion Paragraph Rubric to Analyze the Model

Did you notice that the model on page 239 points out some key elements of an opinion paragraph? As she wrote "Learning About the Past," Eva Sanchez used these elements to help her express her opinion and try to convince others. She also used the 6-point rubric on pages 240–241 to plan, draft, revise, and edit the writing. A rubric is a great tool to evaluate writing during the writing process.

To get started, look at the top score for each trait as you study the model. Do you agree that Eva has earned a 6 for each trait?

- **The opinion is clear.**
- **It is supported by strong reasons and facts.**

The paragraph clearly states the writer's opinion. Eva believes we can learn about the past from older people. She supports her opinion with strong reasons and facts. Eva includes sentences that give reasons we should talk about the past with our grandparents. Here are some of the sentences that support her opinion.

> They can tell about things they didn't have in their daily lives, like computers and cell phones. They can describe what they ate, how they lived, and what they did for fun.

- **The paragraph has a main idea sentence and supporting detail sentences.**
- **Useful linking words and phrases guide the reader from one idea to the next.**

The paragraph is well organized and sticks to one main idea. Linking words and phrases like *Another reason* and *because* help show how ideas are connected. They also help the reader understand the reasons that support the writer's opinion.

Another reason to ask about the past is to get closer to older people. You will feel closer to them because you know more about them.

- **The writer uses a sincere voice to convince the audience.**

A sincere voice helps convince the reader. I felt like Eva was speaking directly to me when she said that I could learn about history from older people in my family. I had never really thought about history coming from anywhere but a book. Eva stated her opinion in a sincere voice. I thought, "Maybe that is true. I want to read her reasons to see if I agree."

If you are interested in learning about the past, talk to your grandparents or other older people. You will learn about things that are not in history books.

Using the Opinion Paragraph Rubric to Analyze the Model

- **Specific words support the writer's opinion.**

Eva speaks with confidence. She sounds like she knows what she is talking about and that makes me want to think about her ideas. She uses specific words, such as *photos* and *letters*, that help convince me.

> They might have photos to show you and letters to share. You will probably hear some good stories. If you want to learn about the past, visit some older folks!

- **Strong, clear sentences support the purpose for writing.**

Eva uses different kinds of sentences that are clear and easy to understand. They all support the purpose of her writing, which is to convince. Here are some examples.

> Grandparents can tell us a lot about history, too. Do your grandparents remember the first walk on the moon in 1969? Did they celebrate in 1976? The United States had a big birthday party that year. It turned two hundred!

- **Proper nouns begin with an uppercase letter.**
- **Pronouns are used correctly.**

Eva proofread her paragraph carefully. She doesn't have any errors in grammar or spelling. She also capitalized proper nouns and used pronouns correctly.

The United States had a big birthday party that year. It turned two hundred!

Presentation The paragraph is legible and placed neatly on the page.

My Turn!

Now I'm going to write my own opinion paragraph. I'll use the rubric and good writing strategies. Follow along to see how I do it.

Prewrite

Focus on **Ideas**

The Rubric Says The opinion is clear. It is supported by strong reasons and facts.

Writing Strategy Use interviews to gather information that will help support your opinion. Take notes and combine the information.

When my teacher asked us to write an opinion paragraph, I knew right away what I wanted to write about. Every year I go to a celebration called Juneteenth. Juneteenth is the oldest known celebration of the ending of slavery. The very first celebration was held in Texas. Juneteenth got its name from the fact that the slaves were freed in Texas on June 19th. I've heard about other Juneteenth parties, but in my opinion, ours is one of the best!

Writer's Term

Opinion

An **opinion** is a belief that is based on reasons. Unlike a fact, an opinion cannot be proven to be true.

I know a lot about Juneteenth celebrations, but I wanted to find out more. I decided to talk to some people in my grandparents' town, Mexia, Texas. My strategy was to interview them to get more information. I interviewed two people, my grandpa and my friend Bob. Here are my questions and their answers.

My Interview With My Grandpa

1. Question: How is Mexia's Juneteenth different from other Juneteenth celebrations?

Answer: Our Juneteenth is special because the first celebration was held right here in Texas in 1898.

2. Question: What can you tell me about how the Juneteenth celebration got started in Mexia?

Answer: Juneteenth celebrates the freedom of the slaves. The freed slaves bought land here in Mexia. They used that piece of land to hold the first Juneteenth celebration. So, today, we use this same piece of land to hold our celebration. It is very historical and special.

3. Question: Do you think Mexia has one of the best Juneteenth celebrations? Why or why not?

Answer: It is one of the biggest Juneteenth celebrations anywhere in the world. One year 20,000 people came.

4. Question: What do you do at the Juneteenth celebration?

Answer: Our Juneteenth celebration is fun, and it's educational, too. We learn new songs and hear stories about the first Juneteenth celebration.

My Interview With Bob

1. Question: How is Mexia's Juneteenth different from other Juneteenth celebrations?

Answer: It is better here than anywhere else because it started here.

2. Question: What can you tell me about how the Juneteenth celebration got started in Mexia?

Answer: We have our celebration on the exact same spot as the freed slaves did.

3. Question: Do you think Mexia has one of the best Juneteenth celebrations? Why or why not?

Answer: It is one of the biggest celebrations anywhere.

4. Question: What do you do at the Juneteenth celebration?

Answer: All of my friends come to the celebration. It is fun being together, playing games, and eating.

Write

Think of a topic for an opinion paragraph. Write interview questions for one or two people. Then conduct your interview. Take notes and combine the information.

Prewrite

Focus on **Organization**

The Rubric Says	The paragraph has a main idea sentence and supporting detail sentences.
Writing Strategy	Make a Main Idea Table from your notes.

A Main Idea Table will help me organize my paragraph. My opinion is the main idea of the paragraph. My reasons are the supporting details. The answers I got to my interview questions helped me determine some of my reasons. My reasons explain why I have an opinion.

Writer's Term

Main Idea Table

A Main Idea Table shows how a main idea is supported by details. The details "hold up" or support the main idea.

Main Idea Table

Main Idea

The best Juneteenth celebration is in Mexia, Texas.

Supporting Detail	Supporting Detail	Supporting Detail	Supporting Detail
Juneteenth began in Texas, so it's special here.	Mexia, Texas, has celebrated Juneteeth since 1898, so it means a lot to the town.	The party is one of the biggest anywhere!	There are many exciting things to do.

Analyze

Look at Marcus's Main Idea Table. How do the details from the interviews support his main idea? How will the organizer help him write his opinion paragraph?

Write

Use your interview notes to make a Main Idea Table. List the details that support your main idea.

Draft

Focus on **Ideas**

The Rubric Says The opinion is clear. It is supported by strong reasons and facts.

Writing Strategy State your opinion and use details to explain it.

Now I can start writing. From the rubric I know that the first sentence should state my opinion for the reader. That's my main idea, so I can take that sentence straight from my Main Idea Table. The middle of my paragraph has to support my opinion. I can take the supporting details (my reasons) from my Main Idea Table, too. Then I'll explain each reason in my draft. I'll end my paragraph with a sentence that states my opinion in a different way.

As I write, I'll do my best with grammar and spelling, but I won't worry about mistakes. I'll have a chance to fix them later.

Proofreading Marks

Indent	Take out something
Make uppercase	Add a period
Make lowercase	New paragraph
Add something	Spelling error

[DRAFT]

Juneteenth in Mexia

One of the best places to go for Juneteenth is Mexia, Texas. Juneteenth started in texas. Juneteenth is named for june 19, 1865, and slavery ended in Texas on that day, and the day is special in Texas, and it is extra special in mexia. The holiday has been held here for such a long time. My grandmother is very old, too. Slaves who were freed in Mexia joined together, and they bought land, and they used the land to celebrate Juneteenth, and that took place in 1898. Mexia is a small town. Today people still use the same land for Juneteenth. Mexia's Juneteenth is one of the best because it is so big. It might be the biggest event anywhere. I think that one year 20,000 people came. Them ate, sang, and had a big party. Juneteenth is possibly a lot of fun. Juneteenth in mexia, texas, is perhaps one of the biggest and best celebrations in the world.

clearly stated opinion

reasons

restatement of opinion

Analyze

Read the draft. Is Marcus's opinion clear? How well did he use strong reasons and facts to support his opinion?

Write

Use your Main Idea Table to write a draft of your opinion paragraph. Remember to state your opinion clearly and then give reasons and facts to support it.

Revise

Focus on Organization

The Rubric Says Useful linking words and phrases guide the reader from one idea to the next.

Writing Strategy Add linking words and phrases to help make the paragraph easy to understand.

The rubric reminds me to add linking words and phrases to my writing. They can act like signals to help the reader understand my paragraph better.

Writer's Term

Linking Words and Phrases

Linking words and phrases help tie ideas together. They guide the reader from one idea to another. Here are some linking words and phrases that are used as signals in opinion writing.

- **as a result**
- **because**
- **for this reason**
- **in fact**
- **one reason is that**
- **that is because**
- **this is why**
- **therefore**

[DRAFT]

One reason is that

One of the best places to go for Juneteenth is Mexia, Texas. ^ Juneteenth started in texas. Juneteenth is named for june 19, 1865, and slavery ended in Texas on that day, and the day is special in Texas, and it is extra special in mexia. That is because ^ The holiday has been held here for such a long time.

added linking phrases

Write

Read your draft. Find places where you can add linking words and phrases to guide the reader.

Revise

Focus on **Voice**

The Rubric Says The writer uses a sincere voice to convince the audience.

Writing Strategy Make sure the writing sounds convincing.

The rubric reminds me to use a sincere voice to convince the audience. That means I need to sound positive in stating my opinion about my topic. I read my draft aloud to hear if I sound convincing all the way through the paragraph. I decided to revise the ending because I want the reader to agree with me. Do you agree with my changes?

[DRAFT]

I ~~think~~ know that one year 20,000 people came. Them ate, sang, and had a big party. Juneteenth is ~~possibly~~ definitely a lot of fun. In my opinion, Juneteenth in mexia, texas, is ~~perhaps~~ absolutely one of the biggest and best celebrations in the world.

used a more convincing voice

Analyze

Look at the revisions. How did Marcus make the paragraph sound more convincing and sincere?

Write

Read your draft carefully. See if you have used a sincere, convincing voice. Find places where you can improve your voice and convince the audience.

Revise

Focus on **Word Choice**

The Rubric Says Specific words support the writer's opinion.

Writing Strategy Replace boring words with strong, convincing words.

The rubric reminds me to use convincing words so that I can encourage my reader to agree with my opinion. Words like *big* and *event* are boring. They won't convince many people. I can replace them with more convincing words.

[DRAFT]

Mexia's Juneteenth is one of the ~~best~~ [most outstanding] because it is so ~~big~~ [gigantic]. It might be the biggest ~~event~~ [celebration] anywhere.

used convincing words

Write

Read your draft carefully. Make sure you use strong, convincing words. Use a dictionary or online thesaurus to replace weak words.

Edit

Focus on **Conventions**

The Rubric Says Proper nouns begin with an uppercase letter. Pronouns are used correctly.

Writing Strategy Check that all proper nouns are capitalized and pronouns are used correctly.

Now I need to proofread for errors. First, I'll check spelling, punctuation, and capitalization. I always do that. Then, I'll reread my paragraph to make sure I capitalized all proper nouns and used pronouns correctly.

Writer's Term

Proper Nouns

A **proper noun** is the name of a specific person, place, or thing. Proper nouns are always capitalized. Capitalize

- a specific person: **P**resident **L**incoln
- a specific place: **S**an **A**ntonio
- specific days of the week: **F**riday
- specific months of the year: **J**une
- specific things: **R**io **G**rande **R**iver

[DRAFT]

came. ~~Them~~ They ate, sang, and had a big party. Juneteenth is a lot of fun. Juneteenth in mexia, texas, is one of the biggest and best celebrations in the world.

used pronoun correctly

capitalized proper nouns

Analyze

Look at Marcus's edits. Did he capitalize all the proper nouns in the sentences and correct all the pronouns? How do his edits make his writing clearer for the reader?

Write Conventions

Be sure you have begun each proper noun with an uppercase letter. Did you use pronouns correctly? Check your spelling, punctuation, and grammar.

For more practice with capitalization and pronouns, use the exercises on the next two pages.

Proper Nouns

Know the Rule

Proper nouns are the names of specific people, places, or things. Proper nouns are always capitalized.

- Capitalize a person's first and last names.
  Example: Sarah Lopez
- Capitalize each important word in the names of streets, towns, countries, parks, lakes, rivers, oceans, and mountains.
  Examples: Glen Drive, Columbus, England, Rocky Mountain National Park, Bear Lake, Ohio River, Pacific Ocean, Smoky Mountains

Practice the Rule

Number a separate sheet of paper 1–12. Rewrite each sentence that has an error in the capitalization of proper nouns. If there are no errors, write **Correct**.

1. Last week our teacher, Mrs. clark, gave us some homework.
2. We were to go to maplewood memorial library.
3. This big library is at the corner of main street and Bay Street.
4. Mrs. Clark said to ask the librarian to help us make a list of celebrations held in the united states.
5. Everyone knows about Thanksgiving Day and independence day.
6. However, did you know about delaware Day?
7. It celebrates the day the first state approved the constitution.
8. In oklahoma, november 4 is Will rogers Day, a day named for the famous actor and humorist.
9. The birthday of Susan B. anthony is a holiday in parts of florida.
10. Many states celebrate arbor day by planting trees.
11. Some schools celebrate benjamin franklin's birthday on January 17.
12. He once said that a penny saved is a penny earned.

Pronouns for People

Know the Rule

A **pronoun** takes the place of one or more nouns. Some singular pronouns are and Some plural pronouns are and

Examples:

Mark said **he** would come to the game.

Mary shouted, "Give the ball to **me**!"

"**We** would like to see the movie," said **John and Michael**.

My **dog** and **cat** thought the treats were for **them**.

Practice the Rule

Number a sheet of paper 1–10. Choose the pronoun in ( ) that correctly completes each sentence.

1. Last April my sister and (I/me) went to a great celebration in Boston.
2. (Her/She) told me that it is called Patriot's Day since it recalls the battle that started the Revolutionary War.
3. People called re-enactors performed for (we/us) and pretended to have a battle.
4. (They/Them) also re-enacted the ride of Paul Revere.
5. It was exciting to watch (him/he) and some others race around the area on their horses.
6. As they raced to warn people, they shouted to (they/them) that the British soldiers were coming!
7. Now there is another big race on Patriot's Day that (us/we) call the Boston Marathon.
8. (Me/I) would like to run in this big race sometime with 20,000 other runners.
9. Paul Revere would be impressed to see all of (they/them) run.
10. It is a grand sight that I wish (he/him) could see!

Publish

+Presentation

Publishing Strategy Post the paragraph on a Class Opinions bulletin board.

Presentation Strategy Balance the amount of white space and text.

My opinion paragraph is finished! Now it's time to publish it. There are many ways to publish an opinion paragraph. My classmates and I have a lot of views about different topics, so we decided to make a bulletin board of all our opinion paragraphs. We will be able to read each other's ideas and discuss whether we agree or disagree with our friends' opinions. Since it will be on display, I want to make sure my paragraph looks neat and is easy to read. I checked to see that I used good margins and included an equal amount of space above and below the paragraph. Finally I checked my paper carefully one last time.

My Final Checklist

Did I—

- ✔ capitalize all proper nouns?
- ✔ use pronouns to take the place of nouns correctly?
- ✔ use neat handwriting or word processing?
- ✔ put my name and the title at the top of my paper?

Write

Use Marcus's list to evaluate your opinion paragraph. Then make a final draft to display on a bulletin board.

Juneteenth in Mexia
by Marcus

One of the best places to go for Juneteenth is Mexia, Texas. One reason is that Juneteenth started in Texas. Juneteenth is named for June 19, 1865. Slavery ended in Texas on that day. The day is special in Texas, and it is extra special in Mexia. That is because the holiday has been held here for such a long time. In fact, slaves who were freed in Mexia joined together. They bought land, and they used the land to celebrate Juneteenth. That took place in 1898. Today people still use the same land for Juneteenth. Mexia's Juneteenth is one of the most outstanding because it is so gigantic. It might be the biggest celebration anywhere. I know that one year 20,000 people came. They ate, sang, and had a big party. Juneteenth is definitely a lot of fun. In my opinion, Juneteenth in Mexia, Texas, is absolutely one of the biggest and best celebrations in the world.

Analyze

Did Marcus follow all the traits of good writing in his paragraph? Use the rubric to check his paragraph. Don't forget to use the rubric to check your own opinion paragraph too.

What's an Opinion Essay?

It's a longer piece of writing that gives the writer's opinion about a topic and his or her reasons for the opinion.

What's in an Opinion Essay?

My Opinion

That's what I think or how I feel about something. It's not a fact. I can't prove that it's true. In my opinion, baseball is the best team sport!

An Introduction, Body, and Conclusion

The introduction is my first paragraph. It's where I state my opinion and get my reader interested in the topic. The next two paragraphs are the body. That's where I give reasons and facts to support my opinion. The conclusion is my last paragraph. It's where I restate my opinion and sum up my support for it.

Supporting Reasons

I can't prove that I am right, but I'll try to convince my reader to agree with me. To do that, I'll support my opinion. I'll explain my reasons and give facts to back them up.

Why write an Opinion Essay?

The main reason to write an opinion essay is to convince a person or group to think a certain way or to do something. Here's why someone might write one.

To Convince

Organizations often hold contests for the most convincing essays by students. The organizations choose topics that their members care about. They want students to think about a topic and understand why it is important. Essay contests often give awards and prizes to the winners.

Some clubs ask members to write their opinions about which arts and crafts projects, field trips, fund-raising activities, and community service projects to do.

Students who want to form a student council at their school might write an opinion essay to the principal. They might explain why a student council is important and give facts about the success of student councils at other schools.

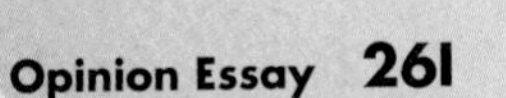

Linking Opinion Writing Traits to an Opinion Essay

In this chapter, you will state your opinion and give your reasons. This type of writing is called an opinion essay. Marcus will guide you through the stages of the writing process: Prewrite, Draft, Revise, Edit, and Publish. In each stage, Marcus will show you important writing strategies that are linked to the Opinion Writing Traits below.

Opinion Writing Traits

	• a clearly stated opinion • reasons that are supported by examples and details
	• a strong introduction, body, and conclusion • organized paragraphs that each stick to one main idea • linking words and phrases that show how ideas are related
	• a voice and tone that are perfect for the piece of writing
	• strong words that convince the reader • no unnecessary words
	• varied sentences that flow
	• no or few errors in spelling, punctuation, and capitalization

Before you write, read Emily Jackson's opinion essay on the next page. Then use the opinion essay rubric on pages 264–265 to decide how well she did. (You might want to look back at What's in an Opinion Essay? on page 260, too!)

A Great Career

by Emily Jackson

the writer's opinion

People should think hard when they decide on a career. They should choose a job they will like. They should choose a job that is important and needed. For people who like to help others, nursing is a great career.

introduction

One reason to choose nursing is that it is very important work. When someone is sick, a nurse often takes care of the person. A nurse is with a patient much more often than a doctor is. Without nurses to take care of patients, doctors would not be able to do their jobs. Because they watch over patients, nurses can get a person emergency help if it is needed. Nurses often affect how fast people get well. A nurse's good care and kind attitude can help a patient heal. In some cases, nurses save lives.

body

supporting reasons

A second reason to choose nursing is that nurses are needed in many different places. It is easy to find work. Nurses work in hospitals and in doctors' offices. They work at health agencies and in schools. Some nursing jobs are in the military. Others are in industry. Many jobs are in home health care. Sometimes a nurse chooses to teach nursing. Some nurses give advice on how to live a healthy life.

Nursing is a job that matters. We can imagine the world without some jobs, but we cannot imagine the world without nurses. Almost everyone needs a nurse at some time in life. A career in nursing can make a person proud.

conclusion

Opinion Essay Rubric

Use this rubric to analyze the model. Then use it to plan and score your own opinion essay.

	6	5	4
Ideas	The essay has a clear opinion. The reasons are backed up with convincing facts.	The essay has a clear opinion with some supporting details. Most reasons are backed up with convincing facts.	The essay has an opinion. Some reasons are backed up with convincing facts.
Organization	The essay has a strong introduction, body, and conclusion. The conclusion sums up the opinion.	The essay has an introduction, body, and conclusion. The conclusion could be stronger.	The essay has an introduction, body, and conclusion. The conclusion is weak.
Voice	The writer's voice is sincere and businesslike. It convinces the reader.	The writer's voice attempts to convince the reader with appropriate tone.	The writer's voice convinces the reader some of the time. The writer's tone does not always sound sincere.
Word Choice	The writer uses specific words that support the message.	Most of the time, the writer uses specific words that support the message.	The writer's use of specific language is inconsistent and affects the reader's understanding of the message.
Sentence Fluency	Sentences vary in length and flow easily.	Most of the sentences are varied in length, and the piece flows smoothly.	Only a few sentences are varied in length, and the flow is somewhat choppy.
Conventions	All subjects and verbs agree. All pronouns are used correctly.	Most of the subjects and verbs agree. Most pronouns are used correctly.	There are a few errors in agreement or with pronouns. The meaning is clear.

+Presentation The essay is neat and legible.

	3	2	1
Ideas	The essay has an opinion, but the details are weak or not true.	The essay has a weak opinion with some vague or untrue details.	The essay has no clear opinion and lacks details.
Organization	The introduction and conclusion are weak.	The introduction is very weak. The conclusion is missing.	The writing is not organized into paragraphs.
Voice	The writer's tone is inconsistent and is unlikely to convince the reader.	The voice is distant or too informal in places and does not convince the reader.	The voice is weak and does not connect with the reader.
Word Choice	More specific language is needed to convey the message.	The language is too general or casual. The reader must reread to understand the meaning.	The language is so vague that it prevents the reader from understanding the message of the writer.
Sentence Fluency	Too many sentences are the same length, and the flow is very choppy.	Sentences are not varied or may be incomplete, which interrupts the flow of the piece.	This piece is a challenge to read aloud due to choppiness and repetition.
Conventions	Some of the subjects and verbs agree, but the reader must reread for understanding.	There are many errors in agreement or with pronouns. The reader is confused.	Too many errors distract the reader from the meaning.

See Appendix B for 4-, 5-, and 6-point opinion rubrics.

Using the Opinion Essay Rubric to Analyze the Model

Did you notice that the model on page 263 points out some key elements of an opinion essay? As she wrote "A Great Career," Emily Jackson used these elements to express her opinion and try to convince others. She also used the 6-point rubric on pages 264–265 to plan, draft, revise, and edit the writing. A rubric is a great tool to evaluate writing during the writing process.

To get started, look at the top score for each trait as you study the model. Do you agree that Emily has earned a 6 for each trait?

- **The essay has a clear opinion.**
- **The reasons are backed up with convincing facts.**

Emily states her opinion about nursing as a career very clearly. She gives two good reasons to be a nurse. Then she writes a paragraph with convincing details to explain each reason. Take a look at two reasons.

> One reason to choose nursing is that it is very important work.

> A second reason to choose nursing is that nurses are needed in many different places.

- The essay has a strong introduction, body, and conclusion.
- The conclusion sums up the opinion.

Emily's introduction is strong, and the ideas are easy to follow. Take a look at the way she gives her opinion in the introduction and summarizes it in the conclusion.

People should think hard when they decide on a career. They should choose a job they will like. They should choose a job that is important and needed. For people who like to help others, nursing is a great career.

Almost everyone needs a nurse at some time in life. A career in nursing can make a person proud.

- The writer's voice is sincere and businesslike.
- It convinces the reader.

The writer uses a sincere voice to convince the reader that nursing is an important career. She includes facts to support her opinion, and her tone is clear and businesslike. Look at how she uses details to convince the reader that nursing is a great career.

It is easy to find work. Nurses work in hospitals and in doctors' offices. They work at health agencies and in schools. Some nursing jobs are in the military.

Using the Opinion Essay Rubric to Analyze the Model

- **The writer uses specific words that support the message.**

Emily uses specific words that support her opinion. She gives specific examples of the places a nurse can work. These examples support her message that nursing is a great career with many opportunities.

> Many jobs are in home health care. Sometimes a nurse chooses to teach nursing. Some nurses give advice on how to live a healthy life.

- **Sentences vary in length and flow easily.**

Emily uses a variety of sentence lengths to make her essay flow smoothly. Essays are more interesting and easier to follow when the sentences are of different lengths. This pattern makes it easier for me to follow the writer's thinking.

> Because they watch over patients, nurses can get a person emergency help if it is needed. Nurses often affect how fast people get well. A nurse's good care and kind attitude can help a patient heal. In some cases, nurses save lives.

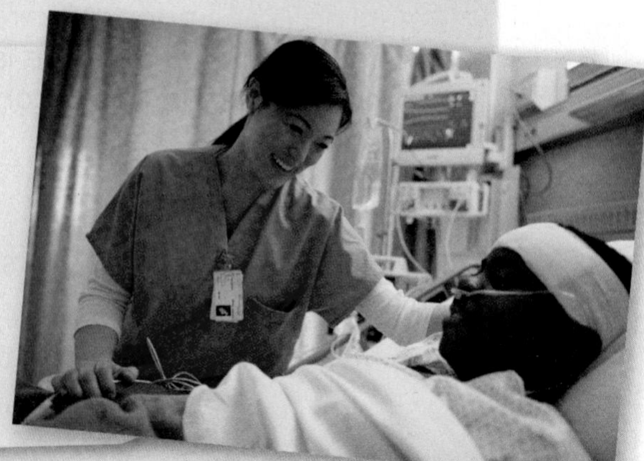

- **All subjects and verbs agree.**
- **All pronouns are used correctly.**

Emily did a good job of proofreading her essay. I couldn't find any errors. She uses all pronouns correctly, and all of her subjects and verbs agree. In the second paragraph Emily uses the singular noun *nurse* and the plural noun *nurses*. The verb *takes* agrees with *nurse*. The verb *save* agrees with *nurses*.

When someone is sick, a nurse often takes care of the person.

In some cases, nurses save lives.

+Presentation The essay is neat and legible.

My Turn!

Now it's my turn to write an opinion essay. I'll use the rubric and good writing strategies to help me do a good job. Read along to see how I do it.

Prewrite

Focus on **Ideas**

The Rubric Says The essay has a clear opinion. The reasons are backed up with convincing facts.

Writing Strategy Choose a topic about which you have a strong opinion. Make notes about the reasons.

My teacher said we should choose an opinion we feel strongly about and can support with reasons. I could write about how much I enjoy running. My mom and I run every morning before school. I think it's the best exercise anyone can do. I'll make notes on the reasons I believe running is the best exercise.

Writer's Term

Reasons

Reasons tell why. They explain the writer's opinion. Good reasons help convince the reader to agree with the writer's opinion.

My Opinion: Running is the best exercise.

My Reasons:

- no gym fees
- can be done almost anytime
- only need running shoes (no other equipment)
- can be done almost anywhere
- not that expensive

Write

Brainstorm some ideas and choose an opinion that you think will interest other students. Then make a list of reasons that support your opinion.

Prewrite

Focus on **Organization**

The Rubric Says The essay has a strong introduction, body, and conclusion.

Writing Strategy Use a Network Tree to organize your essay.

The rubric reminds me that my essay needs to have a strong introduction, body, and conclusion. I will use a Network Tree to organize my notes. I know that my opinion should be stated in the introduction, so I will put it at the top of my Network Tree. Reasons and facts make up the body of my essay. They come next.

Writer's Term

Network Tree

A **Network Tree** organizes information. For an opinion essay, the opinion goes at the top of the tree. Reasons for the opinion come next with supporting facts under each one.

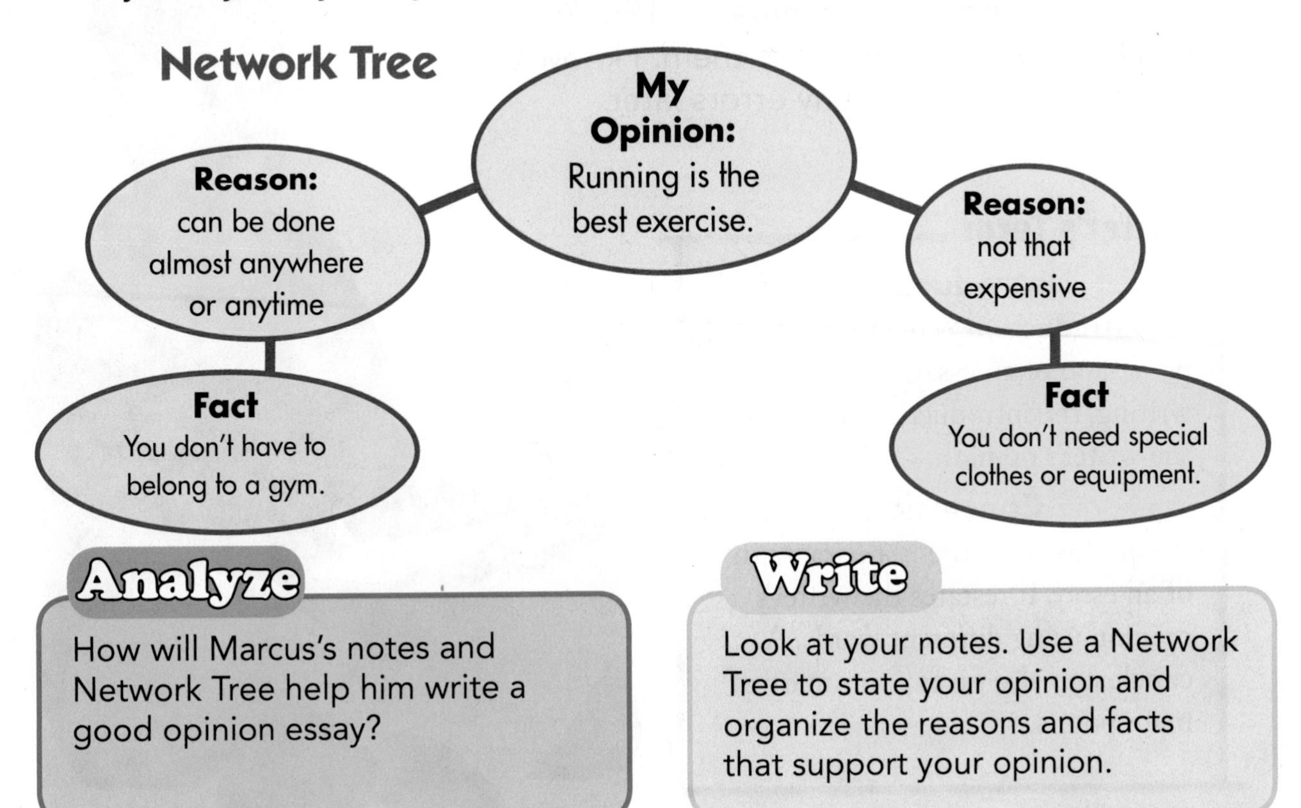

Analyze

How will Marcus's notes and Network Tree help him write a good opinion essay?

Write

Look at your notes. Use a Network Tree to state your opinion and organize the reasons and facts that support your opinion.

Draft

Focus on **Organization**

The Rubric Says The essay has a strong introduction, body, and conclusion.

Writing Strategy Begin the essay with an introduction and end it with a conclusion.

My Network Tree is finished. Now I'm ready to write my draft. I know from the rubric that I need to be especially sure to have a very strong beginning and ending for my essay. I'll write the introduction first.

Then I'll use my Network Tree to help me write the body of my opinion essay. My graphic organizer will help me list my reasons and the facts that support them. The last thing I will write is my conclusion. That's where I will restate my opinion.

I'll do my best with grammar and spelling, but I won't take a lot of time with them. I know that I'll have a chance to fix any errors later.

Writer's Term

Introduction

An **introduction** is the first paragraph of an essay. In opinion writing, the introduction includes the writer's opinion.

Conclusion

A **conclusion** is the last paragraph of an essay. It restates the writer's opinion using different words. A conclusion also gives a summary of main points.

Proofreading Marks

Indent	Take out something
Make uppercase	Add a period
Make lowercase	New paragraph
Add something	Spelling error

[DRAFT]

The Best Exercise

strong introduction

Exercise is important. Adults needs exercise, and yunger people do, too. Yung people can't always do the same exercise that adults do, though. They need something easy and cheap. Running is the best exercise for students.

writer's opinion

Running is an excellent exercise for students because it can always be done anywhere and at any time. Runners don't have to belong to a gym. Students who run don't need a soccer field. They don't need a basketball court. They don't need a pool. All they ever need is a safe place to run. That place might be right outside their door. It might be just down the street or it might be just around the corner. On weekends they can run in the middle of the day.

body paragraphs

Another reason running is the coolest sport for kids is that it is big time cheap. The only important item are a pair of good running shoes. Once a kid has these, there are no other costs. Runners don't need anything special.

Running, like most sports, has many benefits. It helps people stay in shape. A student just can't find a better exercise than running.

conclusion restates writer's opinion

Analyze

Read the draft. How strong are Marcus's introduction, body, and conclusion? How did Marcus connect his introduction and conclusion?

Write

Use your Network Tree to write a draft of an opinion essay. Include a strong introduction and body and a conclusion that restates your opinion.

Revise

Focus on **Voice**

The Rubric Says The writer's voice is sincere and businesslike. It convinces the reader.

Writing Strategy Use a formal tone all through the essay.

The rubric tells me that my essay should sound sincere and businesslike. A formal tone is appropriate for my audience and the purpose for writing. I want my audience to take my opinion seriously. So I'll read my draft aloud to hear how my voice comes across. I found one paragraph where I sound too casual. I'll revise it now.

Writer's Term

Formal Tone

A **formal tone** is the way you would speak to an adult or someone you don't know well. It is polite but not casual or too friendly.

[DRAFT]

used a formal tone

Another reason running is ~~the coolest sport~~ a good sport for ~~kids~~ students is that it is ~~big time cheap!~~ not expensive. The only important item are a pair of good running shoes. Once a ~~kid~~ person has these, there are no other costs.

Write

Read your draft aloud. Listen for a formal tone. If needed, revise your essay so that its tone matches your audience and purpose.

Revise

Focus on **Word Choice**

The Rubric Says	The writer uses specific words that support the message.
Writing Strategy	Replace general words with specific words.

The rubric reminds me to be sure to use specific words to support my message. As I read my essay again, I see some words that are too general or overused. I'll replace them with more specific words that will help convince my reader. I want my reader to take my message seriously.

[DRAFT]

uniforms or other specific running clothes. Most people do just fine in a shirt and a pair of shorts.

Runners don't need ~~anything special.~~

added specific words

Analyze

Look at Marcus's changes. How do the specific words make his writing more convincing?

Write

Read your draft again. Look for places where you can make your writing more convincing by replacing general words with specific words.

Revise

Focus on Sentence Fluency

The Rubric Says Sentences vary in length and flow easily.

Writing Strategy Use some long sentences and some short ones.

The rubric reminds me to vary my sentence lengths. I found a place in my essay where I used too many short sentences in a row. I'll revise them so my ideas flow better.

varied sentence lengths

[DRAFT]

Students who run don't need a soccer field~~. They don't need a~~ , a basketball court~~. They don't need~~ , or a pool. All they ever need is a safe place to run. That place might be right outside their door. It might be just down the street or ~~it might be just~~ around the corner.

Write

Check your draft. Revise your essay to include both long and short sentences.

Edit

Focus on **Conventions**

The Rubric Says All subjects and verbs agree. All pronouns are used correctly.

Writing Strategy Check that all subjects and verbs agree. Use pronouns correctly.

I always check my writing for spelling, capitalization, and punctuation. The rubric reminds me to check subject-verb agreement and the use of pronouns, too.

Writer's Term

Subject-Verb Agreement

A **subject** and **verb** must **agree.** These sentences have subjects and verbs that agree.

- The **park is** a beautiful place to run.
- **Families exercise** together on the trails.

[DRAFT]

Exercise is important. Adults need~~s~~ exercise, and ~~yunger~~ younger people do, too. ~~Yung~~ Young people can't always do the same exercise that adults do, though.

corrected spelling errors

fixed subject-verb agreement

Analyze

Look at Marcus's edits. Are mistakes in subject-verb agreement fixed correctly? How will Marcus's changes clarify his writing?

Write

Conventions

Edit your draft for spelling, capitalization, and punctuation. Be sure all subjects and verbs agree and that pronouns are used correctly.

For more practice with subject-verb agreement and correct use of pronouns, use the exercises on the next two pages.

Conventions **Grammar, Usage & Mechanics**

Subject-Verb Agreement

Know the Rule

The subject and verb in a sentence must agree in number.

- Add **-s** or **-es** to a regular verb in the present tense when the subject is a singular noun or **he, she,** or **it**.
- Do not add **-s** or **-es** to a regular verb in the present tense when the subject is a plural noun or **I, you, we,** or **they**.
- Use **is** or **was** after a singular subject.
- Use **are** or **were** after a plural subject.

Practice the Rule

Number a sheet of paper 1–14. Read each sentence. Write the subject of the sentence and the verb in ( ) that correctly completes it.

1. Many children (is/are) active in sports.
2. Soccer (is/are) one of the most popular sports.
3. Players (need/needs) little equipment to get started.
4. Two nets (stand/stands) at the end of a flat field.
5. A soccer ball (weigh/weighs) about 15 ounces.
6. Players (wear/wears) special shoes and leg guards.
7. A player (kick/kicks) the ball.
8. He (hit/hits) the ball with his head or body.
9. A player called a goalie (guard/guards) the net.
10. Goalies (touch/touches) the ball with their hands.
11. Other players (do/does) not touch the ball with their hands at any time.
12. The player (try/tries) to put the ball into the net.
13. A player (get/gets) one point for each goal.
14. Sports (is/are) good exercise for children.

Subject Pronouns

Know the Rule

A **subject pronoun** takes the place of one or more nouns in the subject of a sentence. *I, you, he, she,* and *it* are singular subject pronouns. *We, you,* and *they* are plural subject pronouns.

Examples:
I like to play soccer.
My parents watched the championship game. **They** are loyal soccer fans.

Practice the Rule

Number a sheet of paper 1–10. Read the following sentences. Choose the pronoun in ( ) that correctly completes each numbered sentence.

Did you know that nearly every country in the world plays soccer?

1. (It/They) was played in the 1900 Olympic Games for the first time.
2. Today (it/they) is an important sport in the Summer Olympics.

The Olympic Games are not the only time people watch soccer games.

3. (It/They) are televised and watched by millions of people every year.
4. (It/They) inspire many young people to play the game.

Pelé is one of the most famous soccer athletes of all time.

5. (He/They) helped make soccer a world-class sport.
6. (They/He) is best known for leading Brazil to the World Cup three times.
7. (They/It) is the highest achievement in the sport.

Thousands of boys and girls in the United States enjoy playing soccer.

8. (We/They) play on teams in practically every American community.
9. (He/They) may dream about winning the World Cup!
10. (They/He) would be very excited to be at a World Cup game.

Publish + Presentation

Publishing Strategy Publish the essay on the class website.

Presentation Strategy Choose one or two readable fonts.

My opinion essay is finished! It's time to publish it now. I think I'll publish it on the class website. That means I'll need to carefully prepare my essay on the computer. I'll make sure that I've done everything on my final checklist.

My Final Checklist

Did I—

- ✔ make sure that all subjects and verbs agree?
- ✔ use subject pronouns correctly?
- ✔ edit and proofread carefully?
- ✔ use neat word processing?
- ✔ put the title and my name at the top of the page?

Write

Use Marcus's checklist to check your own opinion essay. Then make a final copy to post on your class website.

The Best Exercise

by Marcus

Exercise is important. Adults need exercise, and younger people do, too. Young people can't always do the same exercise that adults do, though. They need something easy and cheap. Running is the best exercise for students.

Running is an excellent exercise for students because it can be done anywhere and at any time. Runners don't have to belong to a gym. Students who run don't need a soccer field, a basketball court, or a pool. All they ever need is a safe place to run. That place might be right outside their door. It might be just down the street or around the corner. Also, running is a sport that can be done at any time of day. For example, most swimmers can swim only when a pool is open, but runners can run at any time. On weekdays students can run early in the morning or after school. On weekends they can run in the middle of the day.

Another reason why running is a good sport for students is that it is not expensive. The only important item is a pair of good running shoes. Once a person has these, there are no other costs. Runners do not have to buy tickets the way skiers do. They don't have to own high-cost items like bicycles or golf clubs. They also don't have to pay to go to some faraway place. Runners don't need uniforms or other specific running clothes. Most people do just fine in a shirt and a pair of shorts.

Running, like most sports, has many benefits. It helps people stay in shape. It's affordable and fun! I believe that no one could find a better way to exercise.

Analyze

Use the rubric to see if Marcus included all the traits of a good opinion essay. Remember to use the rubric to check your own opinion essay, too.

What's a Response to Literature?

It's a piece of writing that tells if I liked a book or not and explains why I feel that way. One way I can respond to my reading is to write a book review.

What's in a Response to Literature?

My Opinion
That's how I feel about the book. I love many of the books I read! Some books I don't like at all.

Examples and Details
I'll have to explain why I feel the way I do about my book. I'll give examples and details from the book to support my opinion. It's fun to write about a book I like a lot. I want to convince my friends to read it, too!

A Friendly Tone
I want to use a friendly tone when I tell my classmates my opinion of the book and my reasons for liking it. They are my audience. If I use a friendly tone, they may be more interested.

Why write a Response to Literature?

There are many reasons to respond to literature. Here are some that I thought of.

To Convince
People respond to literature to share their feelings about a book. They might want to convince others to read it or not to read it.

To Inform
A good response to literature gives interesting information about the book. I might decide to read the book even though the reviewer didn't like it. The book review might tell me enough to get me curious. Not everyone likes the same TV shows, movies, or books.

To Entertain
It is fun to learn about different kinds of books and different topics of books.

Linking Opinion Writing Traits to a Response to Literature

In this chapter, you will respond to a book. One way to do this is to write a book review. Marcus will guide you through the stages of the writing process: Prewrite, Draft, Revise, Edit, and Publish. In each stage, Marcus will show you important writing strategies that are linked to the Opinion Writing Traits below.

Opinion Writing Traits

	• a clearly stated opinion • reasons that are supported by examples and details
	• a strong introduction, body, and conclusion • organized paragraphs that stick to one main idea • linking words and phrases that show how ideas are related
	• a voice and tone that are perfect for the piece of writing
	• strong words that convince the reader • no unnecessary words
	• varied sentences that flow
	• no or few errors in spelling, punctuation, and capitalization

Before you write, read Tom Keller's book review on the next page. Then use the response to literature rubric on pages 286–287 to decide how well he did. (You might want to look back at What's in a Response to Literature? on page 282, too!)

Mr. Popper's Penguins

by Richard and Florence Atwater

by Tom Keller

opinion

a friendly tone

If you like stories about animals, faraway places, or funny people, *Mr. Popper's Penguins* by Richard and Florence Atwater is the book for you.

Mr. Popper's life goes crazy when someone sends him a penguin. Then Mr. Popper gets another penguin. After that his two penguins turn into twelve penguins! He opens his windows and doors so the house will be cold for the penguins. Then he fills his basement with ice.

I know that a penguin wouldn't be a good pet, but this book made me want to have a penguin of my own! I think Mr. Popper felt the same way. It says in the book, "Often, too, he thought how different his life had been before the penguins had come to keep him occupied."

details and examples from the book

I like the people in the story. Mrs. Popper was always worried about money, and Mr. Popper was always spending money. She loved Mr. Popper anyway. Mr. Popper did a lot of silly things, but in the end he took good care of the penguins and his family.

The drawings in the book are great. The best one shows Mr. Popper taking a penguin for a walk. The rope he tied to the penguin has gotten wrapped around a lady. She looks angry, and she's dropping all her bags. Mr. Popper looks like he doesn't know what to do. The penguin looks like he's laughing. I think the pictures make the story even funnier.

I really liked the fact that the story was full of surprises. I think families would enjoy reading this book together.

opinion

Response to Literature Rubric

Use this rubric to analyze the model. Then use it to plan and score your own response to literature.

	6	5	4
Ideas	The writer's opinion of the book is clear. Quotes and examples support the opinion.	The writer's opinion is clear. One or two more quotes or examples would help support the opinion.	The writer's opinion is clear. Few quotes or examples are present.
Organization	The reasons are well organized. Linking words and phrases help the reader follow the ideas.	The reasons are organized. Linking words and phrases are used to help the reader follow the ideas.	The reasons are mostly organized. Some linking words and phrases are present and used correctly to support the reader.
Voice	The writer's voice is friendly in tone and reaches out to the reader.	The writer's voice is friendly and reaches out to the reader most of the time.	The writer's voice is friendly and reaches out to the reader some of the time.
Word Choice	The writing has just the right number of words to give the information.	The writing has some words that are not necessary for meaning.	The writing contains many extra words that confuse the reader and are not necessary for meaning.
Sentence Fluency	A variety of sentence patterns makes the writing flow smoothly. The review is fun to read.	Sentences are varied most of the time to make the writing flow easily.	More variety of sentences would make the writing flow better.
Conventions	Quotation marks and apostrophes are used correctly. The meaning is clear.	Quotation marks and apostrophes are mostly used correctly. The meaning is clear.	There are a few punctuation errors with quotations and apostrophes, but the meaning is clear.

+Presentation The paragraphs are indented.

3	2	1	
The writer's opinion is somewhat clear. Too few quotes and examples support an opinion.	The opinion is not clear. Quotes and examples may be unrelated or confusing.	The opinion is not clear. Quotes and examples are not used.	Ideas
The reasons are weakly organized. Linking words and phrases are lacking, and the reader must reread to understand.	The reasons are not well organized and lack linking words and phrases. The reader must reread to understand.	The reasons are not organized and leave the reader confused. Linking words and phrases are missing.	Organization
The voice sounds too formal and does not reach out to the reader.	The writer's voice is barely present and does not involve the reader.	Little or no voice is present.	Voice
The writing has many words that are not necessary for meaning.	The writing is wordy and confusing, making it difficult to read.	The writing is wordy, and the meaning is lost in the extra words.	Word Choice
Similar sentence patterns make reading predictable and dull for the reader.	Sentence fluency is minimal due to a lack of sentence variety. This makes the piece hard to read.	Sentences are incomplete or follow the same pattern, which makes the writing choppy and predictable.	Sentence Fluency
Many errors cause the reader to reread for meaning.	The writing contains serious errors. It is very difficult to read and understand.	A number of errors stop the reader. The writing has not been edited.	Conventions

See Appendix B for 4-, 5-, and 6-point opinion rubrics.

Using the Response to Literature Rubric to Analyze the Model

Did you notice that the model on page 285 points out some key elements of a response to literature? As he wrote the review of *Mr. Popper's Penguins*, Tom Keller used these elements to help him convince people to read the book. He also used the 6-point rubric on pages 286–287 to plan, draft, revise, and edit the writing. A rubric is a great tool to evaluate writing during the writing process.

To get started, look at the top score for each trait as you study the model. Do you agree that Tom has earned a 6 for each trait?

- **The writer's opinion of the book is clear.**
- **Quotes and examples support the opinion.**

The writer clearly expresses his opinion that people will like reading *Mr. Popper's Penguins*. He also gives examples to support his opinion. Tom starts his fourth paragraph with an example and tells why it supports his opinion.

> I like the people in the story. Mrs. Popper was always worried about money, and Mr. Popper was always spending money. She loved Mr. Popper anyway. Mr. Popper did a lot of silly things, but in the end he took good care of the penguins and his family.

- **The reasons are well organized.**
- **Linking words and phrases help the reader follow the ideas.**

The writer includes reasons that are well organized and easy to follow. He also uses linking words and phrases to help the reader understand how ideas are connected. For example, in the sentence below, he uses the word *but* to connect two ideas that are different.

> Mr. Popper did a lot of silly things, but in the end he took good care of the penguins and his family.

- **The writer's voice is friendly in tone and reaches out to the reader.**

The beginning of the review sounds like the writer is talking to a friend about a book. He talks directly to the reader. When I read the first paragraph, I thought, "Yes, I like animal stories. Maybe I would like this book. I want to find out more."

> If you like stories about animals, faraway places, or funny people, *Mr. Popper's Penguins* by Richard and Florence Atwater is the book for you.

Using the Response to Literature Rubric to Analyze the Model

- **The writing has just the right number of words to give the information.**

The writer gives lots of information to support his opinion, but his sentences are not too wordy. They have just the right number of words to explain why *Mr. Popper's Penguins* is a good book to read.

> Mr. Popper's life goes crazy when someone sends him a penguin. Then Mr. Popper gets another penguin. After that his two penguins turn into twelve penguins! He opens his windows and doors so the house will be cold for the penguins. Then he fills his basement with ice.

- **A variety of sentence patterns makes the writing flow smoothly.**

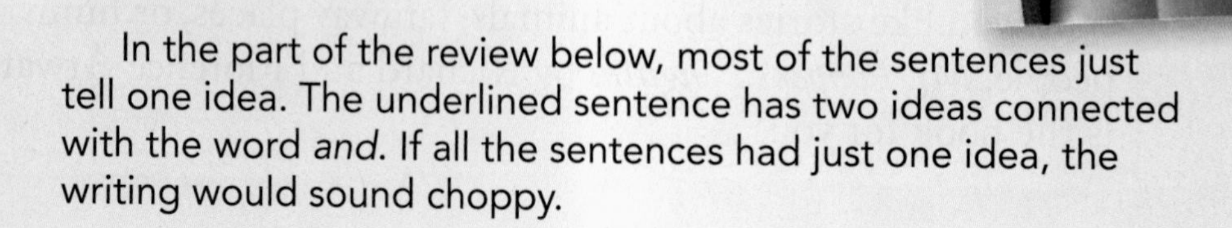

In the part of the review below, most of the sentences just tell one idea. The underlined sentence has two ideas connected with the word *and.* If all the sentences had just one idea, the writing would sound choppy.

> The drawings in the book are great. The best one shows Mr. Popper taking a penguin for a walk. The rope he tied to the penguin has gotten wrapped around a lady. She looks angry, and she's dropping all her bags. Mr. Popper looks like he doesn't know what to do.

- **Quotation marks and apostrophes are used correctly.**

Tom did a great job editing his book review. There are no errors in spelling, capitalization, or punctuation. He also uses apostrophes correctly. In these two examples, apostrophes are used for different reasons. Do you know what they are?

Mr. Popper's life goes crazy when someone sends him a penguin.

Mr. Popper looks like he doesn't know what to do.

+Presentation The paragraphs are indented.

My Turn!

Now it's my turn to write a review about a book I've read. I'll use the rubric and good writing strategies to help me. Follow along to see how I do it.

Prewrite

Focus on **Ideas**

The Rubric Says The writer's opinion of the book is clear. Quotes and examples support the opinion.

Writing Strategy Choose a book you have read. List the reasons why you like or do not like the book.

My teacher asked us to write a book review, so I need to select a book. I just finished reading *Prairie School* by Avi. This book was very good. I want to tell my classmates about it because some of them may like it, too.

Before I write my review, I'll reread the names of the chapters and look at the pictures again. That will help me remember more details about the story. Then I'll list some reasons why I liked the book.

Reasons I Like Prairie School

- ✔ about a boy my age
- ✔ likes being outside like I do
- ✔ feels the way I used to feel about reading
- ✔ takes place in a different time
- ✔ has an interesting aunt
- ✔ gives an important message about reading and books
- ✔ has surprising details
- ✔ has a happy ending

Write

Think about books you have read recently. Choose one you would like to review. Decide whether or not you would recommend this book to others to read. Write some reasons why you would or wouldn't recommend the book.

Prewrite

Focus on **Organization**

The Rubric Says The reasons are well organized.

Writing Strategy Use a Web to organize your reasons and plan a response.

I know from the rubric that I have to organize the reasons for my opinion. A Web will help me organize my ideas about the book so they will be easy for my readers to understand.

Writer's Term

Web

A **Web** organizes information. The center circle tells the topic and main idea. The outer circles show the supporting details.

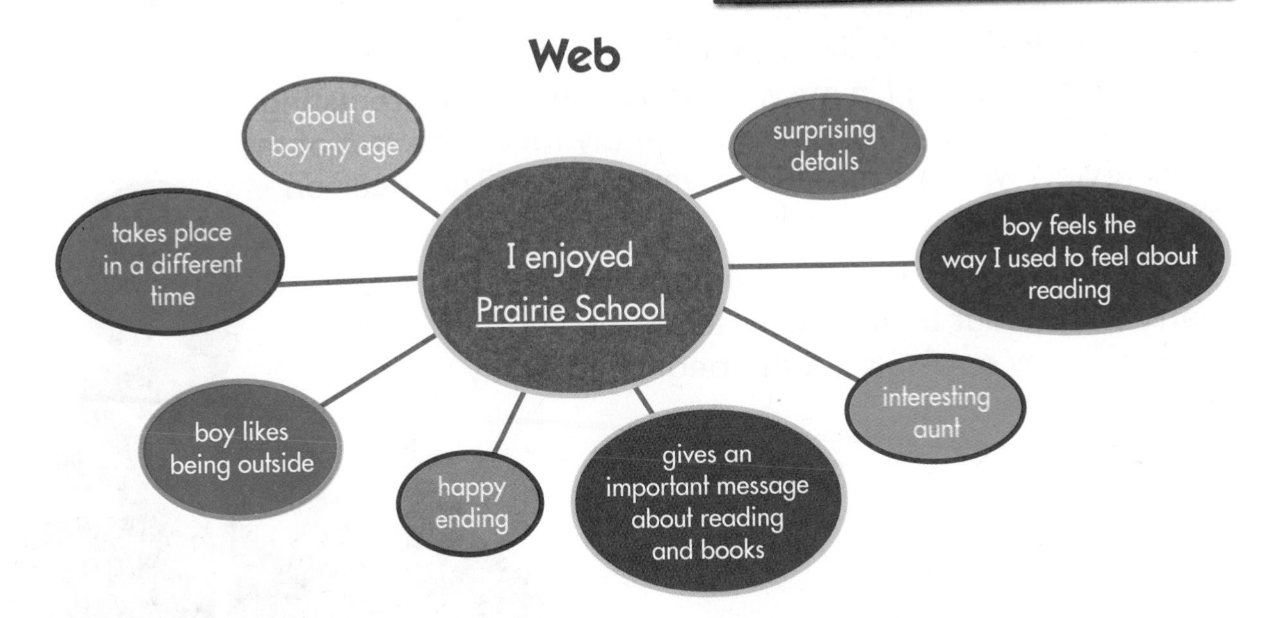

Analyze

Look at Marcus's Web. How does it help him organize his ideas about the book he likes?

Write

Look at your notes. Use a Web to organize the reasons for your opinion.

Draft

Focus on **Voice**

The Rubric Says The writer's voice is friendly in tone and reaches out to the reader.

Writing Strategy Choose details that will interest the reader. Use *I* to connect with the reader.

Writer's Term

Tone

Tone is the writer's attitude toward the topic of his or her writing. A writer's tone can be serious, funny, sad, businesslike, or friendly.

Now it's time to write my book review. I'll use my Web to help me write a draft.

I know that my opinion of the book is very important. The rubric says I should state my advice in a friendly tone. I want to make sure that my review sounds like I am talking directly to the audience. Using *I* in my writing and choosing interesting details will also give my review a friendly tone. The rest of my book review will give reasons for my opinion. The ideas on my Web will help me do that.

I'll do my best with grammar and spelling, but I won't worry a lot about them now. Later, when I edit, I'll take time to fix my errors. Read the beginning of my draft on the next page.

Proofreading Marks

- Indent
- Make uppercase
- Make lowercase
- Add something
- Take out something
- Add a period
- New paragraph
- Spelling error

[DRAFT]

Prairie School by Avi
review by Marcus

I enjoyed the book Prairie School by Avi so much that I think other people would, too. It tells the story about a boy named Noah. He lives on a farm in Colorado. His life changes when he is nine years old. Noah loves the prairie. He spends a lot of time outside. Everyone in his family works very hard. Noah's dad and mom want him to have a better life. They want him to learn to read and write.

stated opinion in a friendly tone

Analyze

Read the beginning of Marcus's draft. How does his tone of voice reach out to the reader?

Write

Use your Web to write a draft of a book review. Remember to state your opinion clearly and use a friendly tone that sounds as if you are talking directly to your audience.

Revise

Focus on **Ideas**

The Rubric Says Quotes and examples support the opinion.

Writing Strategy Support the opinion with a brief quote from the book.

I finished my draft. Then I looked back at the rubric. It says to use quotes from the book to support my opinion. When I reread my draft, I noticed that I said Aunt Dora likes to read. I remember something she says in the book that shows her love of reading. I can find that part and quote it. I think her words will make my readers want to read the book, too.

Writer's Term

Quote

A **quote** states the exact words of an author. A quote is placed within quotation marks to show that the words belong to someone else.

[DRAFT]

wheelchair. She was in an accident. She can't walk anymore.

Aunt Dora is a schoolteacher, so it is easy to see why she likes to read. I liked it when she told Noah, "My mind can go farther with books than my body can go with my legs." This is the most important idea in the book. The author is saying that being able to read makes your life better.

added a memorable quote

Write

Read your draft. Revise your writing by adding short quotes from the book that support your opinion.

Revise

Focus on **Word Choice**

The Rubric Says The writing has just the right number of words to give the information.

Writing Strategy Take out unnecessary words.

The rubric reminds me to check my writing to make sure I use just the right number of words. I want my review to be easy to read and understand. As I read my draft again, I found a spot where I repeated some information. This could confuse my reader, so I'll take out the unnecessary words.

[DRAFT]

Then Aunt Dora comes to the farm to teach Noah how to read ^and write. ~~She also comes to the farm to teach Noah how to write.~~ Noah doesnt want to learn how to read ^or write. ~~He doesn't want to learn how to write either.~~ He hates being inside the house. ~~I mean, he really hates being inside the house!~~

took out unnecessary words

Analyze

Look at Marcus's revisions. Did he take out repetitious words? How does this affect his writing?

Write

Read through your draft. Take out words that repeat what has already been said.

Revise

Focus on Sentence Fluency

The Rubric Says A variety of sentence patterns makes the writing flow smoothly. The review is fun to read.

Writing Strategy Fix choppy sentences.

Now I'll read my draft aloud to check my sentences. I want to make sure that my sentences are not all the same length. I want to include both long and short sentences so that my writing will flow smoothly.

As I read the first paragraph, I noticed it sounded choppy. See how I fixed the problem?

Writer's Term

Choppy Sentences

Choppy sentences express complete thoughts, but by combining these sentences, the writing will flow better.

Choppy Sentences:

- Prairies are in the Midwest.
- Prairies are covered with grass.
- Prairies don't have trees.

Better Sentence:

- Prairies in the Midwest are covered with grass but don't have trees.

[DRAFT]

Noah. He lives on a farm in Colorado. His life changes when he is nine years old. Noah loves the prairie~~. He~~ and spends a lot of time outside. Everyone in his family works very hard.

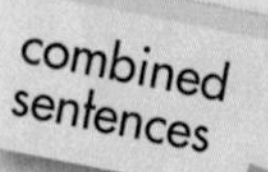

Write

Read your draft. Revise your writing for smooth flow by combining choppy sentences.

Edit

Focus on **Conventions**

The Rubric Says Quotation marks and apostrophes are used correctly. The meaning is clear.

Writing Strategy Make sure all apostrophes are used correctly.

I know from the rubric that I should be sure that apostrophes are used correctly. I'll also check to be sure other punctuation marks and spelling are correct. I'll check my proper nouns, too.

Writer's Term

Apostrophe

An **apostrophe** is a punctuation mark ('). It can be used to show that someone owns something, such as **Aunt Dora's wheelchair**. In a contraction, an apostrophe shows where the word has been shortened, such as using **she'll** for **she will**.

added apostrophe

Every time Noahs aunt tries to teach him something, he thinks of something he has to do and runs outside. At the begining of the book Noah says, Reading is as much use on the prairie as the stars!

[DRAFT]

Analyze

Look at Marcus's edits. Are apostrophes used correctly? Are other punctuation errors fixed? How do Marcus's edits clarify his writing?

Write

Conventions

Edit your draft for spelling, punctuation, and capitalization.

For more practice with apostrophes and quotation marks, use the exercises on the next two pages.

Apostrophes

Know the Rule

An **apostrophe** (') is used to show possession. A possessive noun is the name of an owner.

- When there is one owner, add **'s** to the word.
  Example: Avi**'s** story was about Noah.
- When there are two or more owners and the word ends in **-s,** add an apostrophe after the **-s**.
  Example: His parents' home is on the prairie.

An apostrophe is also used to show where a letter or letters have been taken out in a contraction.

Example: At first Noah didn't like reading.
Example: I've read *Prairie School,* too.

Practice the Rule

Number a sheet of paper 1–10. Read each sentence. Rewrite each sentence and add any missing apostrophes. If a sentence has no errors, write **Correct** after the number.

1. A prairies land is flat and grassy.
2. North America's prairies stretch from Texas to Canada.
3. Grasses arent the only plants on prairies.
4. The flowers colors are red, yellow, orange, and purple.
5. Many animals homes are on the prairie.
6. Jackrabbits, deer, and prairie dogs are a few prairie animals.
7. Prairie dogs dont belong to the dog family.
8. Some prairie creatures homes are burrows dug into the ground.
9. Many birds live on the prairie, too.
10. A birds nest is usually made from plants on the prairie.

Quotation Marks

Know the Rule

Use **quotation marks** to show someone's exact written or spoken words. Quotation marks go around the beginning and end of a **direct quotation**. Do not use quotation marks when the word *that* comes before someone's words.

Examples:

Evan said, "Prairie dogs live in burrows in the ground."

"I never knew," said Oliver, "that they make sounds much like a dog's bark."

John said **that** prairie dogs eat mostly plants and a few grasshoppers.

Practice the Rule

Number a sheet of paper 1–10. Read each sentence. Rewrite each sentence that uses quotation marks incorrectly. If a sentence has no errors, write **Correct** after the number.

1. "Prairie dogs can be found from Canada to Mexico," said Lucas.
2. They don't come out at night, replied Danny.
3. Matt said, They like to come out during the day and eat.
4. Hasan said that prairie dogs live in groups of up to 500.
5. "Their enemies," said Oliver, "include American badgers, coyotes, and hawks."
6. When an enemy comes near, said Curtis, a prairie dog makes a loud sound.
7. "They don't go into the ground until the enemy gets close," replied Michael.
8. Evan said that prairie dogs are interesting rodents to study.
9. Ms. Dexter said, I'm glad you enjoyed learning about prairie dogs.
10. Next week, Ms. Dexter continued, we will learn about owls.

Publish

+Presentation

Publishing Strategy Present your review to the class.

Presentation Strategy Indent each paragraph.

Now that my book review is finished, it's time to publish it. Everyone in my class wants to hear about the books that we have read. We decided to read our book reviews to the class. Before I present my review, I need to check to see if I indented all of my paragraphs correctly. This helps to separate the paragraphs and ideas. It will help me when I read aloud. I will also use a map of Colorado as a prop. It will make my review more interesting if I use the map to point out where Noah lived. Here is the final checklist I used.

My Final Checklist

Did I—

- ✔ use correct spelling, capitalization, and punctuation?
- ✔ use apostrophes correctly?
- ✔ use quotation marks to show someone's exact words?
- ✔ indent each paragraph to separate the ideas?
- ✔ write my name and the title of my book at the top of my paper?

Write

Make your own checklist to check your response to literature. Then make a final copy to present to your class. Display the book and a prop that has to do with the book.

Prairie School by Avi
a book review by Marcus

I enjoyed the book Prairie School by Avi so much that I think other people would, too. It tells the story about a boy named Noah, who lives on a farm in Colorado. His life changes when he is nine years old. Noah loves the prairie and spends a lot of time outside. Everyone in his family works very hard. Noah's dad and mom want him to have a better life. For this reason, they want him to learn to read and write.

Then Aunt Dora comes to the farm to teach Noah how to read and write. Noah doesn't want to learn how to read or write. He hates being inside the house. Every time Noah's aunt tries to teach him something, he thinks of something he has to do and runs outside. At the beginning of the book, Noah says, "Reading is as much use on the prairie as the stars!" Will he ever learn to read?

Aunt Dora is a very interesting character. She uses a wheelchair because she was in an accident. She can't walk anymore. Aunt Dora is a schoolteacher, so it is easy to see why she likes to read. I liked it when she told Noah, "My mind can go farther with books than my body can go with my legs." This is the most important idea in the book. The author is saying that being able to read makes your life better.

In the book Prairie School, Noah learns to read and write. He also learns that reading is fun. At the end of the book he writes a letter to Aunt Dora. He writes, "I live on the prairie, but now I can read the whole world." I didn't always like to read, so I know how Noah felt. I think many people will enjoy this book. I would recommend this book to anyone.

Analyze

Use the rubric to evaluate Marcus's writing. Remember to use the rubric to check your own response to literature, too.

What's a Brochure?

It's a folded flyer or booklet that gives information to convince people to make certain choices.

What's in a Brochure?

Details
Details are the facts and examples that support my purpose. In a brochure, my purpose is to convince someone to do something, such as visit a place or vote for a particular person.

Positive Words
These are words that will convince the reader to agree with my opinion. For example, I might use the word *cozy* instead of *small* to describe a hotel I like.

Graphics
Graphics include photographs, appealing headings, and attractive art. These are combined in a way that makes the very best impression on a reader.

Organization
The text, graphics, and photos are laid out in an organized way that helps readers clearly understand the information in the brochure.

Why write a Brochure?

There are many reasons to write a brochure. Here are some of them.

To Advertise
A brochure can let people know about an event or place and show why you would want to go. The best brochures get the full attention of the reader and leave a positive impression.

To Convince
Words, pictures, and text can convince readers to do what the brochure suggests, such as go to a particular place. If a brochure is attractive and fun to read, it'll have the best chance of convincing people.

To Inform
A good brochure gives readers accurate information that will be useful and reliable. It helps readers decide what to do.

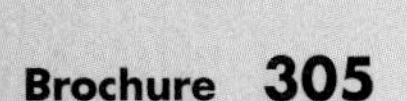

Linking Opinion Writing Traits to a Brochure

In this chapter, you will tell your opinion in a short piece of writing. This type of opinion writing is called a brochure. Marcus will guide you through the stages of the writing process: Prewrite, Draft, Revise, Edit, and Publish. In each stage, Marcus will show you important writing strategies that are linked to the Opinion Writing Traits below.

Opinion Writing Traits

Trait	Description
	• a clearly stated opinion • reasons that are supported by examples and details
	• a strong introduction, body, and conclusion • organized paragraphs that each stick to one main idea • linking words and phrases that show how ideas are related
	• a voice and tone that are perfect for the piece of writing
	• strong words that convince the reader • no unnecessary words
	• varied sentences that flow
	• no or few errors in spelling, punctuation, and capitalization

Before you write, read Nora Chen's brochure on the next three pages. Then use the brochure rubric on pages 310–311 to decide how well she did. (You might want to look back at What's in a Brochure? on page 304, too!)

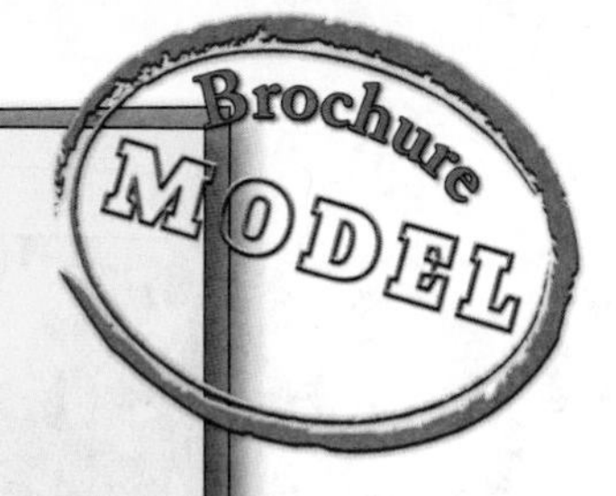

Brochure created by
Nora Chen

PLIMOTH
PLANTATION

When you are in Massachusetts, be sure to visit

Plimoth Plantation

This is your chance to travel back in time almost four hundred years. Once you get there, you will know what life was like through all five senses and with your own active mind!

Find out a few of the many amazing things you will see, hear, touch, taste, and smell at Plimoth Plantation.

graphics

positive words

Brochure MODEL

interesting details

positive words

Interpreter and visitors at the Wampanoag Homesite

See two special sites with homes and activities that recreate the lives of the English colonists and the Native Wampanoag who lived there in 1627. Look inside boats and buildings where people will welcome you and tell you fascinating stories.

Hear words as they were spoken then. The interpreters at the 1627 English Village speak the language of the 1620s. At the Wampanoag Homesite, real native people show visitors what life was like for their ancestors who lived on the land at that time. Talk with people at both sites, and they will tell you about their adventures, hopes, and chores.

Touch tools, tables, cradles, bowls, bags, and baskets like the ones used by people who lived in those times. You can try out their garden tools, try on Pilgrim clothes, and play their games.

Bags

good organization

Smell herbs, farm animals, and cooking fires that were part of daily village life in 1627. You won't smell fumes of cars, trucks, trains, or tractors because that was before any of those had been invented.

Taste corn pudding, venison burgers, stew, and other delicious dishes. Find out favorite recipes of colonists and native people.

Learn from many exhibits that very clearly explain the lives of colonists and native people almost four centuries ago. You will not forget these exhibits because they get you involved.

Think and ***imagine*** how it would be for you to live long ago and how your days would be different from your usual life in the present. Now you are set for your day at Plimoth Plantation.

good organization

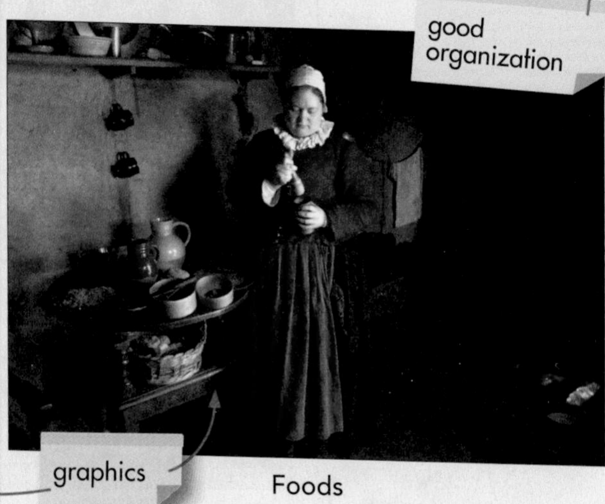

graphics

Foods

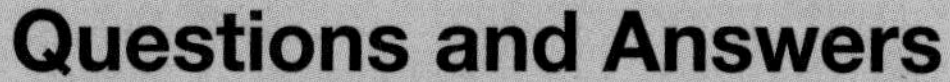

Questions and Answers

Q: Why is this place called *Plimoth Plantation*?

A: *Plantation* meant "colony" or "settlement" at the time when people from England came to settle in North America. They planted crops on the land, and some called themselves "planters."

Q: What does *Wampanoag* mean?

A: *Wampanoag* means "People of the First Light." In the early 1600s, there were more than sixty Wampanoag villages on what is now the southeast coast of Massachusetts.

Q: What is a wetu?

A: A *wetu* is a dome-shaped home on a frame of bent trees. The *wetu* is covered in tree bark and has a hole in the top for smoke from cooking fires.

Q: What did children do at Plimoth Plantation in 1627?

A: Children in both Wampanoag and English settler families helped adults with most daily work, such as planting, fishing, tending animals, and preparing food. They also studied and played. Find out much more when you visit!

good organization

Ask your own questions,
and real people will answer you at

Plimoth Plantation!

Brochure Rubric

Use this rubric to analyze the model. Then use it to plan and score your own brochure.

	6	5	4
Ideas	The opinion is clear. Interesting details support the reasons.	The opinion is clear. Most details are interesting and support the reasons.	The opinion is clear. Some details are interesting and support the reasons.
Organization	Clear headings organize the information. Linking words and phrases connect the details clearly.	Clear headings organize the information. One or two more linking words and phrases are needed.	Clear headings organize the information. More linking words and phrases are needed.
Voice	The writer's voice is strong and speaks to the reader all the way through.	The writer's voice is fairly strong and speaks to the reader.	The writer's voice is strongest in the beginning but then fades.
Word Choice	Strong words convince the reader.	One or two weak words could be replaced with more convincing words.	Some of the words are very weak. More convincing words are needed.
Sentence Fluency	A variety of sentence patterns adds interest and flow.	A few sentences share the same pattern.	Several sentences in a row share the same pattern.
Conventions	There are no errors. *Very* and *real* are used correctly. There are no double negatives.	A few minor errors are present. Adverbs are used correctly.	Several errors may confuse the reader. Adverbs are used correctly.

+Presentation The brochure catches the reader's attention.

	3	2	1
Ideas	The opinion may not be clear. Details may not belong together.	The opinion is not clear. Details are not provided.	The opinion is not provided.
Organization	The information is not well organized. Several linking words and phrases may be confusing.	The information is hard to follow. Linking words and phrases are confusing or missing.	The writing is not organized as a brochure. Linking words and phrases are not used.
Voice	The writer's voice is distant. It does not speak to the reader.	The voice is confusing or inconsistent.	The voice is very weak or absent. The reader does not know who is speaking.
Word Choice	Most of the words are weak and not convincing.	The words are too general or overused.	Words are used incorrectly.
Sentence Fluency	Most sentences share the same pattern.	All sentences share the same pattern.	Sentences are incomplete or incorrect.
Conventions	Many errors confuse the reader. Some adverbs may be used incorrectly.	Serious errors stop the reader. Adverbs are used incorrectly.	The writing has not been edited.

See Appendix B for 4-, 5-, and 6-point opinion rubrics.

Using the Brochure Rubric to Analyze the Model

Did you notice that the model on pages 307–309 points out some key elements of a brochure? As she wrote "Plimoth Plantation," Nora Chen used these elements to help her convince people to visit the plantation. She also used the 6-point rubric on pages 310–311 to plan, draft, revise, and edit the writing. A rubric is a great tool to evaluate writing during the writing process.

To get started, look at the top score for each trait as you study the model. Do you agree that Nora has earned a 6 for each trait?

- **The opinion is clear.**
- **Interesting details support the reasons.**

It is clear that the writer thinks Plimoth Plantation is full of amazing things to experience through our senses. She lists the five senses and then follows up with details about what people see, hear, touch, smell, and taste there.

> Find out a few of the many amazing things you will see, hear, touch, taste, and smell at Plimoth Plantation.

- **Clear headings organize the information.**
- **Linking words and phrases connect the details clearly.**

The opening paragraph catches the reader's attention. The linking phrase *Once you get there* connects the idea of "then" and "now" for the reader.

This is your chance to travel back in time almost four hundred years. Once you get there, you will know what life was like through all five senses and with your own active mind!

- **The writer's voice is strong and speaks to the reader all the way through.**

Nora begins each paragraph with a verb that urges readers to get to know Plimoth Plantation in different ways. She has a strong voice, but she also keeps it friendly by using *you* and *your*.

Think and ***imagine*** how it would be for you to live long ago and how your days would be different from your usual life in the present. Now you are set for your day at Plimoth Plantation.

Using the Brochure Rubric to Analyze the Model

- **Strong words convince the reader.**

To bring the plantation to life, Nora uses strong words that engage the reader's senses. Her words help convince the reader that a trip to the plantation is like going back in time.

> ***Smell*** herbs, flowers, farm animals, and cooking fires that were part of daily village life in 1627. You won't smell fumes of cars, trucks, trains, or tractors because that was before any of those had been invented.

- **A variety of sentence patterns adds interest and flow.**

Nora's sentences vary in length and pattern, so the reader will stay interested. Compare the length and pattern of the two sentences below.

> ***Hear*** words as they were spoken then. The interpreters at the 1627 English Village speak the language of the 1620s.

- There are no errors.
- *Very* and *real* are used correctly.
- There are no double negatives.

I don't see any errors in Nora's brochure. She must have checked carefully for punctuation, capitalization, and spelling. Nora has used the word *very* correctly in the first sentence below. In the second sentence, she has used one negative, so her meaning makes sense.

Learn from many exhibits that very clearly explain the lives of colonists and native people almost four centuries ago. You will not forget these exhibits because they get you involved.

+Presentation The brochure catches the reader's attention.

My Turn!

Now it's my turn to write a brochure. I'll use the rubric and good writing strategies to help me. Follow along to see how I do it.

Prewrite

Focus on **Ideas**

The Rubric Says The opinion is clear. Interesting details support the reasons.

Writing Strategy Choose a place and find out details about it.

Our class has been studying major landforms and bodies of water in the United States. Now we will each write a brochure about a landform or body of water that we choose. Our brochures should tell positive things and important details that would make people want to visit the places.

I wanted to write about the Rio Grande River. From doing web research about it, I learned that more than a hundred miles of the river are part of Big Bend National Park. I'll use details about the park's mountains, desert, and river to convince my audience that this is a great place to visit!

Interesting Details About Big Bend National Park

- ✔ unique animals in Chisos Mountains
- ✔ flowering cactus plants in Chihuahuan Desert
- ✔ big bend in Rio Grande River
- ✔ camping, hiking, and nature activities

Write

Think about a landform or body of water you would recommend to others. Use reference books and reliable websites to learn more. Then make a list of interesting details about the place.

Prewrite

Focus on **Organization**

The Rubric Says Clear headings organize the information.

Writing Strategy Use a Spider Map to plan the brochure.

My teacher suggested using a Spider Map to organize the information for my brochure. I'll name the park on the front cover and list the park activities on the back cover. On the inside pages, I'll include the three main ideas about my topic. I need to be sure I group related details together. Here's my map.

Writer's Term

Spider Map

A **Spider Map** organizes information about a topic. Write the topic in the center of the "spider," the main ideas on the spider's "legs," and the details on the connecting lines.

Spider Map

My Topic: Big Bend National Park

- Chisos Mountains
  - unique animals
  - trees and rocks
  - mountain lookouts
- Chihuahuan Desert
  - different kinds of cactus
  - glorious flowers
  - desert animals
- Rio Grande River
  - big bend in river
  - rafting on river
  - adventure trips
- Park Activities
  - hiking
  - camping
  - biking
  - exploring

Analyze

Look at the Spider Map. How did Marcus organize his ideas? Could he have organized his ideas differently? How will the Spider Map help Marcus write his draft?

Write

Use your notes to make a Spider Map for your brochure. Place your topic in the center of the "spider." List main ideas on the "legs." List the details on the connecting lines.

Draft

Focus on **Word Choice**

The Rubric Says Strong words convince the reader.

Writing Strategy Use strong adjectives to describe the place.

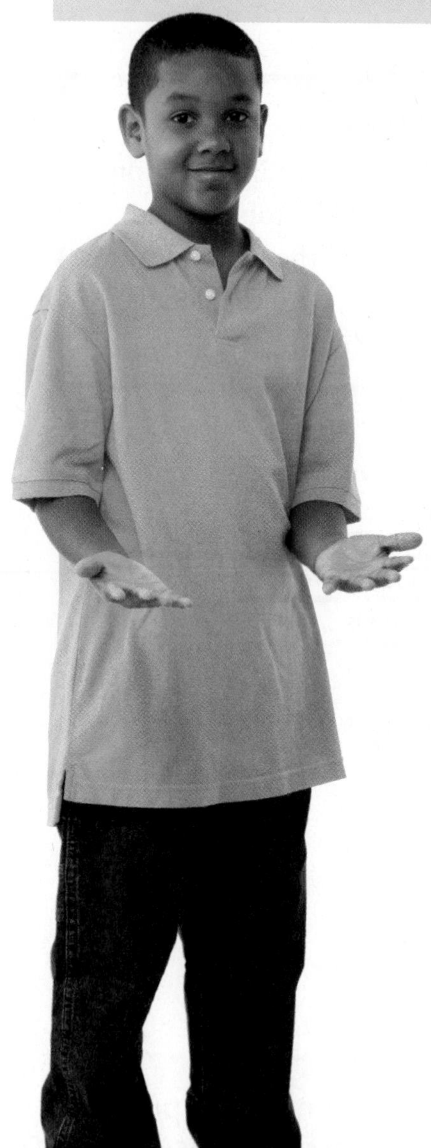

I am ready to use my notes and Spider Map to start writing my brochure. I won't put in pictures yet, but my Spider Map reminds me where I'll want them.

I know that my brochure should give interesting details about my place. The purpose of my brochure is to convince readers to learn more about Big Bend National Park. I hope they'll want to visit it someday! So I'll use strong adjectives in my writing to describe it. I won't worry about spelling and grammar now. I know that I can come back and fix those things later. Here is the start of my draft.

Writer's Term

Strong Adjectives

Adjectives describe, or tell more about, nouns. Strong adjectives help the reader picture what the writer is describing.

Examples:

Weak adjectives: They restored the old wood cabin in the park.

Strong adjectives: They restored the historic log cabin in the park.

Proofreading Marks

⊐	Indent	ℓ	Take out something
≡	Make uppercase	⊙	Add a period
/	Make lowercase	¶	New paragraph
∧	Add something	(sp)	Spelling error

[DRAFT]

BIG BEND National Park

is like *three* wonderful parks in *one*—

the Chisos Mountains, the Rio Grande River, the Chihuahuan Desert!

strong words

Look inside for real special views of all three! Then you will not want to never miss this huge and fascinating park.

Big Bend National Park is one of the biggest national parks in the United States. Located in southwest Texas, it includes more than 800,000 acres of land, ranging from majestic mountains to vast deserts. One of it's borders is 118 miles of the Rio Grande River. Big Bend National Park is great for other reasons besides being big. Here are some fantastic ways to have fun in different parts of the park.

strong words

As you hike the Chisos Mountains, watch for lots of animals. You might even see a black bear or a mountain lion, but don't get too close! The different trees and rocks have long histories that you can learn from park rangers or self-guided tours. Mountain lookouts will give you nice views of the desert, high waterfalls, and the daytime sky.

Analyze

Read the draft. What are some strong words that Marcus uses? How do they help convince the reader?

Write

Use your Spider Map and notes to write your brochure. Include strong words to convince your audience.

Revise

Focus on **Ideas**

The Rubric Says Interesting details support the reasons.

Writing Strategy Add details that will surprise and please the reader.

My draft is done. Now the rubric reminds me to support my reasons with interesting details. I want to surprise and please readers so they will want to visit Big Bend National Park.

As I read through my draft, I realized that I had not included an interesting detail about the animals that live in the Chisos Mountains. I'll add it now. Does it surprise you, too?

added surprising details

[DRAFT]

falcons, rare types of deer, and other animals you won't see anywhere else in the United States.

As you hike the Chisos Mountains, watch for ~~lots of animals~~. You might even see a black bear or a mountain lion, but don't get too close!

Write

Read your draft. Think of interesting details that you can add. Use them to surprise and please your readers.

Revise

Focus on **Organization**

The Rubric Says Linking words and phrases connect the details clearly.

Writing Strategy Use linking words and phrases to connect ideas.

The rubric reminds me that linking words and phrases can help connect ideas. These words and phrases are like signs telling the reader to follow a certain path. Words like *first, next,* and *last* are signs that show the order of information.

When I read over my draft, I found places to connect ideas with a few linking words and phrases.

Writer's Term

Linking Words and Phrases

Linking words and phrases connect ideas and guide the reader. Use **also, another, as well as, for example,** and **of course** to add information.

connected ideas

Of course,

One of it's borders is 118 miles of the Rio Grande River. ^ Big Bend National Park is great for other reasons besides being

For example,

big. ^ Here are some fantastic ways to have fun in different parts of the park.

[DRAFT]

Analyze

Look at Marcus's revisions. How do the linking words and phrases connect his ideas? How do they improve his writing?

Write

Read the draft of your brochure again. This time look for places to add linking words and phrases that connect ideas and guide the reader.

Revise

Focus on Sentence Fluency

The Rubric Says A variety of sentence patterns adds interest and flow.

Writing Strategy Start sentences in different ways.

This time the rubric reminded me to revise for a variety of sentence patterns. I want my brochure to be fun to look at and to read. So I'll check now to make sure all my sentences are interesting. I found a place where I can revise the way they begin. This will improve the flow.

Writer's Term

Sentence Patterns

One way to use a variety of **sentence patterns** is to begin sentences in different ways. Varying sentence beginnings keeps the writing flowing and holds the reader's interest.

[DRAFT]

Most of the park land is desert, which has about sixty different kinds of cactuses! In springtime, many have glorious flowers. ~~There are~~ Look for some incredible desert animals.

changed sentence beginnings

Write

Read through the draft of your brochure to make sure you have used a variety of sentence patterns. To add variety, begin your sentences in different ways.

Edit

Focus on **Conventions**

The Rubric Says There are no errors. *Very* and *real* are used correctly. There are no double negatives.

Writing Strategy Check the wording of the sentences.

From the rubric, I know it is time to check spelling, capitalization, and punctuation. Also I will correct the way I used *real* and *very*. I will look for negatives so I can make corrections if I used two negatives and confused readers.

Writer's Term

Negatives

A **negative** is a word that means "no" or "not at all." **No, not, nothing, none,** and **nobody** are negatives. Do not use two negatives in the same sentence.

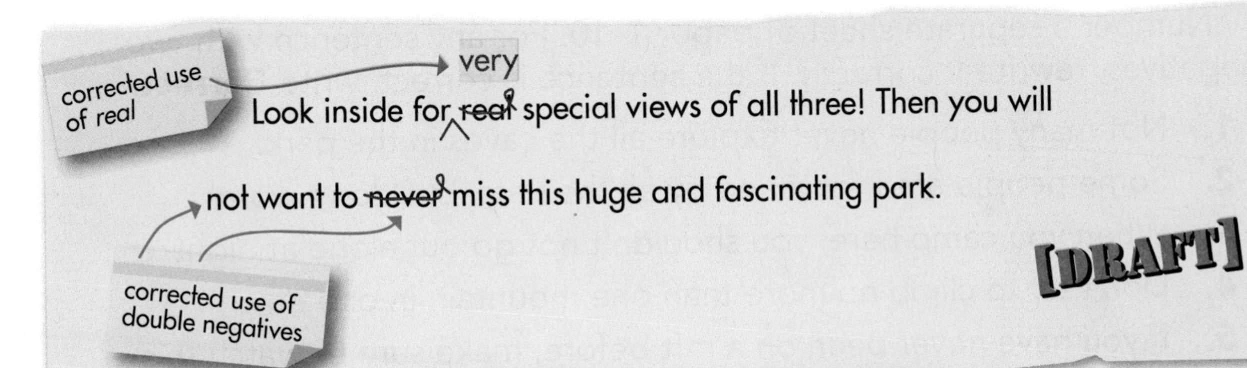

Analyze

Look at Marcus's edits. How did they improve this part of the draft? How will they add to Marcus's final product?

Write

Conventions

Edit your draft for spelling, punctuation, and capitalization. Correct any misuses of negatives and any confusions of the words *very* and *real*.

For more practice avoiding double negatives and using *real* and *very* correctly, use the exercises on the next two pages.

Negatives

Know the Rule

A **negative** is a word that means "no" or "not at all." *No, not, nothing, none, never, nowhere,* and *nobody* are negatives.

Example: You will **never** see a more beautiful desert.

Words that have *not* in them, like *can't* and *don't,* are negatives, too.

Example: Visitors **don't** always know that they should have drinking water with them on the trail.

Do not use two negatives in the same sentence.

Example: You will **not** find these birds **nowhere** else in the country.
Corrected: You will **not** find these birds anywhere else in the country.

Practice the Rule

Number a separate sheet of paper 1–10. For any sentence with two negatives, rewrite it correctly. If the sentence is correct, write **Correct**.

1. Not many people never explore all the caves in the park.
2. Some people are frightened by all the bats, but don't worry.
3. When you camp here, you shouldn't not go out alone at night.
4. Don't try to climb no more than one mountain in one day.
5. If you have never been on a raft before, make sure to watch this helpful video.
6. Nobody should not miss a view of the canyons.
7. You cannot rent horses in the park, but you can ride horses that you bring in.
8. Most people have not heard nothing about the historic ranches, mines, and wall paintings in the park.
9. No bike riding is not permitted on the trails, but you can ride on the roads.
10. None of the parks I know are as much fun as Big Bend National Park.

Very and Real

Know the Rule

When you write, do not use ***real*** to mean "very." Use ***real*** to mean "actual" or "true."

Example: You can find **real** fossils if you go with the park ranger.

Use ***very*** to mean "to a high degree."

Example: The visitor center has **very** helpful exhibits for families.

Practice the Rule

Number a separate sheet of paper 1–10. Decide if **real** or **very** should go in the blank. Write the word that best completes each sentence.

1. Visitors are always _____ excited about taking raft trips on the Rio Grande River.
2. You have to paddle _____ fast when you come to the bend.
3. The river is _____ wide between those two points.
4. The _____ story about this mountain is better than any you could make up.
5. This trail is steep, but the views are _____ special.
6. You don't have to go far before you see a _____ tall waterfall.
7. The animals in the exhibit look _____, but they are not quite like the animals you will see on the trail.
8. The changing weather can be a _____ problem for visitors.
9. Even if you are a _____ good swimmer, you must be careful in this river.
10. Some hikers saw a _____ panther, but they called it a mountain lion.

Publish

+Presentation

Publishing Strategy Publish copies of the brochure for a library display.

Presentation Strategy Use graphics that go well with the text.

After revising and editing my draft, I am going to publish my brochure. We will put our completed brochures on display in the library, so children and adults can read them. Presentation is very important for a brochure because the pictures, headings, and design can make a strong impression on readers. If the words, map, and photos in my brochure look great together, people will want to visit the park.

My Final Checklist

Did I—

✔ use *very* and *real* correctly?

✔ use negatives, such as *not* and *never*, correctly?

✔ correct punctuation, capitalization, and spelling?

✔ include attractive, helpful visuals and graphics?

✔ fold the brochure correctly?

Write

Make a checklist for your own brochure, including words, graphics, and photos. Use it to go over the design and wording of your final copy. Then display and share your brochure.

Brochure by Marcus

Big Bend National Park

is like *three* wonderful parks in *one*—

the Chisos Mountains,

the Rio Grande River,

the Chihuahuan Desert!

Look inside for very special views of all three! Then you will not want to miss this huge and fascinating park.

Big Bend National Park

Big Bend National Park is one of the biggest national parks in the United States. Located in southwest Texas, it includes more than 800,000 acres of land, ranging from majestic mountains to vast deserts. One of its borders is 118 miles of the Rio Grande River. Of course, Big Bend National Park is great for other reasons besides being big. For example, here are some fantastic ways to have fun in different parts of the park.

Chisos Mountains

Chisos Mountains

As you hike the Chisos Mountains, watch for falcons, rare types of deer, and other animals you won't see anywhere else in the United States. You might even see a black bear or a mountain lion, but don't get too close! The different trees and rocks have amazing histories that you can learn from park rangers or self-guided tours. Mountain lookouts will give you super views of the desert, surprising waterfalls, and the brilliant sky.

Rio Grande River

Rio Grande River

The park is named for a very big bend, where the river sharply changes its course. Floating or paddling a raft is one really cool way for you to enjoy this exciting river, especially when the desert is too hot for hiking. You can go out for half a day or longer with guides who take you on safe adventures.

Chihuahuan Desert

Most of the park land is desert, which has about sixty different kinds of cactus plants! In springtime, many have glorious flowers. Look for some incredible desert animals. Learn how they have adapted to the extreme heat and long stretches of time without water.

Chihuahuan Desert

Now you know why Big Bend National Park is a grand place to go. When will you visit?

Big Bend Park Activities

- ☆ Hiking mountain trails and desert trails
- ☆ Riding horses, if you bring your own
- ☆ Camping in a variety of campsites
- ☆ Paddling or floating along the river
- ☆ Exploring mysterious and historic caves
- ☆ Swimming in hot springs
- ☆ Biking on scenic roads
- ☆ Seeing and finding fossils
- ☆ Learning about wildlife from park rangers
- ☆ Viewing animals you've never seen before

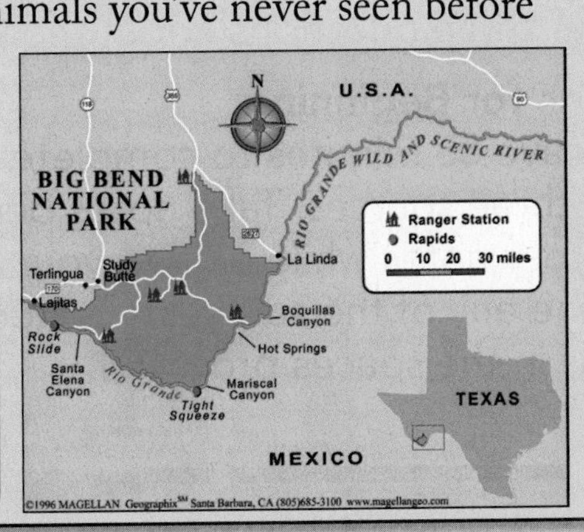

Analyze

Use the rubric to evaluate "Big Bend National Park." Then use the rubric to check your own brochure. What score did you give yourself?

PART 1

Next Generation Opinion Assessment

Writing assessments test you on your ability to write in different ways. The assessments are made to be like real-life writing experiences. For example, you might be asked to give your opinion on a topic. First, you will have to read short articles or watch videos on the topic and answer questions. Then you will have to write an essay that states your opinion on the topic.

Now let's analyze each part of this test, so you can really see what the assessment looks like.

Part 1: Close Reading

Your Task

You will examine three sources about different types of public libraries and why they are important. Then you will answer three questions about what you have learned. Later, in Part 2, you will write an opinion essay about why it is important for a community to have a library.

Steps to Follow

In order to plan and write your opinion essay, you will do all of the following:

1. Examine three sources.
2. Make notes about the information from the sources.
3. Answer three questions about the sources.

Directions for Beginning

You will have 55 minutes to complete Part 1. You will now examine three sources. Take notes because you may want to refer to your notes while writing your opinion essay. You can re-examine any of the sources as often as you like. Answer the questions in the spaces provided.

Your Task This part of the directions gives information about the whole test. You will have two parts to complete. In Part 1, you will read and answer questions. In part 2, you will write an opinion essay.

Steps to Follow This section reviews the task as a list. It tells how many sources you will examine. You also find out how many questions you have to answer. In this assessment, you will have to examine three sources and answer three questions.

Directions for Beginning This section gives information about Part 1 only—the reading part. You'll need to decide how you want to take notes. Will you write them on a piece of paper or use a note tool online? This section also tells how long you'll have to complete your task. These directions tell you that you have 55 minutes. Since there are three sources, you'll have about 15 minutes to spend on each source plus a few minutes to check your answers.

TEST TIP

To save time, I read the question before I start reading a text or watching a video. You can do this, too. It will help you know what to focus on when you examine a source.

Source 1: Video

View the video at www.sfw.z-b.com/video/g3.

Why are libraries so wonderful for kids? Write a summary using three details from the video.

TEST TIP

Be careful when reading the directions for taking an assessment. It's important to write about the right things! Look for key words in the writing assignment. These words tell what kinds of details you should give.

This question asked me to summarize the video using three details. Because I have about 15 minutes to answer this question, I can watch the video again. When I hear a detail that answers the question, I will click the pause button so I can type it in the space provided. I will repeat this plan until I have identified all three details. I think this will help me write my summary quickly.

My Response

Libraries are wonderful places for kids. Libraries are full of books written just for children. Some are simply fun to read, and some are helpful for school. All of them can be checked out for free! Librarians are also very helpful. In addition, libraries offer special places for kids to read and learn. Other resources, such as videos and computers, are available to kids too.

Analyze

How well did Marcus use evidence from the video to support his summary? Are there other details he could have included?

Source 2: Text

Reading in Mongolia
by Dashdondog Jamba

It was boiling hot and felt like summer even though it was September. My wife, son, and I were embarking on a new trip across Mongolia with our mobile library minibus. I couldn't remember how many trips I had completed. Over the years I had been doing this, I had covered most of the country.

Sixteen years ago I decided to bring books to the children in the countryside. They didn't have much interest in reading books then. So I gave them candies and read to them while they ate.

With each visit, the children began to like books more and more and more. This time, as we drove across the wide-open treeless land of the steppes, the children rode out on horseback to meet us.

After reading with the children and giving them books, we left the steppes, where it was so hot, and drove toward the mountains. We stopped at local schools where children gathered to read the books we brought. Then we continued on our way. When we crossed a river in the Khangai Mountains, we noticed it was getting colder. The wind was beginning to blow.

Two children riding on a yak approached. We discovered that they could not read. We read to them and gave them books. They told us they would learn to read.

We continued into the mountains. It began to snow. And snow. And snow. We were in the middle of a blizzard! Suddenly, the minibus stopped and wouldn't start again.

We didn't know what to do. But we knew we would freeze to death if we didn't find warmth somewhere. Horses ran past us in the blizzard. This meant that humans were probably nearby. We got out of the minibus and began to walk.

Suddenly, we heard a dog barking. We walked through the snowstorm in the direction of a dog. We came upon a *ger,* a traditional home for a Mongolian herder. The people who lived there invited us inside.

The ger was very warm. We were given cups of hot tea and a plate of dried curds and clotted cream. We read a story to the five-year-old girl who lived in the ger with her family. They invited us to stay overnight.

The next morning, we burned animal droppings under the minibus to warm it up enough to start. Finally, we were able to continue our trip. We noticed the tracks of many different animals on the fresh snow. All at once, we found big tracks, similar to those of a dog, but larger. We followed the tracks until we saw a wolf.

A wolf! The Mongols say that if someone sees a wolf, he or she will easily achieve his or her goal. On the ridge of the mountain, the wolf stood for a while, staring at us, then moved away at a slow trot without any fear.

We drove through the snow covered valleys and gave books to all the children we met. Soon it was time to return home.

Why are mobile libraries helpful to communities? Include three reasons from the text in your answer.

The question asks me to give reasons. I think I already know two good reasons why mobile libraries are helpful, but I will check the text again to confirm my ideas.

My Response

A mobile library takes books to children who don't have them. When children have books, they learn to read. As they read each new book, they love reading more and more.

Analyze

How well did Marcus identify reasons? Would you have used the same reasons? Why or why not?

Source 3: Text

From My Librarian Is a Camel: How Books Are Brought to Children Around the World
by Margriet Ruurs

England

The Blackpool Beach Library brings books directly to people who are enjoying their summer holiday at the beach. The library is a wheelbarrow!

Two library assistants cart the books up and down the beach. Borrowers needn't join the Blackpool Library. When they finish reading the books, they simply return them to the wheelbarrow when it comes by another day. The people at the Blackpool Library believe that it is important to promote the joy of reading. "Libraries are services, not buildings," says one librarian. So, besides donkey rides and lemonade stands, this beach offers books!

England has other types of mobile libraries as well. Share-a-Book is a children's mobile library van in Gloucester, a county in England. A librarian travels with the van to the countryside, where children don't have access to a regular public library. Many children don't have books at home to read and share with their parents.

Share-a-Book has special books for children for whom English is a second language. They also offer toddler story times and take part in special celebrations in the area.

Pakistan

There are not many libraries in Pakistan, and libraries for children are especially rare. Most schools don't have libraries either. That is why the Alif Laila Bookbus Society ran a children's library in an old double-decker bus. But in order to reach more children, they needed to put a mobile library on the road. Thanks to help from the Jersey and Guernsey Trust and the United Kingdom's Save the Children, they now have a very popular bus that travels to schools. The bus is called *Dastangou,* or Storyteller.

The bus carries about six thousand books in English and Urdu (the two official languages of Pakistan) to children in schools. Some schools get a weekly visit, but in most places, the Storyteller can come only once every two weeks. This bus full of books has opened up a whole new world to children.

Afshan, thirteen, says, "I didn't know what a library looked like before! This bus is magic! It brings stories and books. I just wish it came more often or stayed longer!"

Bushna, from eighth grade, says, "When the Storyteller arrives at the gates of our school, we file out of the school in orderly lines and find our books. Then we take them back to our classrooms to read for an hour."

Mrs. Syeda Basarat Kazim is the coordinator of Storyteller. She explains that there aren't enough books to allow the children to take books home. "If we did, there wouldn't be enough books to take to the next school."

Compare and contrast the mobile libraries in England and Pakistan. Use three examples from the text in your response.

I remember some details about the different mobile libraries. I will go back and re-examine the text to find more information about how the libraries are alike and how they are different.

My Response

Both libraries take books to schools and villages. They both have books for children who speak English and for children who don't. In England, some people keep a book until the library comes to get it, but in Pakistan, the children can keep their books for only an hour.

Analyze

How well did Marcus use evidence from the source in his answer? What else can he add?

PART 2

Next Generation Opinion Assessment

Now that Part 1 is complete, it's time to write the opinion essay. Usually you will complete Part 1 on one day and Part 2 on the next day. The directions for Part 2 are longer than those for Part 1. They continue onto a second page. So remember to read all of the directions carefully. Ask questions if you don't understand.

PART 2: Writing to Multiple Sources

Setup

You will now have 70 minutes to review your notes and sources, plan, draft, and revise an opinion essay. You may use your notes and refer to the sources. You may also refer to the answers you wrote to questions in Part 1, but you cannot change those answers. Now read your assignment and the information about how your opinion essay will be scored. Then begin your work.

Your Assignment

Libraries of all types are found in communities throughout the world. Your assignment is to write an opinion essay on this topic. Your position is that having access to a library is important to every community. Support your position with concrete details and examples from each of the sources you have examined. The audience for your opinion essay will be people who can support libraries by giving money to keep them going.

Setup This section lets you know how much time you have to complete Part 2. You can divide the time into the different parts of the writing process. Here's an example of what Marcus plans to do.

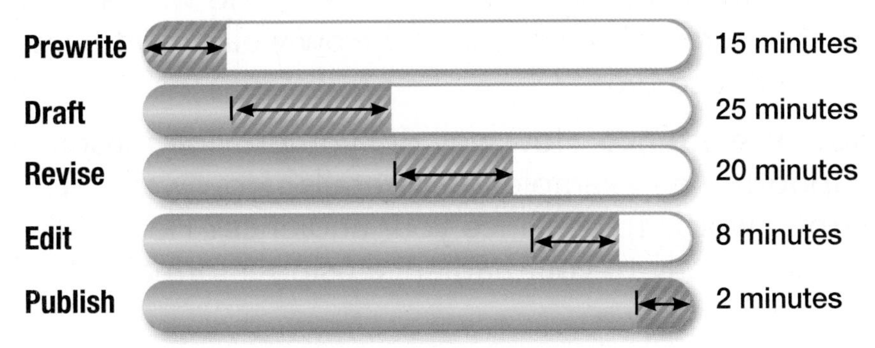

The directions also tell you that you can go back and examine the sources from Part 1, but the answers can't be changed.

Your Assignment This part explains your writing assignment. The topic of your assignment usually appears in the first few sentences of this section. In this case, it's the first three sentences. Finally, you are given a clue to what kind of voice you should use in your opinion essay. Because your audience is adults, you should use a serious and knowledgeable voice.

Scoring Guide

Your opinion essay will be scored on the following criteria:

1. **Statement of purpose/focus and organization** How well did you clearly state your opinion on the topic? How well did you begin with a strong introduction and end with a conclusion that sums up your opinion? How well did you use a variety of sentence types?
2. **Elaboration of evidence** How well did you provide reasons that are supported by examples and details? How well did you use strong words to convince your audience? How well did you speak directly to your audience using a formal voice?
3. **Conventions** How well did you check your grammar, punctuation, capitalization, and spelling?

Now begin work on your opinion essay. Manage your time carefully so that you can:

- plan your essay.
- write your essay.
- revise and edit for a final draft.

Spell check is available to use.

Type your response in the space provided on the following page. Write as much as you need to fulfill the requirements of the task. You are not limited by the size of the response area on the screen.

Writing Traits in the Scoring Guide

The second page of the directions tells you how your opinion essay will be scored. This scoring guide includes all of the writing traits. You can use what you have learned about the writing traits to help you write an effective opinion essay.

1 Statement of purpose/focus and organization

- How well did you use a variety of sentence types?

- How well did you begin with a strong introduction and end with a conclusion that sums up your opinion?

2 Elaboration of evidence

- How well did you provide reasons that are supported by examples and details?

- How well did you speak directly to your audience using a formal voice?

- How well did you use strong words to convince your audience?

3 Conventions

- How well did you check your grammar, punctuation, capitalization, and spelling?

Before you start Part 2, review your plan for how you will divide your time. Remember there is no word limit, but don't feel you have to fill the entire space with your thoughts. Now it's time for Marcus to start writing his opinion essay.

Prewrite

Focus on **Ideas**

Writing Strategy Respond to the assignment.

Prewrite ⟷ 15 minutes

Writers gather information to help them write. This is a key step when you write for an assessment. You can gather a lot of information from the directions. Take another look at the assignment in the directions. The assignment explains what you are supposed to write.

From my assignment, I know I'm supposed to write an opinion essay. I also know the topic.

> Libraries of all types are found in communities throughout the world. Your assignment is to write an opinion essay on this topic. Your position is that having access to a library is important to every community.
>
> topic
> genre

First, I'm going to write a sentence stating my opinion. Then, I'll think about details from the sources that will support my opinion. I can't remember all the details about the sources, but I just want to see what I remember.

My Opinion:

Having access to a library is important to every community.

Sources With Details That Support My Opinion:

The text about the minibus in Mongolia

The text about unusual libraries in England and Pakistan

The video about American public libraries

Prewrite

Writing Strategy Choose a graphic organizer.

Prewrite 15 minutes

I need to start organizing my ideas. A good graphic organizer for an opinion essay is a Main Idea Table. It will help me identify evidence from the sources in Part 1 to support my opinion. I may want to go back now and examine the sources again so I can get more specific.

Main Idea Having access to a library is important to every community.			
Supporting Detail	**Supporting Detail**	**Supporting Detail**	**Supporting Detail**
Public libraries have something for everyone.	Libraries have many resources for kids and grown-ups. They may also have special places for kids.	In some places, children do not have books unless a library can travel to where they live.	Libraries want to spread a love of reading.

Analyze

Does the graphic organizer include enough evidence to support Marcus's opinion? Is there anything he left out?

Draft

Focus on **Ideas**

Writing Strategy Write a topic sentence that tells the opinion. Include reasons and supporting details.

Draft 25 minutes

I need to state my opinion right away so readers know my point of view. So first, I will write a topic sentence that states my opinion. Then I will use my Main Idea Table to remind me of the reasons that support my opinion. I will include details with each reason.

Where can you go if you want to find a book by your favorite author? Where can kids get help with their reports about sea turtles? We can all go to the library, of course! Having access to a library is very important for every community. Let's support a library!

my opinion

Public libraries are important because they are the one free sourse of books for all ages. Kids can do homework, find a book, or work on a computer at a library. Libraries have many other stuff too, such as magazines, CDs, and DVDs. It's simple and it don't cost anything. You need a library card to check out a book, but that's it.

A library doesn't have to be a building. In Pakistan and mongolia, libraries travel to people. Buses take books to vilages and schools. Often, these are the first books children have seen. More people can enjoy books because of these mobile libraries.

Libraries provide many awesome services. Please think about supporting a library. If people would donate time and money to help them operate, they can help libraries spread the joy of reading in the community and around the world.

Analyze

Does the topic sentence clearly state Marcus's opinion? Do all the reasons and details he included support his opinion?

Revise

Focus on **Organization**

Writing Strategy Be sure your essay is well organized.

Revise 20 minutes

Now it's time to check my draft against the scoring guide. I want to be sure I've included all the points that will be scored.

The scoring guide tells me that my opinion essay should include an introduction, a body, and a conclusion. I have all of those, but I notice that the sentences in one of my paragraphs aren't in the correct order. I will rearrange them so they make sense.

Public libraries are important because they are the one free sourse of books for all ages. ~~Kids can do homework, find a book, or work on a computer at a library.~~ Libraries have many other stuff too, such as magazines, CDs, and DVDs. Kids can do homework, find a book, or work on a computer at a library. It's simple and it don't cost anything. You need a library card to check out a book, but that's it.

changed sentence order

Analyze

Did Marcus's draft make sense before his revision? How is his writing clearer after his revision?

Revise

Focus on **Voice**

Writing Strategy Speak directly to your audience using a formal tone.

Revise 20 minutes

The scoring guide reminds me to speak directly to my audience. Since my audience is adults, I need to use a formal tone. As I read my draft again, I see a place where I can replace casual language to make my writing sound more serious. I also see a couple of places where I can speak directly to the audience.

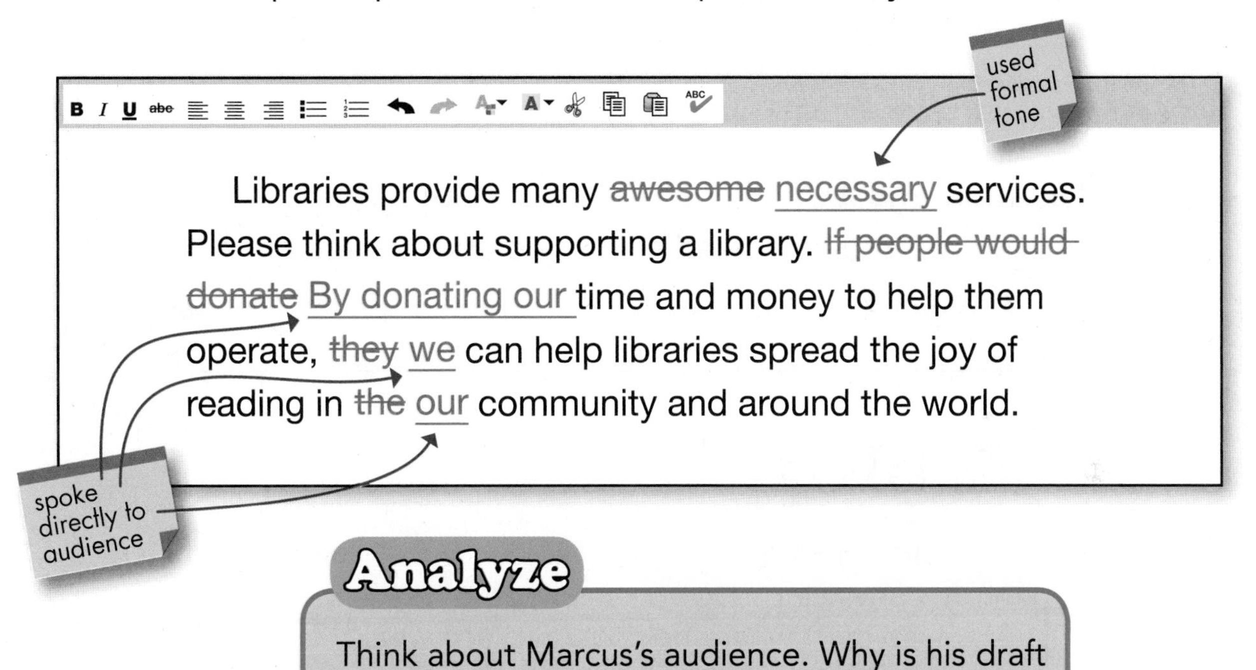

Analyze

Think about Marcus's audience. Why is his draft better after these revisions?

Revise

Focus on **Word Choice**

Writing Strategy Replace weak, boring words with convincing ones.

Revise 20 minutes

The scoring guide reminds me that a good opinion essay uses words that match my purpose for writing. I'm writing to convince the reader that libraries are important. I'll revise my draft to make sure my words are strong and convincing.

~~It's simple and it don't cost anything.~~ And all this is fast, easy, and free. You only need a library card to check out a book~~, but that's it~~.

clear convincing language

Analyze

How do Marcus's revisions make his sentences more convincing? Do you see another place in Marcus's draft where he could replace weak words with stronger ones?

Writing Strategy Check grammar, spelling, capitalization, and punctuation.

The scoring guide reminds me to check and correct my grammar and spelling. To save time, I can use the spell-check feature. I need to make sure I've used capitalization and punctuation correctly. I also need to check for subject-verb agreement errors. I'm glad I have time to check for all of this!

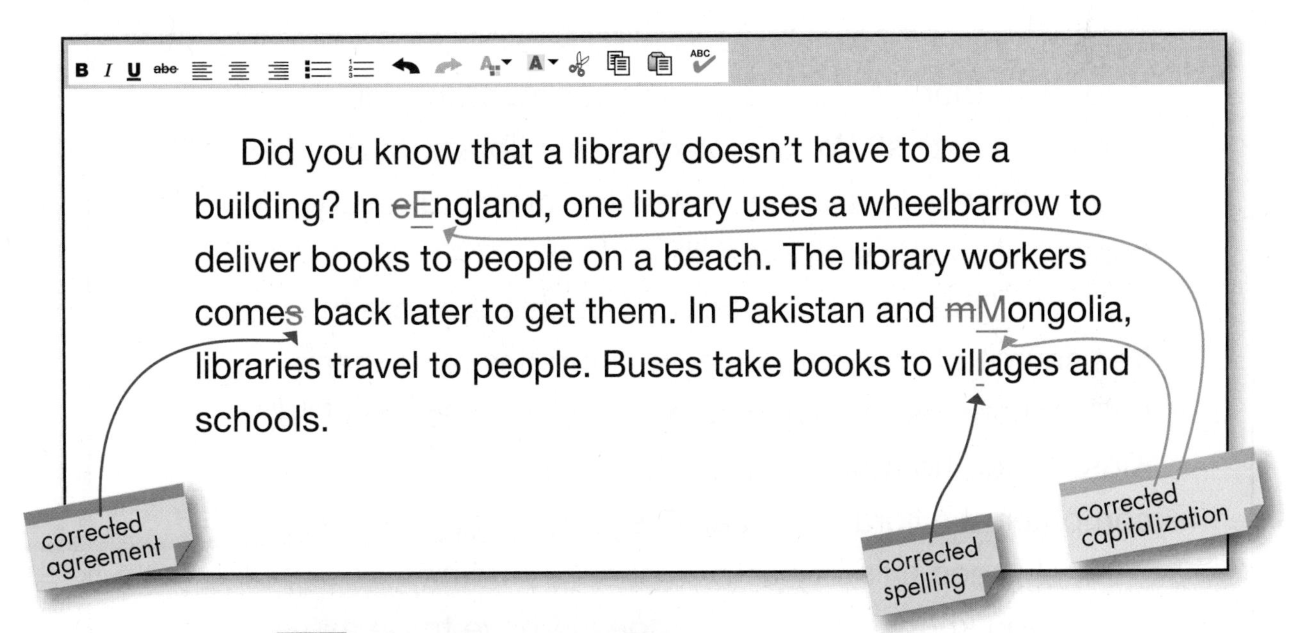

TEST TIP

If you spell a word correctly but use it incorrectly, the spell-check tool won't catch your error. Be sure to reread your writing carefully after spell-checking. Look closely at each word.

Publish

Publishing Strategy Submit the final draft of your opinion essay.

Publish 2 minutes

I am almost done with my assessment. I used information in the scoring guide and the writing traits to complete my opinion essay. Now I am going to use the spell-check feature once more to make sure I didn't miss any spelling errors. Then I will submit my final draft.

Where can you go if you want to find a book by your favorite author? Where can kids get help with their reports about sea turtles? We can all go to the library, of course! Having access to a library is very important for every community. Let's support a library!

Public libraries are important because they are the one free source of books for all ages. Libraries have many other resources too, such as magazines, CDs, and DVDs. Kids can do homework, find a book, or work on a computer at a library. And all this is fast, easy, and free. You only need a library card to check out a book.

Did you know that a library doesn't have to be a building? In England, one library uses a wheelbarrow to deliver books to people on a beach. The library workers come back later to get the books. In Pakistan and

Mongolia, libraries travel to people. Buses take books to villages and schools. Often, these are the first books children have seen! More people can enjoy books because of these mobile libraries.

Libraries provide many necessary services. Please think about supporting a library. By donating our time and money to help them operate, we can help them spread the joy of reading in our community and around the world!

Now It's Your Turn

Don't forget all the advice Marcus gave you during his assessment. Now, it's your turn to practice taking an opinion assessment.

More Writing Practice

Descriptive Elements in the Text Types

Descriptive Paragraph

Informative/Explanatory

Description of a Process

Informative/Explanatory

Descriptive Essay

Informative/Explanatory

Poem

SCIENCE CONNECTION

Why do good writers use Descriptive Elements?

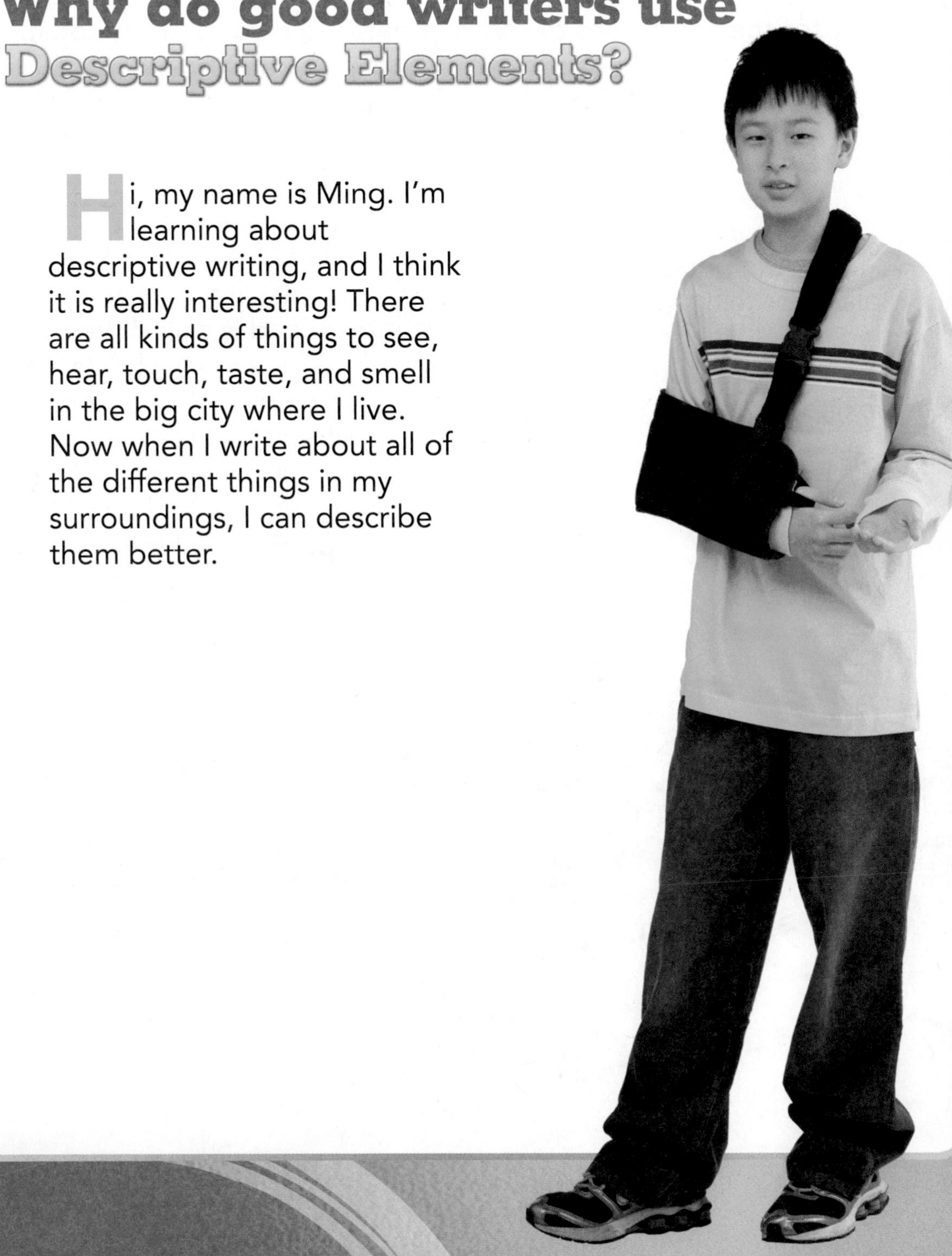

Hi, my name is Ming. I'm learning about descriptive writing, and I think it is really interesting! There are all kinds of things to see, hear, touch, taste, and smell in the big city where I live. Now when I write about all of the different things in my surroundings, I can describe them better.

What's a Descriptive Paragraph?

A descriptive paragraph describes a person, place, or thing. The writer often uses the five senses to create a detailed picture of the topic.

What's in a Descriptive Paragraph?

Topic
That's the person, place, or thing I am writing about. I will choose something I can spend time looking at, like my pet kitten.

Main Idea
This is usually told in the first sentence and is called the topic sentence. It will tell what is most interesting about my topic. The details I write will support that main idea. If I write about my kitten, I might say, "When Kitty sleeps, she is a limp, purring puffball."

Sensory Details
These are what I write when I describe how my topic looks, sounds, smells, tastes, or feels. I can use my five senses to help my reader get a clear picture of my topic.

Why write a Descriptive Paragraph?

There are many reasons to write a descriptive paragraph. Here are a few good reasons.

To Inform

Scientists and researchers record and describe their observations. They write descriptions to share the results of experiments.

Reporters often share their observations and conclusions with readers. They might describe special topics such as remote animal habitats or special environments like outer space or the Arctic.

To Entertain

Authors of storybooks and novels write descriptive paragraphs. They describe what characters look like. They describe the noises that animals make. They describe places so we can see them in our mind's eye.

To Advertise

Advertisers describe their products. They write descriptions hoping we will buy these products.

Linking Descriptive Writing Traits to a Descriptive Paragraph

In this chapter, you will describe something you have seen. This type of descriptive writing is called a descriptive paragraph. Ming will guide you through the stages of the writing process: Prewrite, Draft, Revise, Edit, and Publish. In each stage, Ming will show you important writing strategies that are linked to the Descriptive Writing Traits below.

Descriptive Writing Traits

	• a clear, focused topic • sensory details that tell readers what they want to know about the topic
	• a strong beginning, middle, and end • details that are arranged in an order that makes sense • linking words and phrases that connect ideas
	• a voice that is appropriate for the purpose and audience
	• clear, specific words that make a picture for the reader
	• sentences that are easy to read aloud because they flow smoothly
	• no or few errors in spelling, punctuation, and capitalization

Before you write, read Rachel Cohen's descriptive paragraph on the next page. Then use the descriptive paragraph rubric on page 358 to decide how well she did. (You might want to look back at What's in a Descriptive Paragraph? on page 354, too!)

Descriptive MODEL Paragraph

Lady Liberty

topic

main idea

sensory details

sensory details

a clear picture of the topic

by Rachel Cohen

The Statue of Liberty in New York Harbor takes your breath away. From the top of her head to her feet, she measures just over 111 feet tall. The huge statue of a woman stands for freedom. Her mighty right arm stretches 42 feet toward the sky. Her right hand holds a glowing golden torch. On the woman's head is a crown with seven sharp points. The points stand for the world's seven seas and seven continents. The woman's face looks serious and calm. In her left hand, she holds a flat tablet. A date in Roman numerals is written on the tablet: July 4, 1776. The woman wears a long Roman gown with many graceful folds. At her feet is a broken chain, which stands for the freedom the United States won from England. The base of the statue sits inside the walls of an old fort. The fort is covered with rough granite. Did you know that it is more than 305 feet from the ground to the tip of the torch? That makes the Statue of Liberty one of the largest statues in the world.

Descriptive Paragraph Rubric

Use this rubric to analyze the model. Then use it to plan and score your own descriptive paragraph.

	6	5	4
Ideas	The topic sentence is clear. All details develop the topic and answer the reader's questions.	The topic sentence is clear. Most details support the topic and answer the reader's questions.	There is a topic sentence. Details are limited, but they relate to the topic.
Organization	The first sentence introduces the topic and grabs the reader's attention. The paragraph is organized by order of location.	The first sentence introduces the topic but does not grab the reader's attention. The paragraph is organized by order of location.	The first sentence does not introduce the topic. The paragraph is organized by order of location.
Voice	The writer's voice sounds appealing and interested in the topic. It connects with the reader.	The writer's voice sounds interested and appealing. It connects with the reader most of the time.	The writer's voice sounds interested and appealing some of the time. The reader often has to guess how the writer feels about the topic.
Word Choice	Carefully chosen adjectives create a clear picture for the reader.	Most of the adjectives are well chosen and help to create a clear picture for the reader.	Some adjectives are used to help create a clear picture for the reader. More adjectives could be added.
Sentence Fluency	The writer uses a pleasing variety of sentence types, including questions, to keep the reader's interest.	The writer uses several different sentence types, including questions. The writing is easy to read.	Many sentence types are the same. A question would add interest.
Conventions	All sentences begin with an uppercase letter and end with appropriate punctuation.	Just a few minor errors are present. The writing is still easy to understand.	Some minor errors are present. They should not cause a problem for the reader.

+Presentation The paragraph is placed neatly on the page.

3	2	1	
There is a topic sentence. The details are too general to answer the reader's questions.	The reader can guess what the topic is but only by rereading. The details are general and often confusing.	It is not clear what the topic is, and the details do not tell about a main idea.	Ideas
The first sentence does not introduce the topic. Most of the paragraph is organized by order of location.	The first sentence does not introduce the topic. The paragraph is not organized by order of location.	The first sentence does not introduce a topic. The writing is not a paragraph.	Organization
The writer's voice does not come through clearly or show much interest in the topic.	The writer's voice is very weak. The reader can't tell what the writer thinks about the topic.	The piece lacks a writer's voice. The writer seems indifferent or not involved.	Voice
Adjectives used in the writing are too general, and the reader must reread to get a clear picture.	There are not enough adjectives used, and many are used incorrectly.	The writer does not use adjectives. The reader cannot form a clear picture.	Word Choice
All the sentences are of the same type. The writing is not interesting.	Many sentences are used incorrectly, making the writing difficult to read.	Sentences are incomplete or incorrect.	Sentence Fluency
Some end punctuation is incorrect or missing. The reader might be confused by the errors.	Many words and sentences are written incorrectly. The reader will have difficulty in understanding the paragraph.	Serious, frequent errors will cause the reader to stop reading.	Conventions

See Appendix B for 4-, 5-, and 6-point descriptive rubrics.

Descriptive Paragraph Using the Rubric to Analyze the Model

Did you notice that the model on page 357 points out some key elements of a descriptive paragraph? As she wrote "Lady Liberty," Rachel Cohen used these elements to help her write a description of the Statue of Liberty. She also used the 6-point rubric on pages 358–359 to plan, draft, revise, and edit the writing. A rubric is a great tool to evaluate writing during the writing process.

To get started, look at the top score for each trait as you study the model. Do you agree that Rachel has earned a 6 for each trait?

- **The topic sentence is clear.**
- **All details develop the topic and answer the reader's questions.**

When I read the first sentence, I knew Rachel's topic. It's the Statue of Liberty! Whenever I look at pictures, I wonder how tall the statue really is. I'm glad she answered my question.

The Statue of Liberty in New York Harbor takes your breath away. From the top of her head to her feet, she measures just over 111 feet tall.

- **The first sentence introduces the topic and grabs the reader's attention.**
- **The paragraph is organized by order of location.**

Rachel caught my attention right away! She describes the statue from top to bottom. Putting details in order of location makes the paragraph easy to follow.

At her feet is a broken chain, which stands for the freedom the United States won from England.

- **The writer's voice sounds appealing and interested in the topic. It connects with the reader.**

I can tell that Rachel likes her topic and knows a lot about it. She sounds interested in sharing facts with her reader, too!

Did you know that it is more than 305 feet from the ground to the tip of the torch?

Using the Descriptive Paragraph Rubric to Analyze the Model

- **Carefully chosen adjectives create a clear picture for the reader.**

Rachel uses describing words like *Roman* and *graceful* to help me picture the Statue of Liberty. Rachel could have written *beautiful gown*, but the reader's picture would not have been clear.

> The woman wears a long Roman gown with many graceful folds.

- **The writer uses a pleasing variety of sentence types, including questions, to keep the reader's interest.**

Rachel asks a question in her description. This keeps the paragraph moving along and holds the reader's interest.

> The fort is covered with rough granite. Did you know that it is more than 305 feet from the ground to the tip of the torch?

- **All sentences begin with an uppercase letter and end with appropriate punctuation.**

Every sentence begins with an uppercase letter and ends with an appropriate punctuation mark. Here are two examples.

Did you know that it is more than 305 feet from the ground to the tip of the torch? That makes the Statue of Liberty one of the largest statues in the world.

+Presentation The paragraph is placed neatly on the page.

My Turn!

Now it's my turn to write. I'm going to write my own descriptive paragraph. I will use the rubric to help me. Follow along to see how I use good writing strategies, too.

Prewrite

Focus on **Ideas**

The Rubric Says The topic sentence is clear.

Writing Strategy Make a list of interesting things you have seen. Choose one for your topic.

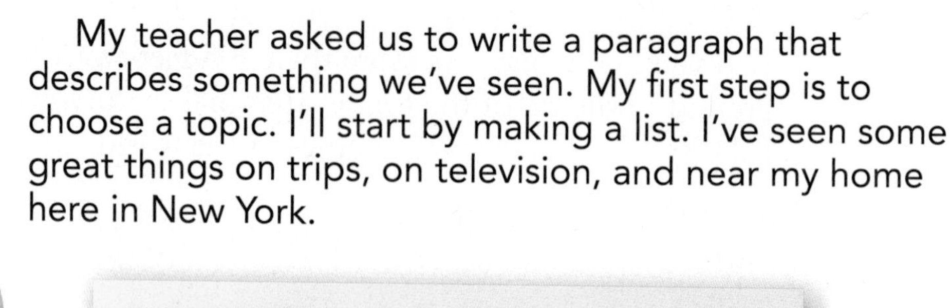

My teacher asked us to write a paragraph that describes something we've seen. My first step is to choose a topic. I'll start by making a list. I've seen some great things on trips, on television, and near my home here in New York.

Interesting Things I Have Seen

- baby elephant
- covered wagon
- redwood tree
- street performer
- solar-powered car
- huge pumpkin

I read the ideas on my list and picked one. I think I'll write about a redwood tree I saw on a trip to California. Redwood trees grow much taller than any tall tree in Central Park! That's just one interesting detail I can use. Most of my classmates have never seen a redwood tree. I think they would like to hear a description of one.

Write

Make a list of interesting things you have seen. Pick one that you would like to describe to your classmates.

Prewrite

FOCUS ON 

The Rubric Says The paragraph is organized by order of location.

Writing Strategy Make an Observation Chart to organize your notes.

The rubric reminds me to organize my description by order of location. I will describe the giant redwood tree I saw from bottom to top. I'll begin by listing the details I remember best. Then I can put them in order as I write.

Writer's Term

Observation Chart
An **Observation Chart** organizes details by using the five senses: sight, sound, touch, taste, and smell.

Observation Chart

My Topic: Redwood Tree

Sight	Sound	Touch	Taste	Smell
almost 300 feet high	soft rustling sound	bumpy	(didn't taste it)	fresh
wide trunk		rough		clean
grooves in bark		jagged		cedar chest
reddish-brown trunk				
gleaming needles				

Analyze

Read Ming's chart. How will it help him write a good descriptive paragraph?

Write

Think about the topic you chose. Organize your details in an Observation Chart.

Draft

Focus on **Ideas**

The Rubric Says The topic sentence is clear. All details develop the topic and answer the reader's questions.

Writing Strategy Write a clear topic sentence and use details that interest the reader.

My Observation Chart is finished. I'm ready to write my draft. I know from the rubric that I need an interesting topic sentence that explains what my paragraph will be about. I'll write that sentence first.

Next I'll use my Observation Chart to help me write the rest of my paragraph. I want to make sure my details answer the questions my reader might have about my topic. I'll do my best with grammar and spelling, but I won't take a lot of time with them. I know that I will have a chance to fix my errors later.

Writer's Term

Topic Sentence

The **topic sentence** tells the reader the main idea of a paragraph. The topic sentence is often the first sentence in the paragraph.

Proofreading Marks

Indent	Take out something
Make uppercase	Add a period
Make lowercase	New paragraph
Add something	Spelling error

[DRAFT]

topic sentence

sensory details

A Very Old Friend

Last summer I met a real wooden giant in California. It is really a huge redwood tree that is almost three hundred feet high I stood beside its wide trunk. Its thik bark had many deep grooves. It felt bumpy. I looked up at the big tree. The reddish-brown trunk seemed to go on forever The treetop was so far away that it seemed to touch the sky. The tree was covered with many needles that gleamed in the sunlight. they sounded like made a soft rustling sound as the wind blew through them. I took a deep breath. I liked the fresh smell of the needles. They reminded me of my grandma's old cedar chest. I really don't like the smell of mothballs. my new giant friend isn't just very tall. He is very old, too. It's hard to imagine this giant has stood here for over two thousand years.

Analyze

Read Ming's draft. Did he write a clear topic sentence? Does his opening sentence make you want to read further? Why?

Write

Use your Observation Chart to write your own draft. Remember to begin with a clear topic sentence.

Revise

Focus on **Organization**

The Rubric Says The paragraph is organized by order of location.

Writing Strategy Use order of location to organize details.

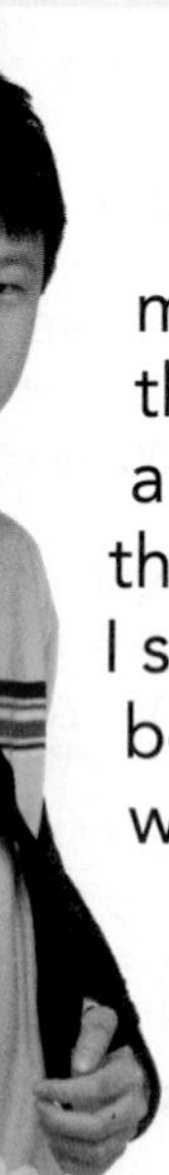

Now I want to improve my paragraph! I know from the rubric that I need to arrange the details in an order that is easy to follow. I started my description at the bottom of the tree and worked my way up to the top.

I see where I can add details in the beginning to help my reader follow my description better. Do my changes help you picture the tree and me?

Writer's Term

Order of Location

Order of location means that the details are arranged in the order in which you would look at something, for example, from top to bottom or from left to right.

[DRAFT]

Bending my head back, , and up, and up

I looked up at the big tree.

arranged details

Write

Read your draft. Revise your writing so that your details are arranged by order of location.

Revise

FOCUS ON

The Rubric Says The writer's voice sounds appealing and interested in the topic. It connects with the reader.

Writing Strategy Show interest in the topic.

The rubric reminds me to show that I'm interested in my topic. I can add sentences in the beginning to let my reader hear how I feel about the giant redwood and share another fact about it.

Writer's Term

Voice

A **voice** is a writer's individual and unique writing style. It shows the writer's knowledge and interest in a topic. An enthusiastic voice connects with the reader.

[DRAFT]

My giant isn't a person. It is the tallest living thing in the world.

Last summer I met a real wooden giant in California. It is really a huge

redwood tree that is almost three hundred feet high

added voice

Analyze

Look at Ming's revision. How does his voice connect better with the reader after his change?

Write

Read your draft again. Revise your writing for an enthusiastic voice that reaches out to the reader.

Revise

Focus on **Word Choice**

The Rubric Says Carefully chosen adjectives create a clear picture for the reader.

Writing Strategy Add exact adjectives.

I know from the rubric that it's important to choose adjectives carefully.

I see where I can add exact adjectives about the tree. Words like *big* and *many* don't really describe what I saw. I'll remember to use an online dictionary or thesaurus to look for exact adjectives when I need them. I want my reader to picture the tree.

Writer's Term

Exact Adjective

An **exact adjective** is a describing word that tells what you are writing about very clearly. For example, **towering** is more exact than **big**.

[DRAFT]

Bending my head back, I looked up, and up, and up at the ~~big~~ towering tree.

added exact adjectives

away that it seemed to touch the sky. The tree was covered with ~~many~~ tiny green needles that gleamed in the sunlight.

Write

Read your draft. Add exact adjectives to create a clear picture for your reader.

Edit

Focus on **Conventions**

The Rubric Says All sentences begin with an uppercase letter and end with appropriate punctuation.

Writing Strategy Check that every sentence begins with an uppercase letter and ends with the correct punctuation mark.

I always check spelling, capitalization, and punctuation. The rubric reminds me that I should pay attention to the way each sentence begins and ends. If my sentences don't begin and end correctly, my paragraph will be confusing and hard to read.

Writer's Term

Writing Sentences Correctly

All sentences begin with an uppercase letter. **Declarative sentences** end with a period. **Interrogative sentences** end with a question mark. **Imperative sentences** end with a period. **Exclamatory sentences** end with an exclamation point.

[DRAFT]

my new giant friend isn't just very tall. He is very old, too. It's hard to imagine this giant has stood here for over two thousand years. !

used an uppercase letter to begin a sentence

used an exclamation point

Analyze

Look at Ming's revisions on the previous page. How do his additions help you picture the scene? Now look at Ming's edits. How do they improve his writing?

Write

Conventions

Edit your draft for spelling. Start every sentence with an uppercase letter and end it with the correct punctuation.

For more practice with capitalization and punctuation, use the exercises on the next two pages.

Conventions Grammar, Usage & Mechanics

Writing Sentences Correctly

Know the Rule

Begin each sentence with an uppercase letter.
Put a period (**.**) at the end of a declarative sentence and an imperative sentence.
Example: Do not cut down that apple tree**.**
Put a question mark (**?**) at the end of an interrogative sentence.
Example: How long did the forest fire last**?**
Put an exclamation point (**!**) at the end of an exclamatory sentence.
Example: Wow, that is an old tree**!**

Practice the Rule

Rewrite each incorrect sentence to fix any errors in capitalization or punctuation. If a sentence has no errors, write **Correct** after the number.

1. Trees can grow to be very large.
2. people measure them in different ways.
3. California has many tall redwoods and sequoias
4. how can you tell them apart
5. redwoods have longer needles than sequoias.
6. Where do sequoias grow
7. they grow in the mountains of California.
8. what a huge tree trunk that is
9. When I stood at the base and looked up, I was truly amazed?
10. when will you see the giant redwoods.
11. Is Sequoia National Park in California!
12. scientists measure the age of a tree by its rings

Types of Sentences

Know the Rule

A **declarative sentence** makes a statement. It ends with a period.

Example:
Ming wrote down his questions.

An **interrogative sentence** asks a question. It ends with a question mark.

Example:
Do you think he found answers?

Remember: Both types of sentences begin with an uppercase letter.

Practice the Rule

Number a sheet of paper 1–10. Read each sentence. Write **declarative** or **interrogative** for each one.

1. How long can redwoods live?
2. They can live for more than 2,000 years.
3. How large are the seeds?
4. Some seeds are as small as wheat grains.
5. How tall do they grow?
6. A redwood can grow to be about 300 feet tall.
7. How thick is its bark?
8. The bark can grow to over 12″ thick.
9. People walk through the tunnel tree in Yosemite National Park.
10. Would you like to do that someday?

Publish

+Presentation

Publishing Strategy Read the descriptive paragraph aloud to the class.

Presentation Strategy Add extra space between lines.

I've finished my descriptive paragraph! Because so many of my friends were interested in my topic, I wanted to read my paragraph to the whole class. I'll add extra space between the lines of my descriptive paragraph so it's easy to read. Here's the checklist I used to get my paragraph ready.

My Final Checklist

Did I—

- ✔ check my spelling?
- ✔ capitalize and punctuate sentences correctly?
- ✔ use neat handwriting or word processing?
- ✔ add extra space between lines?
- ✔ put my name and the title of my paragraph on my paper?

Write

Make a checklist for your own descriptive paragraph. Then make a final copy to read aloud to your class. Bring a picture or object that relates to your paragraph to show after you read.

A Very Old Friend
by Ming

Last summer I met a real wooden giant in California. My giant isn't a person. It is the tallest living thing in the world. Can you guess what the giant is? It is really a huge redwood tree that is almost three hundred feet high! I stood beside its wide trunk. Its thick bark had many deep grooves. It felt bumpy. Bending my head back, I looked up, and up, and up at the towering tree. The reddish-brown trunk seemed to go on forever! The treetop was so far away that it seemed to touch the sky. The tree was covered with tiny green needles that gleamed in the sunlight. They made a soft rustling sound as the wind blew through them. I took a deep breath. I liked the fresh smell of the needles. They reminded me of my grandma's old cedar chest. My new giant friend isn't just very tall. He is very old, too. It's hard to imagine this giant has stood here for over two thousand years!

Analyze

Use the rubric to evaluate the paragraph. Were all the traits of a good descriptive paragraph used? Then use the rubric to check your own paragraph.

What's a Description of a Process?

It tells each stage in a process that I watched happen.

What's in a Description of a Process?

Steps
A process has steps that must be followed in sequence. Let's say that I'm describing the process of getting ready for a family vacation. The first step could be making a list of clothing to bring along. The last step could be saying good-bye to my friends.

Temporal Words
These make the order of steps clear. Use temporal words like *first, next, then,* and *last.*

Sensory Details
These are what I include in my writing when I describe how my process looks, sounds, smells, tastes, or feels. I use my five senses to help my reader picture all the steps.

Why write a Description of a Process?

People have different reasons for writing a description of a process. Here are two good reasons.

To Inform

A scientist writes a description of a process to record what she observes in nature or in her own experiments.

A person who manufactures things writes a detailed description of the process of making a product. Studying all of the steps helps the manufacturer save time and money.

A teacher writes a description of a process to teach students the steps in writing a research paper.

To Entertain

Steps in a process can be serious or funny. An adventure story might include a description of a process like rock climbing or clearing a path through the jungle. A funny story might tell each tiny error a character made in the process of making a big mistake.

Linking Descriptive Writing Traits to a Description of a Process

In this chapter, you will write about a process for doing something. This type of descriptive writing is called a description of a process. Ming will guide you through the stages of the writing process: Prewrite, Draft, Revise, Edit, and Publish. In each stage, Ming will show you important writing strategies that are linked to the Descriptive Writing Traits below.

Descriptive Writing Traits

Ideas	• a clear, focused topic • sensory details that tell readers what they want to know about the topic
Organization	• a strong beginning, middle, and end • details that are arranged in an order that makes sense • temporal words that connect ideas
Voice	• a voice that is appropriate for the purpose and audience
Word Choice	• clear, specific words that make a picture for the reader
Sentence Fluency	• sentences that are easy to read aloud because they flow smoothly
 Conventions	• no or few errors in spelling, punctuation, and capitalization

Before you write, read Ethan Curtis's description of a process on the next page. Then use the description of a process rubric on page 380 to decide how well he did. (You might want to look back at What's in a Description of a Process? on page 376, too!)

From Trash to Art

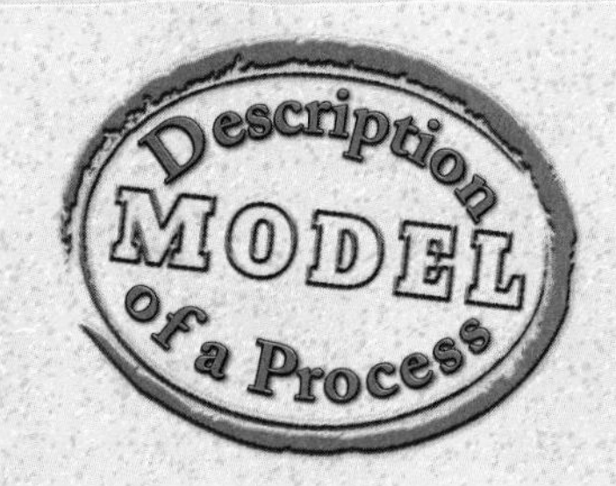

by Ethan Curtis

Today I met someone who uses other people's trash to make art. I went to the Fiber Arts Studio to watch artist Kerry Jackson at work. She makes beautiful handmade paper out of old newspapers, magazines, and phone books from the garbage dump.

temporal words

Walking into Jackson's workspace was like walking into a recycling center. Cluttered rows of paper-filled bins lined the studio. Heaps of magazines spilled over onto the counters. Tubs of water made the shop smell musty, like wet clothes that had stayed damp too long.

First, Jackson showed me one tub of wet paper pieces that had soaked overnight. It contained everything from torn notebook paper to shreds from a phone book. Jackson scooped up the soaked paper in her hands, then swiftly carried the dripping mass over to a blender. The wet paper mound fell into the blender jar with a thump.

sensory details

After adding some water, Jackson turned the blender on. The motor started with a low hum and then squealed to a stop. Kerry added still more water until the blender's motor ran smoothly. I touched the pulp after it was completely blended. It felt as though I had stuck my hand into a bowl of cold oatmeal.

steps

Then, Jackson scraped the pulp into a dishpan filled with water and mixed it. Next, she plunged the side of a small framed screen into the pan. She held the screen flat under the water and slowly raised it. The pulp clung thinly to the top side of the screen like a layer of frost. Water dripped from the frame, and Jackson dabbed the pulp lightly with a sponge. She sprinkled flecks of foil and bright paper onto the damp sheet.

Finally, Jackson flipped the frame onto a thin cloth. The sheet of paper gently fell free. As it was drying, I studied the paper's rich detail. Its dots of dazzling color made it perfect for a party invitation.

Description of a Process Rubric

Use this rubric to analyze the model. Then use it to plan and score your own description of a process.

	6	5	4
Ideas	The writing describes the writer's important observations. Details are complete.	The writing describes the writer's observations. Details are mostly complete.	The writing tries to describe the writer's observations, but the details are too general.
Organization	The writing has a strong beginning, middle, and end. Well-chosen temporal words guide the reader through the steps of the process.	The writing has a beginning, middle, and end. Well-chosen temporal words guide the reader through some of the steps.	The beginning, middle, and end are weak. Few or no temporal words are used.
Voice	The writer's voice speaks directly to the reader.	The writer's voice generally speaks directly to the reader.	The writer's voice occasionally speaks directly to the reader.
Word Choice	Carefully chosen adjectives create a clear picture.	Adjectives create a clear picture most of the time.	Adjectives may be overused or too general, but they still create a picture.
Sentence Fluency	A variety of sentence patterns makes the writing flow smoothly.	Most sentences are varied. The writing generally flows smoothly.	Many sentences follow the same pattern. The writing often does not flow well.
Conventions	The writing is error free. Subjects and verbs agree. Commas follow words in a series.	The writing contains occasional errors. Subjects and verbs generally agree.	A few minor errors are present, but they do not confuse the reader.
+Presentation	Pictures or photographs work well with the description.		

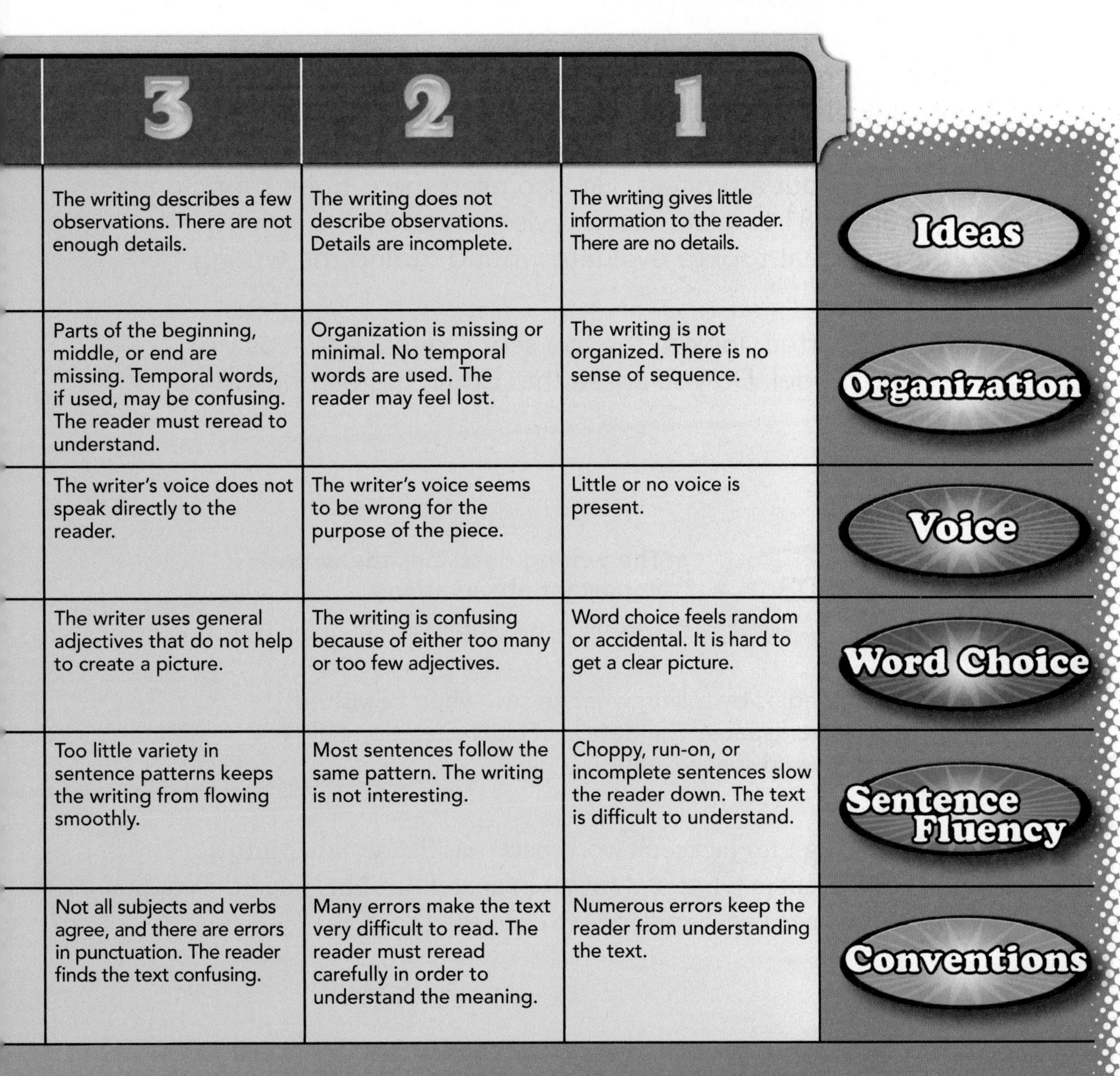

3	2	1	
The writing describes a few observations. There are not enough details.	The writing does not describe observations. Details are incomplete.	The writing gives little information to the reader. There are no details.	Ideas
Parts of the beginning, middle, or end are missing. Temporal words, if used, may be confusing. The reader must reread to understand.	Organization is missing or minimal. No temporal words are used. The reader may feel lost.	The writing is not organized. There is no sense of sequence.	Organization
The writer's voice does not speak directly to the reader.	The writer's voice seems to be wrong for the purpose of the piece.	Little or no voice is present.	Voice
The writer uses general adjectives that do not help to create a picture.	The writing is confusing because of either too many or too few adjectives.	Word choice feels random or accidental. It is hard to get a clear picture.	Word Choice
Too little variety in sentence patterns keeps the writing from flowing smoothly.	Most sentences follow the same pattern. The writing is not interesting.	Choppy, run-on, or incomplete sentences slow the reader down. The text is difficult to understand.	Sentence Fluency
Not all subjects and verbs agree, and there are errors in punctuation. The reader finds the text confusing.	Many errors make the text very difficult to read. The reader must reread carefully in order to understand the meaning.	Numerous errors keep the reader from understanding the text.	Conventions

See Appendix B for 4-, 5-, and 6-point descriptive rubrics.

Using the Description of a Process Rubric to Analyze the Model

Did you notice that the model on page 379 points out some key elements of a description of a process? As he wrote "From Trash to Art," Ethan Curtis used these elements to help him write about a process. He also used the 6-point rubric on pages 380–381 to plan, draft, revise, and edit the writing. A rubric is a great tool to evaluate writing during the writing process.

To get started, look at the top score for each trait as you study the model. Do you agree that Ethan has earned a 6 for each trait?

- **The writing describes the writer's important observations.**
- **Details are complete.**

Ethan begins by telling what he saw when he visited Jackson's workspace. The details in his description help me picture the workspace clearly.

Walking into Jackson's workspace was like walking into a recycling center. Cluttered rows of paper-filled bins lined the studio. Heaps of magazines spilled over onto the counters.

- **The writing has a strong beginning, middle, and end.**
- **Well-chosen temporal words guide the reader through the steps of the process.**

Ethan's description has three parts: a beginning, a middle, and an end. He connects his ideas with words that present all the steps in order. For example, he uses the temporal word *First* to describe the first thing they did.

First, Jackson showed me one tub of wet paper pieces that had soaked overnight. It contained everything from torn notebook paper to shreds from a phone book.

- **The writer's voice speaks directly to the reader.**

Ethan's writing voice sounds like he is speaking directly to me. I sometimes collect ordinary things to recycle into art. Plus, I've always wanted to see a real artist's studio!

Today I met someone who uses other people's trash to make art. I went to the Fiber Arts Studio to watch artist Kerry Jackson at work. She makes beautiful handmade paper out of old newspapers, magazines, and phone books from the garbage dump.

Using the Description of a Process Rubric to Analyze the Model

- **Carefully chosen adjectives create a clear picture.**

Ethan describes the steps of making paper in a way that helps me picture the whole process. His sensory details call on my senses! I can practically smell the studio!

> Tubs of water made the shop smell musty, like wet clothes that had stayed damp too long.

- **A variety of sentence patterns makes the writing flow smoothly.**

The writer used different sentence patterns. He used both short and long sentences. Ethan also began sentences in different ways. This variety makes the essay flow smoothly.

> Finally, Jackson flipped the frame onto a thin cloth. The sheet of paper gently fell free. As it was drying, I studied the paper's rich detail. Its dots of dazzling color made it perfect for a party invitation.

- **The writing is error free.**
- **Subjects and verbs agree.**
- **Commas follow words in a series.**

All the spelling, punctuation, and capitalization is correct. The subjects and verbs agree, too. Ethan uses singular verbs with singular subjects and plural verbs with plural subjects. For example, *she* is a singular subject so Ethan uses *makes*, which is a singular verb. I also noticed that he uses commas correctly with words in a series.

She makes beautiful handmade paper out of old newspapers, magazines, and phone books from the garbage dump.

+Presentation Pictures or photographs work well with the description.

My Turn!

Now it's my turn to write my own description of a process. The rubric and good writing strategies will help me. Read along to see how I do it.

Prewrite

Focus on **Ideas**

The Rubric Says The writing describes the writer's important observations. Details are complete.

Writing Strategy Think of things you have watched people do. Make a list of them.

My teacher asked us to write a description of a process. I'll think about things I have watched people do. I'll try to think of ideas that have just the right number of details. A topic with too many details in the steps would be hard to describe.

Processes I Have Watched

- ✔ making a pizza
- ✔ checking stream water for pollution
- ✔ building model airplanes
- ✔ making a papier-mache mask
- ✔ teaching a trick to a dolphin
- ✔ planting a vegetable garden

I think I want to write about the process of building model airplanes. My next-door neighbor builds model planes in his garage. They look really cool. I think my classmates would like to know how he makes them.

Write

Make a list of interesting things you have watched people do. Pick one that you would like to describe. Jot down some notes on what you saw.

Prewrite

Focus on **Organization**

The Rubric Says The writing has a strong beginning, middle, and end. Well-chosen temporal words guide the reader through the steps of the process.

Writing Strategy Use a Sequence Chain to organize your notes.

I know from the rubric that my description needs to be well organized. I'll use a Sequence Chain to put the steps in order. When I write my draft, I'll use temporal words like *first, next,* and *finally* so my reader can follow the steps.

Writer's Term

Sequence Chain

A **Sequence Chain** organizes information in a time order. It is made of a series of boxes. Each one tells a step or an event in the order it happens.

Sequence Chain

Topic: Making a Model Plane

First Step: cut out plane parts

Next Step: mixed glue and water

Next Step: made wings

Next Step: glued the body and tail parts together

Next Step: glued the wings to the body

Next Step: cut tissue paper

Next Step: brushed the plane with glue

Final Step: covered the plane with tissue paper

Analyze

Look at the Sequence Chain. What temporal words do you think Ming might use?

Write

Think about the process you watched. Create a Sequence Chain to organize the steps.

Draft

Focus on **Organization**

The Rubric Says The writing has a strong beginning, middle, and end.

Writing Strategy Grab the reader's attention in the first sentence with an interesting fact.

Now it's time for me to describe the whole process. To write a strong beginning, I need an interesting first sentence that grabs attention and makes the reader want to know more. After I introduce the topic, I'll use my Sequence Chain to write the middle part of the description. Finally I'll wrap up my writing with a good conclusion.

I'll do my best with grammar and spelling, but I won't worry about any mistakes yet. I'll fix my errors after I have all my ideas down on paper. Here's the first part of my draft.

Proofreading Marks

⊐ Indent	Take out something
≡ Make uppercase	⊙ Add a period
/ Make lowercase	¶ New paragraph
∧ Add something	(sp) Spelling error

[DRAFT]

strong beginning

Building a Model Plane

My neighbor, Mr. Bergeron, keep airplanes in his garage instead of cars. his lightweight plane swing gently on long, thin strings from the ceiling A bright lamp in the back corner on Mr. B's workbench light the model planes from behind. The outline of the stik frames inside each plane can be seen. Bright tissue paper streches over the frames like a thin, see-through skin. Mr. B offered to demonstrate how to build a plane.

Mr. B cut out the pieces for the plane. He did it carefully. He used wood. It is called balsa wood. He barely pressed the blade of his knife. he pressed it along the pattern lines. He cut with soft, slow strokes. Then he sliced square sticks to the exact lengths called for in the plans.

Analyze

Read the draft. How does Ming's first sentence grab your attention? Does it make you want to find out more? What do you want to know?

Write

Use your Sequence Chain to write your own draft. Remember to start with a good first sentence that grabs your reader's attention.

Revise

Focus on **Voice**

The Rubric Says The writer's voice speaks directly to the reader.

Writing Strategy Use a natural voice and the word *I*.

I've finished my draft. The rubric says my voice should speak directly to the reader. I need to remember that I'm describing Mr. B's process to my classmates.

I'll look for places where I can use the words *I* and *me*. I want my voice to sound like me.

[DRAFT]

I can see ^ ~~The~~ the outline of the stik frames inside each plane ~~can be seen~~. Bright tissue paper streches over the frames like a thin, see-through skin.

When Mr. B asked me if I wanted to watch him build a plane, I said yes!
^ ~~Mr. B offered to demonstrate how to build a plane.~~

added natural voice

Write

Read your draft. Look for places where you can use the words *I* or *me*.

Revise

The Rubric Says Carefully chosen adjectives create a clear picture.

Writing Strategy Choose the right adjectives to help the reader "see" the process.

The rubric reminds me to use adjectives to describe the process. I see places in my draft where I can add helpful ones. I want my readers to "see" the process clearly.

My teacher says it's important that I don't add too many, though. Too many would distract the reader and make my writing too wordy!

[DRAFT]

Mr. B cut out the pieces for the plane. He did it carefully. He used ^a thin, light^ wood. It is called balsa wood. He barely pressed the ^razor-sharp^ blade of his knife.

added helpful adjectives

Analyze

Look at Ming's changes. How do his adjectives help you "see" the process?

Write

Read your draft again. Look for places where your adjectives could be clearer and replace them.

Revise

The Rubric Says A variety of sentence patterns makes the writing flow smoothly.

Writing Strategy Use a variety of sentence patterns.

As I reread the part about Mr. B gluing the pieces, it didn't sound right to me. I noticed that several sentences in a row begin the same way and repeat information. They make that part of my description sound choppy.

If I combine them, I can change the sentence pattern. I'll make sure they're written correctly, too.

Writer's Term

Sentence Pattern

A **sentence pattern** is the order in which the parts of a sentence are arranged. One sentence pattern is subject-verb. Another is subject-verb-object. Phrases and clauses can be added to these basic patterns.

[DRAFT]

varied sentence patterns

Next Mr. B gathered wood glue, a small brush, and some tiny pins. He mixed the glue with water. ~~He~~ [and] brushed the mixture on the pieces. ~~He~~ [h]e wanted to join ~~the pieces~~.

Write

Read your description aloud. Have you used a variety of sentences? Revise your writing to improve the flow.

Edit

Focus on Conventions

The Rubric Says Subjects and verbs agree.

Writing Strategy Check that all subjects and verbs agree.

No matter what kind of writing I do, I always check my spelling. The first two sentences don't sound right. I think it's because my subjects and verbs do not agree. I'll fix that now.

Writer's Term

Subject-Verb Agreement

A subject and verb must agree. Add **-s** or **-es** to a verb in the present tense when the subject is a singular noun or **he, she,** or **it**. Do not add -s if the subject is a plural noun or if the subject is **I, you, we,** or **they**.

[DRAFT]

corrected subject-verb agreement error

My neighbor, Mr. Bergeron, keep^s airplanes in his garage instead of cars. his lightweight plane swing^s gently on long, thin strings from the ceiling^.

Analyze

Look at Ming's revisions on the previous page. How do his changes improve the flow of his writing? Look at Ming's edits. Do the subjects and verbs agree? Are the spelling and punctuation correct? How do Ming's changes clarify his writing?

Write

Conventions

Edit your draft carefully. Be sure all your subjects and verbs agree. Remember to use commas to separate words in a series.

For more practice with subject-verb agreement and using commas to separate words in a series, use the exercises on the next two pages.

Subject-Verb Agreement

Know the Rule

Present tense verbs must agree with the subject of the sentence. Use singular verbs with singular subjects. Use plural verbs with plural subjects.

- Singular nouns and some singular pronouns take verbs that end in *-s* or *-es*.
  Example: The **pilot needs** more fuel for her airplane.
- Plural nouns and plural pronouns take verbs that do not end in *-s* or *-es*.
  Example: The **pilots enjoy** the air show every year.

Practice the Rule

Number a sheet of paper 1–12. Read each sentence. If the subject and verb do not agree, rewrite the sentence correctly. If the sentence is correct, write **Correct.**

1. Model planes comes in many shapes, sizes, and styles.
2. Lots of people build model planes as a hobby.
3. Some scientists uses model planes to test ideas for real planes.
4. A rubber band make some model planes fly.
5. Other model planes fly with engines.
6. Some model planes take off by themselves.
7. People throws other model planes to make them fly.
8. A model builder buys a kit.
9. She glue the parts together.
10. She display the finished plane for people to see.
11. Some model builders enter contests.
12. Judges decide whose plane is best.

Commas in a Series

Know the Rule

A **series** is a list of three or more words or phrases. Use **commas** to separate words in a series.

Example:
Some birds recycle feathers, string, and dryer lint for their nests.

Practice the Rule

Number a sheet of paper 1–10. Read each sentence. Rewrite the sentences that need commas to separate words in a series. Write **Correct** for any sentence that uses commas correctly.

1. We learned a lot about recycling plastic aluminum and glass.
2. Our school will sponsor "Reduce, Reuse, and Recycle Day" next month.
3. Principal Greene wants students teachers and parents involved.
4. Students in the third fourth, and fifth grades will make signs.
5. The cafeteria will collect plastic aluminum and glass containers.
6. The library will collect white paper cardboard and newspapers.
7. Teachers will make announcements on the radio TV and school website.
8. With the money we raise, we can buy recycled paper, pencils, and notebooks.
9. New recycling bins will be placed in the office the lobby, and the library.
10. We hope everyone will learn to reduce, reuse, and recycle.

Publish

+Presentation

Publishing Strategy Publish the paper in a class scrapbook.

Presentation Strategy Add pictures or photographs.

My description of a process is done! Now it is almost time to publish it. I think I should add pictures to my description. They will help my classmates "see" Mr. B's process even more clearly. We're making a class scrapbook of our descriptions for the library. Before I add my writing to the class scrapbook, I will read through it one last time. Here's the final checklist I used.

My Final Checklist

Did I—

- ✔ make sure that my subjects and verbs agree?
- ✔ use commas to separate words in a series?
- ✔ add pictures or photographs?
- ✔ use neat handwriting or word processing?
- ✔ put my name and title at the top of my paper?

Write

Use Ming's checklist to prepare your final copy. Add pictures or illustrations to your description.

Building a Model Plane
by Ming

My neighbor, Mr. Bergeron, keeps airplanes in his garage instead of cars. His lightweight planes swing gently on strings from the ceiling. A bright lamp in the back corner on Mr. B's workbench lights the model planes from behind. I can see the outline of the stick frames inside each plane. Bright tissue paper stretches over the frames like a thin, see-through skin. When Mr. B asked me if I wanted to watch him build a plane, I said yes!

The first thing Mr. B did was to carefully cut out the pieces for the plane. He used a thin, light wood called balsa wood. He barely pressed the razor-sharp blade of his knife along the pattern lines. He cut with soft, slow strokes. Then he sliced square sticks to the exact lengths called for in the plans.

Next Mr. B gathered wood glue, a small brush, and some tiny pins. He mixed the glue with water and brushed the mixture on the pieces he wanted to join. He built the ribbed wings stick by stick on a long board. Then Mr. B gently pushed the pins around the edges to hold his work together while it dried. Next he assembled the main body of the plane and then the tail. Finally he joined the wings and tail to the body.

The next day I came back to watch as Mr. B skillfully covered the airplane frame with tissue paper. First he used scissors to trim the sheer paper into the exact pieces he needed. Then he brushed the airplane frame with glue.

Finally Mr. B stretched the thin tissue over the frame. Although the finished model looked delicate, Mr. B promised me the plane was strong and light—perfect for flying.

Analyze

Use the rubric to evaluate Ming's description. Were all the traits of a good description of a process used? Then use the rubric to check your own writing.

What's a Descriptive Essay?

It's writing that paints a picture of a person, place, or thing. It is a lot like a descriptive paragraph, but longer. A descriptive essay has several paragraphs.

What's in a Descriptive Essay?

Topic
A descriptive essay tells about one topic. I can write a descriptive essay about almost anything I can describe. I'll choose a topic that interests me a lot, like the beauty of nature or the amazing skyscrapers in New York City.

Sensory Details
A descriptive essay gives a lot of details about the topic. I'll use my five senses to tell how my topic looks, sounds, smells, tastes, and feels. Sensory details will help my reader "experience" my topic.

Paragraphs
A descriptive essay has several paragraphs. Writers use paragraphs to organize their ideas. I'll write a topic sentence that will tell the main idea of each paragraph.

Why write a Descriptive Essay?

There are many reasons to write a descriptive essay. Here are two good reasons.

To Inform

Many nonfiction writers describe animals, places, people, objects, and events. Their essays are published in magazines, newspapers, and books. People read descriptive essays to learn about many different topics.

To Entertain

Some people write descriptive essays about works of fiction like novels and movies. Writers can create descriptive essays about people, places, or things that are imaginary. Many people enjoy reading these kinds of descriptive essays to be entertained.

Linking Descriptive Writing Traits to a Descriptive Essay

In this chapter, you will describe an interesting place. This type of descriptive writing is called a descriptive essay. Ming will guide you through the stages of the writing process: Prewrite, Draft, Revise, Edit, and Publish. In each stage, Ming will show you important writing strategies that are linked to the Descriptive Writing Traits below.

Descriptive Writing Traits

Trait	
	• a clear, focused topic • sensory details that tell readers what they want to know about the topic
	• a strong beginning, middle, and end • details that are arranged in an order that makes sense • linking words and phrases that connect ideas
	• a voice that is appropriate for the purpose and audience
	• clear, specific words that make a picture for the reader
	• sentences that are easy to read aloud because they flow smoothly
	• no or few errors in spelling, punctuation, and capitalization

Before you write, read Lee Taylor's descriptive essay on the next page. Then use the descriptive essay rubric on page 404 to decide how well he did. (You might want to look back at What's in a Descriptive Essay? on page 400, too!)

On Top of the World

by Lee Taylor

Some people do not like to go to work. I go to work, and it feels wonderful. In fact, I am on top of the world! That's because I am a construction worker who helps build skyscrapers.

topic

What I enjoy most is the amazing view from a skyscraper! I am like a bird sitting in a steel treetop. I see tiny people hurry along crowded sidewalks. Little cars and trucks move slowly down streets that look like a huge game board. Beautiful parks are bright green islands in a sea of cement. Huge ships look like small twigs that float in and out of the harbor. Sometimes, the whole city is wrapped in rays of pink sunlight.

sensory details

I also like hearing the sounds of the city. Most mornings, honking horns, jackhammers, and train whistles join together to play a city song. Often the sound of the rushing wind is part of the city's music, too.

paragraphs

Other things I enjoy are the feel and the smell of the air high above the ground. I might feel warm, soft breezes. I might have to brace myself against strong gusts of wind. Sometimes damp fog rolls in from the ocean, and I smell salty sea air. What a refreshing smell that is!

I am very lucky to have my job. Many people know the city from the ground up. But not many know it from the top down!

Descriptive Essay Rubric

Use this rubric to analyze the model. Then use it to plan and score your own descriptive essay.

	6	5	4
Ideas	Descriptive details catch the reader's attention. They give the reader a clear picture of the topic.	Most details catch the reader's attention. Most give a clear picture of the topic.	Some details catch the reader's attention. More or stronger details are needed.
Organization	The essay has a beginning, middle, and end. Linking words and phrases guide the reader through the description.	The essay has a beginning, middle, and end. Some linking words and phrases guide the reader.	The essay has a beginning, middle, and end. Few linking words and phrases guide the reader.
Voice	The voice clearly shows that the writer knows and cares about the topic.	Most of the time, the voice shows that the writer knows and cares about the topic.	The voice occasionally shows that the writer knows or cares about the topic.
Word Choice	Specific words make the writing come alive.	The use of many specific words makes the writing interesting.	The use of some specific words makes the writing interesting.
Sentence Fluency	A variety of sentence structures makes the essay flow.	Most of the sentences in the essay flow smoothly.	Some short, choppy sentences interrupt the flow of the essay.
Conventions	The essay has no errors. Sentences are written correctly and are easy to read.	The essay has a minor error. Most sentences are written correctly and are easy to read.	There are a few errors, but they do not confuse the reader.

+Presentation The title and writer's name are clear.

3	2	1	
A few details catch the reader's attention. The reader needs many more to form a picture of the topic.	Details do not catch the reader's attention. Some details are confusing or incomplete.	The topic is not clear. Details are not provided.	Ideas
The essay has a beginning, middle, and end. Linking words and phrases are not used to guide the reader.	The essay lacks parts of the beginning, middle, or end. Linking words and phrases are not used to guide the reader.	The writing is not organized into paragraphs. Linking words and phrases are not used.	Organization
Very little voice is present to show that the writer knows and cares about the topic.	Little or no voice is present. The writer does not seem involved with the topic.	The reader cannot tell if the writer knows or cares about the topic.	Voice
Most words are too general, which keeps the writing from being interesting.	Words are frequently repeated, misused, or wrong for the essay.	Words are too general. Many are repeated or used incorrectly.	Word Choice
Some parts of the essay are easy to read. Other parts do not flow due to choppy or run-on sentences.	There are many choppy and run-on sentences. The essay does not flow.	Short and incomplete sentences keep the reader from understanding the essay.	Sentence Fluency
Some errors confuse the reader, but with rereading the essay can be understood.	Numerous errors make the essay difficult to understand, and the reader must reread it more than once.	Many serious errors keep the reader from understanding the essay.	Conventions

See Appendix B for 4-, 5-, and 6-point descriptive rubrics.

Using the Descriptive Essay Rubric to Analyze the Model

Did you notice that the model on page 403 points out some key elements of a descriptive essay? As he wrote "On Top of the World," Lee Taylor used these elements to help him write a description of a place. He also used the 6-point rubric on pages 404–405 to plan, draft, revise, and edit the writing. A rubric is a great tool to evaluate writing during the writing process.

To get started, look at the top score for each trait as you study the model. Do you agree that Lee has earned a 6 for each trait?

- **Descriptive details catch the reader's attention.**
- **They give the reader a clear picture of the topic.**

Lee's descriptive details really catch my attention. They give me a clear picture of his topic right from the start.

> What I enjoy most is the amazing view from a skyscraper! I am like a bird sitting in a steel treetop. I see tiny people hurry along crowded sidewalks.

- **The essay has a beginning, middle, and end.**
- **Linking words and phrases guide the reader through the description.**

Lee's essay is well organized and easy to follow. Linking words like *sometimes* and *often* guide me through the description.

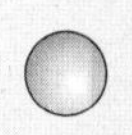

Sometimes damp fog rolls in from the ocean, and I smell salty sea air.

- **The voice clearly shows that the writer knows and cares about the topic.**

Lee's voice sounds very knowledgeable. It's clear that he knows his topic. I like it when he shares his personal feelings about it!

I am very lucky to have my job. Many people know the city from the ground up. But not many know it from the top down!

Using the Descriptive Essay Rubric to Analyze the Model

- **Specific words make the writing come alive.**

Lee uses precise words all the way through the essay. His words describe what he sees, hears, feels, and smells. That helps me picture the city the way he sees it.

Often the sound of the rushing wind is part of the city's music, too.

- **A variety of sentence structures makes the essay flow.**

The sentences in Lee's essay have different structures. He doesn't have any short, choppy sentences. The variety makes the essay easy to read and keeps my interest.

Some people do not like to go to work. I go to work, and it feels wonderful. In fact, I am on top of the world! That's because I am a construction worker who helps build skyscrapers.

- **The essay has no errors.**
- **Sentences are written correctly and are easy to read.**

I read the essay carefully, and I couldn't find any errors. All the spelling, capitalization, and punctuation are correct. Lee has joined compound sentences correctly, too. Here's an example.

Sometimes damp fog rolls in from the ocean, and I smell salty sea air.

+Presentation The title and writer's name are clear.

My Turn!

Now it's my turn to write a descriptive essay! I'll use the rubric and good writing strategies to help me. Follow along to see how I do it.

Prewrite

Focus on **Ideas**

The Rubric Says Descriptive details catch the reader's attention. They give the reader a clear picture of the topic.

Writing Strategy Choose a place to describe. Jot down notes that tell all about the place.

My family took a trip to Yellowstone National Park. It is a beautiful place that's made for picture-taking! I saw amazing things there. When our teacher asked us to write a descriptive essay about a place, I chose Yellowstone as my topic. First I'll jot down notes about what I remember. Then I'll make sure I have the right kind of details.

Yellowstone National Park

- cool lakes
- bubbling mud pots
- an awful smell
- bellowing moose
- loud waterfalls
- deep canyons
- elk with pointed antlers
- sweet-smelling wildflowers
- roaring geysers
- forests—green and thick
- bears with shiny fur
- foaming rivers
- colorful rock steps
- loud swan
- rolling meadows

Write

Think of an interesting place you have visited. Jot down notes about how the place looks, sounds, feels, and smells.

Prewrite

Focus on **Organization**

The Rubric Says The essay has a beginning, middle, and end.

Writing Strategy Make a Spider Map to organize the notes.

My essay should have a beginning, middle, and end. In the beginning I'll introduce my topic—Yellowstone National Park. Then I'll use the middle paragraphs to describe the park. I'll use a Spider Map to help organize the details.

Writer's Term

Spider Map

A **Spider Map** organizes information about a topic. Write the topic in the center of the "spider," the topic sentence ideas on the spider's "legs," and the descriptive details on the lines coming from the "legs."

Spider Map

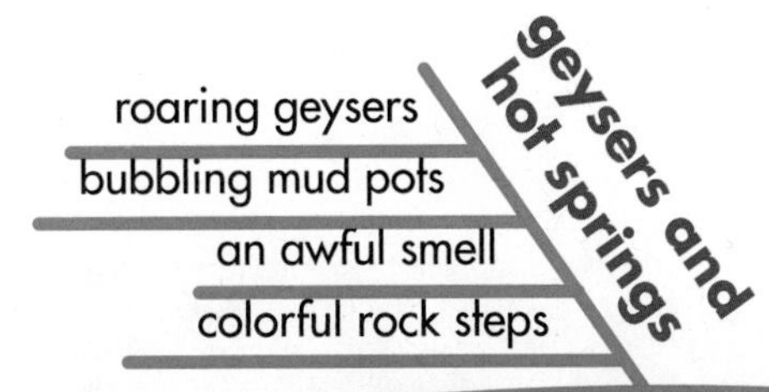

animals
elk with pointed antlers
bears with shiny fur
bellowing moose
loud swan

Yellowstone National Park

scenery
foaming rivers
deep canyons
green forests
rolling meadows

Analyze

Look at the Spider Map. How did Ming use it to organize his details? Why was this the best way to organize his details?

Write

Think about the topic you chose. Use a Spider Map to organize the details for the middle part of your essay.

Draft

Focus on **Voice**

The Rubric Says The voice clearly shows that the writer knows and cares about the topic.

Writing Strategy Use a voice that connects with the reader.

Now I'm ready to write my draft. It helps me to keep my audience in mind as I write. I'll use *I* and *my* so my classmates will know that I'm sharing what I know and how I feel about the park.

I'll do my best with grammar and spelling. I won't worry too much about mistakes now, but I will check again after I finish my draft.

[DRAFT]

My Favorite Place

shows enthusiasm

shows knowledge

Yellowstone National park is the most wonderful place. It has something amazing arownd every corner. People's favorite things about it are the scenery, the animals, and the geysers and hot springs.

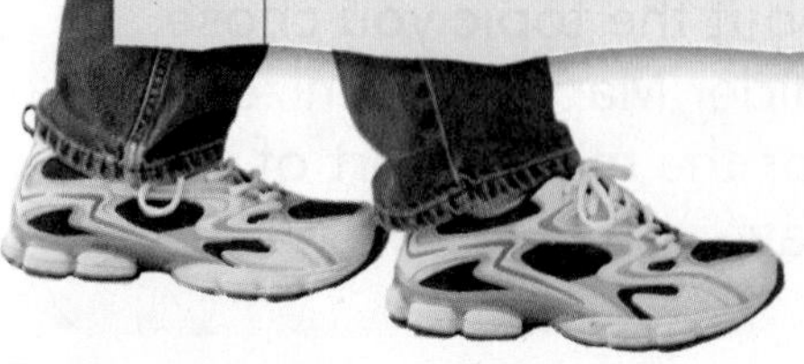

Proofreading Marks

⊐ Indent	Take out something
≡ Make uppercase	⊙ Add a period
/ Make lowercase	¶ New paragraph
∧ Add something	(sp) Spelling error

[DRAFT]

The first thing you notice is the beautiful scenery. Foaming rivers run through canyons. The canyons are deep. Thick green forests grow near cool water and rocks. Rolling meadows are covered with sweet-smelling wildflowers. Huge waterfalls are loud.

writer's facts

Yellowstone is home to many animals. It has elk with long, pointed antlers. shaggy buffalo roam freely. Bears with shiney fur sometimes walk right beside the road! If your lucky, you will hear the bellow of a moose or the loud call of a swan. It is nice to look at the animals don't try to feed them. They are better off eating the food they find naturally.

The park is famous for its geysers and hot springs. Roaring geysers send boiling water shooting high into the air Some hot springs are bubbling mud pots. They look really cool they smell awful! Other springs have colorful rock steps.

writer's feelings

Analyze

Read the draft. How does the writer show he knows and cares about the topic?

Write

Use your Spider Map to write your own draft. Remember to use facts and feelings to show you know and care about your topic.

Revise

Focus on **Ideas**

The Rubric Says Descriptive details catch the reader's attention.

Writing Strategy Add comparisons to strengthen the description.

I finished my draft and took another look at the rubric. It says that the details need to catch my reader's attention. I think I can make my descriptions stronger by adding comparisons. I'll begin with the waterfalls. They sounded like thunder!

I'll make sure that all my sentences begin with an uppercase letter and end with the correct punctuation marks.

Writer's Term

Comparisons

A **comparison** shows how two things are alike.

[DRAFT]

forests grow near cool water and rocks. Rolling meadows are covered with sweet-smelling wildflowers. Huge waterfalls ~~are loud~~ sound like thunder.

added comparison

Some hot springs are bubbling mud pots. They look ~~really cool~~ like steaming soup they smell ~~awful!~~ like rotten eggs!

added comparisons

Write

Read your draft. Revise your writing to add comparisons that will strengthen your description.

Revise

The Rubric Says Specific words make the writing come alive.

Writing Strategy Use exact words to make the description come alive.

The rubric reminds me to use specific words to make my writing come alive. I'll read through my draft again. Then I'll replace any ordinary words with exact ones. I want the reader to picture what I saw.

Writer's Term

Specific Words

A **specific word** gives an exact meaning to help the reader imagine what you are writing about. If you write, **You will hear the sound of a big animal,** your readers will not know what you mean. But if you write, **You will hear the bellow of a moose,** the reader knows exactly what you mean.

[DRAFT]

rivers run through canyons. The canyons are deep. Thick green forests grow near cool ~~water~~ lakes and ~~rocks~~ rocky cliffs.

used exact words

Analyze

Look at the changes. How did you imagine the scene before Ming's changes?

Write

Read your draft again. Replace ordinary words with exact ones. Make sure your descriptions come alive for the reader.

Revise

Focus on **Sentence Fluency**

The Rubric Says A variety of sentence structures makes the essay flow.

Writing Strategy Combine short, choppy sentences.

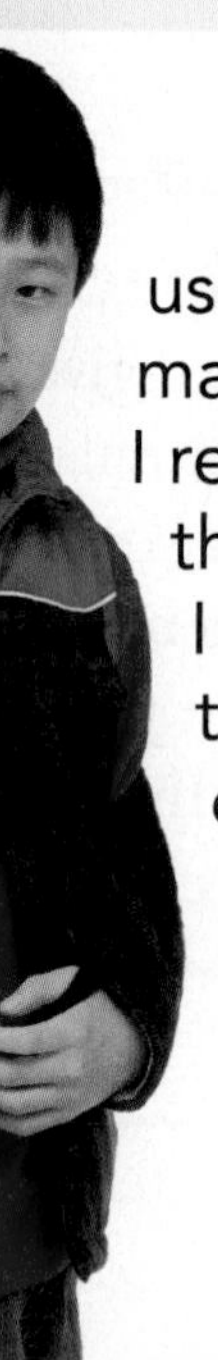

I know from the rubric that I should use a variety of sentence structures to make the sentences in my essay flow. I read my essay out loud to hear how the sentences sounded. As I read, I made a little mark near sentences that sounded choppy. Then I figured out a way to smooth them out. Here is an example of how I combined two short sentences into a longer one.

[DRAFT]

combined short, choppy sentences

The first thing you notice is the beautiful scenery. Foaming rivers run through ^deep canyons. ~~The canyons are deep.~~

Write

Look for short, choppy sentences in your draft. Combine them into one longer, more interesting sentence.

Edit

Focus on **Conventions**

The Rubric Says The essay has no errors. Sentences are written correctly and are easy to read.

Writing Strategy Use a comma and a conjunction to form compound sentences and avoid run-on sentences.

I always check spelling, capitalization, and punctuation. I also need to make sure that compound sentences are correctly joined with a comma and a conjunction.

Writer's Term

Compound Sentences

A **compound sentence** is made of two sentences connected by a conjunction such as **and, but,** or **or**. A comma goes before the conjunction.

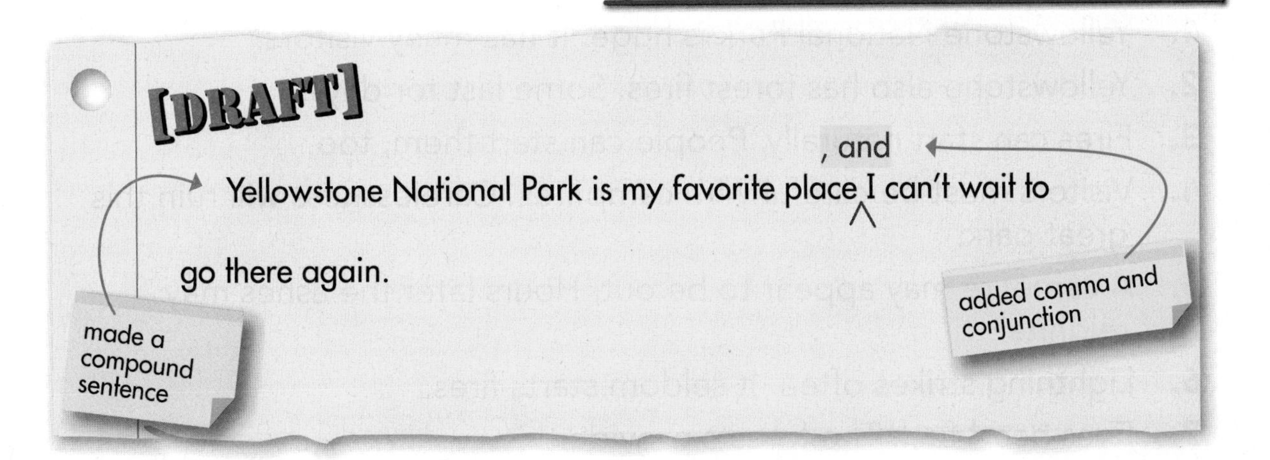

Analyze

Look at Ming's revision on the previous page. How does his simple change affect the flow of his writing? Look at Ming's edit. How did his change clarify his writing? Why is it important to fix run-on sentences?

Write

Conventions

Edit your draft carefully. Fix any run-on sentences you find.

For more practice joining compound sentences correctly, use the exercises on the next two pages.

Compound Sentences

Know the Rule

A **compound sentence** contains two complete thoughts.
A compound sentence is made by joining two simple sentences with a conjunction. A conjunction is a joining word, such as *and, but,* or *or.* A comma is used before the conjunction.

Example:
The park has a large lake**, but** we are not allowed to fish there.

Practice the Rule

Number a sheet of paper 1–10. Read each sentence pair below. Rewrite each as one compound sentence. Remember to use a comma and a conjunction. Underline the conjunction.

1. Yellowstone National Park is huge. It has many visitors.
2. Yellowstone also has forest fires. Some last for days.
3. Fires can start naturally. People can start them, too.
4. Visitors must be careful with campfires. Carelessness will ruin this great park.
5. A campfire may appear to be out. Hours later the ashes may reignite.
6. Lightning strikes often. It seldom starts fires.
7. Fires need fuel. The forests provide this.
8. Fuel might be pine needles. It could be entire trees.
9. Dry weather helps fires form winds. These winds spread the fire.
10. Fire can kill trees. It can also help them.

Run-on Sentences

Know the Rule

Run-on sentences contain two complete sentences that are not joined by a comma and a joining word. A run-on sentence can be corrected by adding a comma and a joining word to make a **compound sentence**. A run-on sentence also can be corrected by making it into two separate sentences.

Examples:

Mike wants to become a firefighter he must pass the tests.

Mike wants to become a firefighter, but he must pass the tests.

Practice the Rule

Number a separate sheet of paper 1–10. Read sentences 1–5 below. Use a comma and the given joining word to rewrite each run-on sentence.

1. Smoke fills the sky (and) flames fill the canyon.
2. An airplane flies overhead (but) it cannot be seen.
3. The plane carries water (and) it also carries smokejumpers.
4. Smokejumpers jump out of the plane (and) they parachute into the forest fire.
5. They have a hard job to do (and) everyone admires their bravery.

Now read sentences 6–10. Correct each run-on sentence by making two separate sentences.

6. Smokejumpers train in real forests they also train on computers.
7. They work hard to stay fit they are in top condition.
8. Off-duty smokejumpers clean forest trails they also teach fire safety.
9. Smokejumping is dangerous it isn't a job for everyone.
10. Fighting fires is what they do smokejumpers love their work.

Publish

+Presentation

Publishing Strategy Post the descriptive essay on the bulletin board.

Presentation Strategy Center the title and the writer's name.

I'm ready to publish my descriptive essay! There are all kinds of ways to publish an essay. I could post it on my school's website, make a book of essays with classmates, or display it on a poster with illustrations. I like the idea of putting it on the class bulletin board. If lots of people will read my paper, I must make sure that my final copy is neat. I'll put the title and my name at the top so that everyone will know that this is my paper. Here's the final checklist I'll use.

My Final Checklist

Did I—

- ✔ write words and sentences correctly?
- ✔ make sure that there are no run-on sentences?
- ✔ write the title and my name clearly?
- ✔ use neat handwriting or word processing?

Write

Use this checklist and prepare a final copy. Make a colorful border or add illustrations before publishing.

My Favorite Place
by Ming

Yellowstone National Park is the most wonderful place I have ever visited. It has something amazing around every corner. My favorite things about it are the scenery, the animals, and the geysers and hot springs.

The first thing you notice is the beautiful scenery. Foaming rivers run through deep canyons. Thick green forests grow near cool lakes and rocky cliffs. Rolling meadows are covered with sweet-smelling wildflowers. Huge waterfalls sound like thunder.

Yellowstone is home to many animals. It has elk with long, pointed antlers. Shaggy buffalo roam freely. Bears with shiny fur sometimes walk right beside the road! If you are lucky, you will hear the bellow of a moose or the loud call of a swan. It is nice to look at the animals, but don't try to feed them. They are better off eating the food they find naturally.

The park is also famous for its geysers and hot springs. Roaring geysers send boiling water shooting high into the air. Some hot springs are bubbling mud pots. They look like steaming soup, but they smell like rotten eggs! Other springs have colorful rock steps.

Yellowstone National Park is my favorite place, and I can't wait to go there again.

Analyze

Use the rubric to evaluate the essay. Were all the traits of a good descriptive essay used? Now use the rubric to check your own descriptive essay.

What's a Poem?

A poem creates a picture in a reader's mind and expresses the writer's feelings about the topic of the poem. Usually poetry uses fewer words than other kinds of writing to say the same thing.

What's in a Poem?

Lines
Most poems are written in lines rather than in complete sentences or paragraphs.

Figurative Language
Figurative language helps readers picture what the writer is describing. Similes and metaphors are examples of figurative language. A simile compares two objects by using *like* or *as*. A metaphor compares the objects without using *like* or *as*.

Sensory Details
Sensory details describe how my topic looks, sounds, smells, tastes, or feels. They help my reader picture the topic.

Form
Some poems follow a certain form. In an acrostic poem, the first letter of each line spells the topic of the poem.

Why write a Poem?

There are many reasons to write a poem. Here are two good ones.

To Inform
Even though some poems are meant to be fun, and even silly, others are serious and tell facts and truths. A poem about a science concept can inform readers if it contains factual information you have learned or researched.

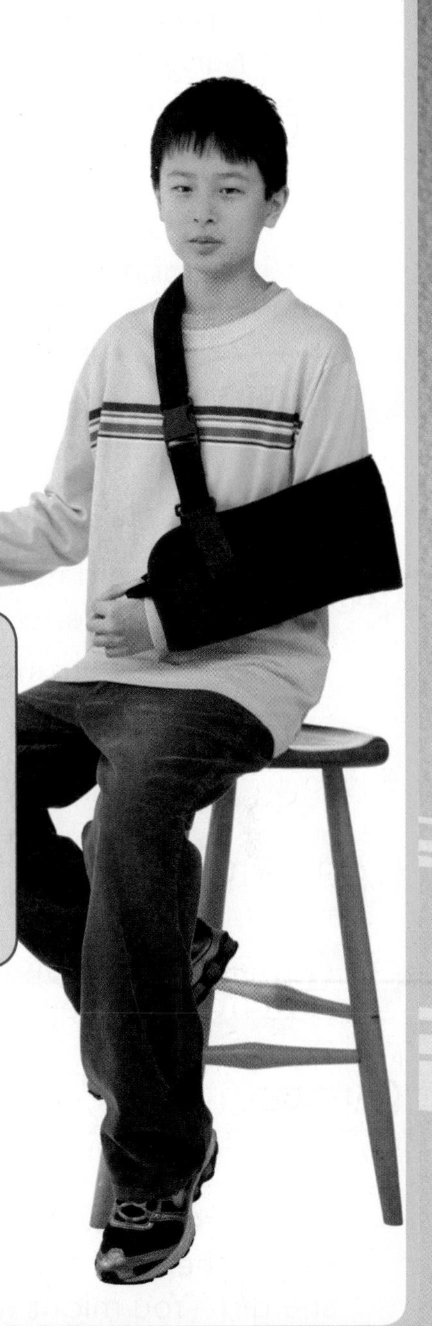

To Entertain
Poets write to entertain their readers by describing an idea, an experience, or an object in an unusual and interesting way. You may have noticed that there are often poems in greeting cards. Sometimes a poem is the best way to express your thoughts!

Linking Descriptive Writing Traits to a Poem

In this chapter, you will write a poem about a science term or idea. Ming will guide you through the stages of the writing process: Prewrite, Draft, Revise, Edit, and Publish. In each stage, Ming will show you important writing strategies that are linked to the Descriptive Writing Traits below.

Descriptive Writing Traits

	• a clear, focused topic • sensory details that tell readers what they want to know about the topic
	• a strong beginning, middle, and end • details that are arranged in an order that makes sense • linking words and phrases that connect ideas
	• a voice that is appropriate for the purpose and audience
	• clear, specific words that make a picture for the reader
	• sentences that are easy to read aloud because they flow smoothly
	• no or few errors in spelling, punctuation, and capitalization

Before you write, read Lupita Martinez's poem on the next page. Then use the poem rubric on page 426 to decide how well she did. (You might want to look back at What's in a Poem? on page 422, too!)

An Unexpected Outcome

by Lupita Martinez

first letters in lines spell out topic

Perhaps you have heard of the amazing life cycle of a butterfly
At the beginning, a caterpillar, not much bigger than a tiny peanut
It grows bigger and bigger, shedding its skin, or molting, as it grows
Nibbling leaves, the caterpillar grows and molts about four times
Then it is time for the caterpillar to make a chrysalis, or pupa, and hide
Even though the brownish pupa looks boring, many changes are occurring
Deep inside, wings form and antennae, too

Look closely—the pupa shakes and jiggles like gelatin
And suddenly a butterfly emerges and slowly spreads its wings!
Delicately opens and closes its wings to dry
You must surely think the butterfly is far more beautiful!

lines, not sentences

sensory details

figurative language

Poem Rubric

Use this rubric to analyze the model. Then use it to plan and score your own poem.

	6	5	4
Ideas	Descriptive details create a clear picture of the writer's topic.	Most details create a clear picture.	Some details create a clear picture.
Organization	The lines follow the form of the poem. The form is ideal for the topic.	One line may be out of order. The form suits the topic most of the time.	Two lines may be out of order. The form may not suit the topic well.
Voice	The writer's personality comes through to the audience.	The writer's personality comes through to the audience most of the time.	The writer's personality comes through to the audience some of the time.
Word Choice	Carefully chosen adjectives and comparisons create a clear picture.	Adjectives and comparisons create a clear picture most of the time.	Adjectives may be overused or too general but the reader still can get a picture.
Sentence Fluency	Each word or line flows into the next. The poem is easy to follow.	Most of the words and lines flow well. Most of the poem is easy to follow.	Some of the words and lines flow well. Some of the poem is hard to follow.
Conventions	The writing is error free. Verbs are used correctly.	The writing contains occasional errors. Verbs are used correctly.	A few minor errors are present, but they do not confuse the reader. Verbs are mostly correct.

+Presentation An illustration or photograph helps convey the message.

	3	2	1
Ideas	Few details form a clear picture.	Details do not form a picture.	Details are incomplete or unrelated.
Organization	Lines in the beginning are in order. The form is not followed.	Lines are not in order. The form is not followed.	The writing is not organized as a poem.
Voice	The writer's personality comes through in the beginning then fades.	The writer's voice is very weak throughout the poem.	The writer's voice is absent. The audience does not know who is speaking.
Word Choice	The writer uses general adjectives that do not help the reader make a picture.	The writing is confusing because of either too many or not enough adjectives.	Word choice feels random or accidental. It is hard to get a clear picture.
Sentence Fluency	Most of the words and lines do not flow well. The poem is hard to follow.	Some of the lines are incomplete or are missing words.	Incomplete lines and missing words make the writing impossible to understand.
Conventions	Many errors confuse the reader. Some verbs may be used incorrectly.	Many errors make the text difficult to read. The reader must fill in the gaps to understand the text.	The writing has not been edited.

See Appendix B for 4-, 5-, and 6-point descriptive rubrics.

Using the Poem Rubric to Analyze the Model

Did you notice that the model on page 425 points out some key elements of a poem? As she wrote "An Unexpected Outcome," Lupita Martinez used these elements to help her describe the life cycle of a butterfly. She also used the 6-point rubric on pages 426–427 to plan, draft, revise, and edit the writing. A rubric is a great tool to evaluate writing during the writing process.

To get started, look at the top score for each trait as you study the model. Do you agree that Lupita has earned a 6 for each trait?

- **Descriptive details create a clear picture of the writer's topic.**

Lupita uses words like *not much bigger than a tiny peanut, brownish pupa*, and *jiggles like gelatin* to describe the changes a caterpillar goes through to become a butterfly. These details help me create a picture in my mind of how the caterpillar and pupa look in each stage of development.

Perhaps you have heard of the amazing life cycle of a butterfly
At the beginning, a caterpillar, not much bigger than a tiny peanut

- **The lines follow the form of the poem.**
- **The form is ideal for the topic.**

Lupita wrote an acrostic poem about her topic, a painted lady butterfly. Each line in her poem gives information about the butterfly. While I read her poem, I noticed the first letter of each line spells out the butterfly's name. Her poem is easy to follow.

Perhaps you have heard of the amazing life cycle of a butterfly
At the beginning, a caterpillar, not much bigger than a tiny peanut
It grows bigger and bigger, shedding its skin, or molting, as it grows
Nibbling leaves, the caterpillar grows and molts about four times
Then it is time for the caterpillar to make a chrysalis, or pupa, and hide
Even though the brownish pupa looks boring, many changes are occurring
Deep inside, wings form and antennae, too

- **The writer's personality comes through to the audience.**

I can tell Lupita is fascinated by her topic. She is obviously very knowledgeable about the life cycle of a butterfly and enjoys sharing what she knows. She speaks directly to her readers, and I feel her excitement when the butterfly finally appears.

Look closely—the pupa shakes and jiggles like gelatin
And suddenly a butterfly emerges and slowly spreads its wings!

Using the Poem Rubric to Analyze the Model

- Carefully chosen adjectives and comparisons create a clear picture.

Lupita uses describing words like *amazing, tiny, four,* and *brownish*. These adjectives help readers get a clear picture of the caterpillar. Look how she compares the size of the caterpillar to a peanut!

> **P**erhaps you have heard of the amazing life cycle of a butterfly
> **A**t the beginning, a caterpillar, not much bigger than a tiny peanut

- Each word or line flows into the next.
- The poem is easy to follow.

Lupita made sure all her words and lines flow smoothly. The poem is easy to follow. In this part of the poem, the exclamations add excitement and emphasis to the lines.

> **L**ook closely—the pupa shakes and jiggles like gelatin
> **A**nd suddenly a butterfly emerges and slowly spreads its wings!
> **D**elicately opens and closes its wings to dry
> **Y**ou must surely think the butterfly is far more beautiful!

- The writing is error free.
- Verbs are used correctly.

Lupita's poem does not include any errors in spelling or punctuation. The verbs she uses are all correct.

Look closely—the pupa shakes and jiggles like gelatin
And suddenly a butterfly emerges and slowly spreads its wings!

+Presentation An illustration or photograph helps convey the message.

My Turn!

Now it's my turn to write. I'm going to write my own acrostic poem. I will use the rubric to help me. Follow along to see how I do it.

Prewrite

Focus on **Ideas**

The Rubric Says Descriptive details create a clear picture of the writer's topic.

Writing Strategy Choose a topic. List details.

We have been studying extinct animals in science class. Now our teacher has asked us to write a descriptive poem about one of the animals we have studied. I'll use what I learned in class and the information I gather at the library to write my poem.

Extinct Animals

- Caspian tiger—lived in parts of Asia
- dodo—a bird that could not fly
- woolly mammoth—possibly killed off by disease
- pteranodon—very large wingspan, not a dinosaur
- golden toad—last seen in 1989

I read over my list of extinct animals and decided to write a descriptive poem about the pteranodon (tuh·**ran**·uh·don). Many people think a pteranodon is a dinosaur, but it is not! I would like to help people understand what a pteranodon is.

Write

Make a list of extinct or endangered animals you have learned about. Choose one that you would like to describe in an acrostic poem.

Prewrite

The Rubric Says The lines follow the form of the poem. The form is ideal for the topic.

Writing Strategy Use a Web to plan the poem.

The rubric says that the lines need to follow the form of the poem. If I write an acrostic poem, I know that the first letter of each line will spell my topic. If I write about a pteranodon, the first word of the first line must start with *p*. The first word of the second line starts with *t*, and so on. I can use a Web to list all the facts and details that I collect about a pteranodon. Then I can choose the ideas that will fit best in my poem.

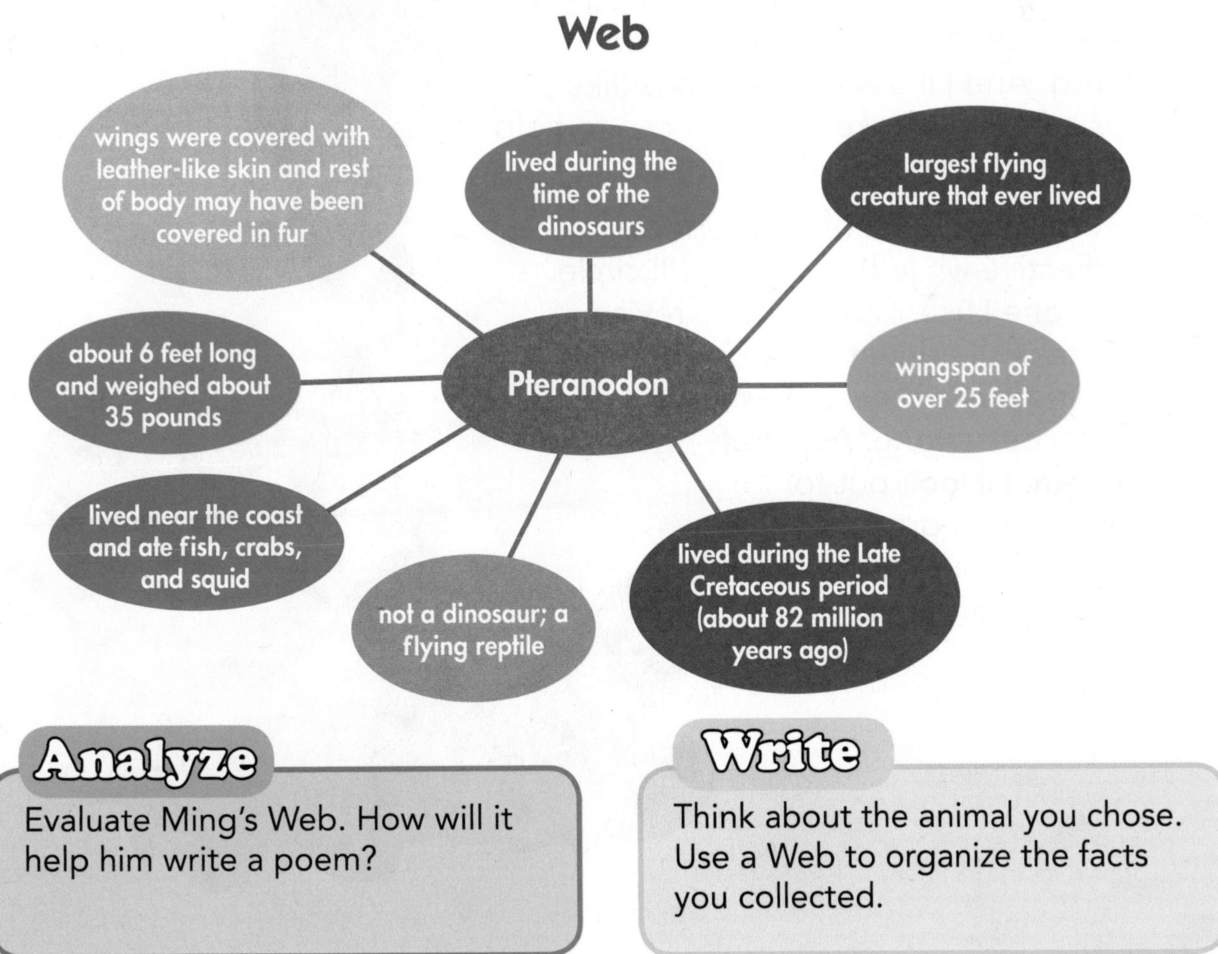

Analyze

Evaluate Ming's Web. How will it help him write a poem?

Write

Think about the animal you chose. Use a Web to organize the facts you collected.

Draft

Focus on **Word Choice**

The Rubric Says Carefully chosen adjectives and comparisons create a clear picture.

Writing Strategy Use exact adjectives.

Now that my Web is finished, I am ready to begin writing a draft of my acrostic poem. Because a poem uses fewer words than a story or essay, every word is important. As I write, I will choose adjectives carefully when describing the information in my Web. And I'll use comparisons (like *soft as a baby's blanket*) where I can to help give the reader a clear picture.

If I can't think of the perfect adjective while I'm writing, I'll circle the one I use. Later, when I revise, I'll take the time to search an online dictionary or thesaurus for a better one. As I draft my poem, I'll look out for mistakes in grammar and spelling, but I know I can fix my draft later.

Proofreading Marks

Indent	Take out something
Make uppercase	Add a period
Make lowercase	New paragraph
Add something	Spelling error

[DRAFT]

The Flying Reptile

Perhaps you have heard of the pteranodon?

Think it were a dinosaur? You're wrong, it were a flying reptile!

Living during the Late Cretaceous period, a dinosaur it is not

Reaching only 35 pounds, its wingspan was over 25 feet

And it was fascinating—a living airplane

metaphor

No other flying creature on Earth has ever being this big

Occupying areas near the coast, it ate fish, crabs, and squid

Do you think it ate vegetables, fruits, and nuts?

One day, look up at the sky and imagine seeing a giant flying reptile

diving like an eagle to get a meal out of the cold water

simile

Never again will you see it any more

Analyze

Read Ming's draft. How does he help readers picture a pteranodon? What are some exact adjectives that Ming used?

Write

Use your Web to write a draft. Begin each line with the next letter in the name of your animal. Use exact adjectives and comparisons to help readers picture the animal.

Revise

Focus on **Ideas**

The Rubric Says Descriptive details create a clear picture of the writer's topic.

Writing Strategy Use simple, descriptive details.

I finished my draft. Now I should find ways to improve my poem. The rubric says that the details should create a clear picture. If I have included details that might confuse my readers, I should take out those details or change them.

I notice that I refer to the Late Cretaceous period. Many readers might not know when that was. I will simplify that detail. I'll also add details to describe the pteranodon's size more clearly.

[DRAFT]

simplified detail

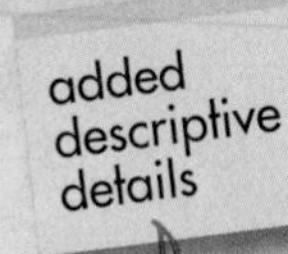

Living during ~~the Late Cretaceous period~~ the time of the dinosaurs, a dinosaur it is not

Reaching only 35 pounds in weight, its wingspan was over 25 feet wide

Read the draft of your poem. Revise your writing to include more descriptive details. Make your details clearer and easier for readers to understand.

Revise

Focus on **Organization**

The Rubric Says The lines follow the form of the poem. The form is ideal for the topic.

Writing Strategy Make sure the order of the lines makes sense.

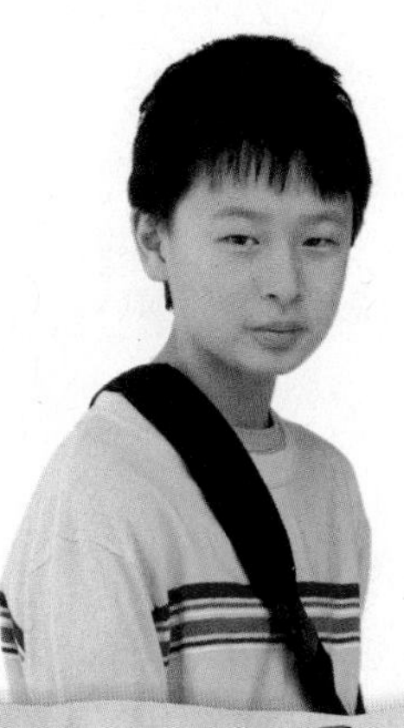

The rubric tells me to be sure that I have followed the form of the poem and that it is ideal for the subject I am writing about. As I read my poem again, I noticed that one line did not follow the form of my poem. I'll change it so all my lines are in order and make sense.

[DRAFT]

changed first word to follow form

Even Living during ~~the Late Cretaceous period~~ the time of the dinosaurs, a dinosaur it is not

Analyze

Look at Ming's change. How does his change help him follow the form of the poem? What other "E" words could he start with?

Write

Read your poem again. Revise any lines that are out of order or don't make sense. Make sure the form is followed throughout the poem.

Revise

Focus on **Sentence Fluency**

The Rubric Says Each word or line flows into the next. The poem is easy to follow.

Writing Strategy Read the poem aloud to listen for flow.

As I revise, I will read the lines of my poem aloud to hear where they could be improved for rhythm and flow. As I read, I'll be listening for ways I can move, add, or delete words to make sure that the writing flows. I'll also add an exclamation point at the end of my last line. Do you think it adds excitement to the line?

[DRAFT]

One day, look up at the sky and imagine seeing a giant flying reptile

diving like an eagle ~~to get a meal out of the cold water~~

Never ~~again~~ will you see it ~~any more~~ again!

took out extra words

moved word to improve flow

used punctuation for effect

Write

Read your draft aloud. Then move, add, or delete words to improve the flow. Use punctuation for the right effect.

Edit

Focus on Conventions

The Rubric Says The writing is error free. Verbs are used correctly.

Writing Strategy Check to make sure that the form of the verb *be* is correct.

I'm ready to check my draft for spelling, capitalization, and punctuation. The rubric reminds me to make sure that I have used the correct forms of the verb *be*, too.

Writer's Term

The Verb *Be*

Use the singular forms **is** and **was** for present and past tenses. Use the plural forms **are** and **were** for present and past tenses. **Be** is also called a linking verb because it links the subject with a noun or adjective.

[DRAFT]

Think it ~~were~~ was a dinosaur? You're wrong, it ~~were~~ was a flying reptile!

Analyze

Read Ming's revisions on the previous page. Do his changes make his writing flow better? Look at Ming's edits. Did he use the correct form of the verb *be*? How do his changes affect his writing?

Write Conventions

Edit your poem for spelling, punctuation, capitalization, and the correct use of the verb *be*.

For more practice with the verb *be*, use the exercises on the next two pages.

The Verb *Be*

Know the Rule

Use **is** or **was** after a singular subject.
Use **are** or **were** after a plural subject.

Examples:
The Caspian tiger **is** an extinct animal.
Caspian tigers **are** extinct animals.

Practice the Rule

Number a sheet of paper 1–10. Next to each number, write the correct form of the verb *be*.

1. Pteranodons (was/were) flying reptiles.
2. A pteranodon (was/is) a meat eater.
3. We (is/are) interested in learning more about pteranodons.
4. Why (is/were) pteranodons unusual?
5. The pteranodon (was/were) the largest flying creature that ever lived.
6. Pteranodon bones (were/was) uncovered in Kansas some years ago.
7. What other animals (was/were) living when pteranodons lived?
8. The pteranodon (is/are) just one of many interesting extinct animals.
9. Did you know that pteranodons (was/were) really as big as small planes?
10. A pteranodon's wingspan (was/were) about 25 feet wide.

Linking Verbs

Know the Rule

A **linking verb** does not show action. It links the subject of a sentence with other words that give information about the subject. The verb *be* is a linking verb. Note how the word *are* links the subject *Tigers* with words that describe them or tell what they are.

Example:

Tigers **are** fierce and wild.

Practice the Rule

Rewrite each sentence below on a sheet of paper. Circle the linking verb and underline the words that describe the subject. Then draw an arrow from the describing words to the subject, as shown in the example.

1. The pteranodon was a large flying reptile.
2. My best friend is the pteranodon's biggest fan.
3. Woolly mammoths were very large.
4. Their coats were thick and protective.
5. The extinct dodo was a bird that couldn't fly.
6. The passenger pigeon is another extinct bird.
7. The giant panda is an endangered animal.
8. Many animals found only in Madagascar are endangered.
9. Every animal on Earth is important.
10. Endangered animals are important and in need of our protection.

Publish

+Presentation

Publishing Strategy Present the poem to the class.

Presentation Strategy Choose interesting photographs or illustrations.

My poem is finished. Now it's time to read our poems to the class. To help my classmates better understand what a pteranodon looked like, I'll display or project images on the board to support my message. This is the list I used to get my poem ready for presentation.

My Final Checklist

Did I—

✔ fix any spelling, capitalization, or punctuation errors?

✔ make sure the forms of *be* are correct?

✔ choose interesting photographs or illustrations?

✔ add a creative title to the poem?

Write

Use Ming's checklist for your poem, too. Have you found interesting pictures or photographs to present along with your poem?

Caution! Low-Flying Reptile
by Ming

Perhaps you have heard of the pteranodon?

Think it was a dinosaur? You're wrong, it was a flying reptile!

Even living during the time of the dinosaurs, a dinosaur it is not

Reaching only 35 pounds in weight, its wingspan was over 25 feet wide

And it was fascinating—a living airplane!

No other flying creature on Earth has filled the sky like a dark thundercloud

Occupying areas near the coast, it ate fish, crabs, and squid

Do you think it ate vegetables, fruits, and nuts? Was it a vegetarian like me?

One day, look up at the sky and imagine seeing a giant flying reptile diving like an eagle

Never will you see it again!

Analyze

Use the rubric to be sure Ming included all the traits of a good poem. Then use the rubric to score your own poem.

Appendix A
Grammar Practice

Simple Sentences

Know the Rule

A **simple sentence** is a group of words that tells one complete thought. One part of a sentence tells whom or what the sentence is about. The other part tells what happened. A sentence begins with an uppercase letter and ends with an end mark.

Examples:
My brother plays many sports.
His favorite sport is hockey.
He loves the fast action!

Practice the Rule

Number a sheet of paper 1–10. Read each group of words. Write **S** if the words make a complete simple sentence. Write **X** if the group of words is not a complete sentence.

1. My whole family loves ice hockey.
2. We think it is an exciting sport.
3. Out on the rink behind the net.
4. Ice hockey was first played in the United States in 1893.
5. When we go to the ice rink.
6. This year my sister's team won many games.
7. They had great skaters and a terrific goalie.
8. Ice hockey can be played inside or outside.
9. Want to be a goalie.
10. To be a forward on the team next year.

Compound and Complex Sentences

Know the Rule

A **compound sentence** contains two complete thoughts. A compound sentence is made of two simple sentences connected by a coordinating conjunction such as *or*, *and*, or *but*. A comma is used before the joining word.

Example: Football is a popular sport, but people love baseball, too.

A **complex sentence** also contains two thoughts, but one is not complete without the other. A complex sentence is made of at least one dependent clause and one independent clause. The dependent clause begins with a subordinating conjunction such as *if*, *because*, *since* or *unless*.

Example: **Unless** it rains, we will go to the game.

Practice the Rule

Number a sheet of paper 1–10. Write whether each sentence is **compound** or **complex.**

1. Opening day is exciting, and many fans enjoy going to the game.
2. You can go to the game if you have a ticket.
3. If you like watching baseball, you might also like to play it.
4. Before you can play a game, you need to learn the basics.
5. Players might play in the outfield, or they may prefer pitching.
6. Because baseballs can cause injury, batters wear helmets.
7. After a game ends, the players shake hands.
8. Many children play baseball, but some children prefer other sports.
9. Our town has a baseball league, but it also has a dance studio and an ice rink.
10. There are lots of things to do if you live in our town.

Imperative and Exclamatory Sentences

Know the Rule

Some sentences give a command. They are called **imperative sentences.** This kind of sentence usually ends with a period. Other sentences express strong feelings. They are called **exclamatory sentences.** This kind of sentence ends with an exclamation point.

Examples:
Make sure the piñata is ready.
Break the piñata open with the stick.
Hurrah, I broke the piñata open!

Practice the Rule

Number a sheet of paper 1–10. Write each sentence. Put a period at the end of each imperative sentence. Put an exclamation point at the end of each exclamatory sentence.

1. Look at the beautiful piñata
2. Wow, it is covered with such brightly colored tissue paper
3. Break it with the stick
4. First you need to put on a blindfold
5. Take turns trying to break it
6. Yay, it's my turn now
7. Be careful not to hit anyone
8. Yippee, I broke the piñata on my first swing
9. Look at all the prizes falling out of it
10. Hey, I need to take off my blindfold now

Grammar, Usage & Mechanics

Abstract and Concrete Nouns

Know the Rule

A **noun** is a word that names a person, place, or thing. A **concrete noun** is a person, place, or thing that can be touched or seen, such as *sunflowers*. An **abstract noun** cannot be recognized through the senses, such as *speed*.

Examples:
Sunflowers turn toward the **sun** when they grow.
These beautiful **flowers** grow at a very fast **speed**.

Practice the Rule

Number a sheet of paper 1–10. Decide which of the two underlined words is a noun. Write that word on your paper. Then write **concrete** or **abstract** after each noun.

1. You can plant the seeds in late spring.
2. After sixty days you may get blooms.
3. When they are mature, their large blooms look like the sun.
4. Sunflowers are some of the largest flowers you can grow.
5. The largest one ever measured was over 25 feet tall!
6. Sunflowers are an important crop for many farmers.
7. The seeds make a healthy and nutritious snack.
8. The seeds are also used to make cooking oil.
9. Did you know that the sunflower is the state flower of Kansas?
10. The sunflower was a favorite subject of the famous painter van Gogh.

Plural Nouns

Know the Rule

A **singular noun** shows "one" (*grape*). A **plural noun** shows "more than one" (*grapes*).

- To make most nouns plural, add *-s* to the singular noun.
  Example: orange/oranges
  - If the noun ends in **s, ch, sh, x,** or **z,** add *-es.*
    Example: beach/beaches
  - For most nouns that end in **y,** change the **y** to **i** and add *-es.*
    Example: berry/berries
  - For nouns that end in a **vowel + y,** just add *-s.*
    Example: toy/toys
  - **Irregular plural nouns** are formed in different ways and must be memorized. Some nouns do not change at all.
    Example: foot/feet; child/children; person/people; knife/knives; loaf/loaves; sheep/sheep

Practice the Rule

Number your paper 1–10. Rewrite each sentence using the correct word. Make the word plural if necessary.

1. To stay healthy, you should eat several servings of fruit every (day).
2. Some (scientist) say that eating fruit helps your memory.
3. Some people think eating fruit will make their (life) longer.
4. Eat different (kind) of fruit.
5. Maybe I should eat some (peach).
6. I could also eat some (blueberry)!
7. Of course, there are other (way) to stay healthy.
8. For example, you should get plenty of (exercise).
9. There are great exercise programs for girls and (boy).
10. You should also sleep about eight (hour) each night.

Possessive Pronouns

Know the Rule

A **pronoun** takes the place of a noun. A **possessive pronoun** shows ownership.

Pronouns	**Possessive Pronouns**
I	my
you	your
he	his
she	her
it	its
we	our
they	their

Examples:
My uncle Jorge's house in New Mexico is called an adobe.
You can make adobe bricks by mixing mud and straw.
It is the oldest building material in the Southwest.

Practice the Rule

Number a sheet of paper 1–10. Find the pronoun in each sentence. Write it next to the number.

1. Adobe homes get their rich, brown color from the soil.
2. I was surprised to learn that adobe construction comes from Native American and Hispanic traditions.
3. You will find adobe houses in dry, desert climates.
4. Their construction style is very energy efficient.
5. My uncle's house has very thick walls.
6. His adobe home always seems to be cool in the summer and warm in the winter.
7. Thick walls would certainly make it energy efficient!
8. He says that an adobe house is both beautiful and practical.
9. Now our family wants to live in an adobe home, too.
10. My mom thinks adobes are the most interesting architectural style.

Action Verbs

Know the Rule

An **action verb** tells what the subject of a sentence does or did.

Examples: My dad and I **take** a cooking class.

We **learn** many different ways to prepare food.

Practice the Rule

Number a sheet of paper 1–10. Decide which of the two underlined words is an action verb. Write that word on your paper.

1. Dad and I love Asian food.
2. We want to learn how to make some new dishes.
3. We have a recipe that uses chicken, broccoli, and carrots.
4. To cook this dish, we need a special kind of pan called a wok.
5. Luckily, our cooking class provides all the dishes and ingredients we need.
6. We carefully chop the broccoli and carrots.
7. Then we toss the vegetables together with the chicken.
8. Dad pours some oil into the wok.
9. He prepares the chicken and vegetables with a little soy sauce.
10. We love eating food we cooked ourselves!

Past Tense

Know the Rule

Past-tense verbs show action that happened in the past. Many past-tense verbs end with *-ed*.

Examples:

Wilma Rudolph **received** many honors for her athletic ability.

She **needed** crutches, braces, and special shoes during her early years.

Practice the Rule

Number your paper 1–10. Write **past tense** if the underlined verb is in the past tense. Write an **X** if the underlined verb is not a past-tense verb.

1. Wilma Rudolph competed in the 400-meter relay in the 1969 Olympics.
2. She also raced in the 100-meter dash and the 200-meter dash!
3. She achieved the honor of being the first American woman to win three gold medals in the Olympics.
4. These achievements would help her become one of the most celebrated female athletes of all time.
5. Wilma achieved many good things for sports and for our country.
6. Her popularity caused women to become more accepted in track-and-field events.
7. Her many honors include election to the Black Sports Hall of Fame and the U.S. Olympic Hall of Fame.
8. She also served as a Goodwill Ambassador to the Friendship Games in Senegal, Africa.
9. Many schools and colleges invited her to speak to their students.
10. Few people will accomplish as much as Wilma Rudolph.

Present Tense

Know the Rule

Present-tense verbs show action that is happening now.

Examples:

My sister Blanca **studies** astronomy in college.
She **likes** to find the constellations in the sky at night.
Astronomers **group** stars into constellations.

Practice the Rule

Number your paper 1–10. Write the present-tense verb in each sentence.

1. Constellations are groups of stars in the night sky.
2. Blanca knows the location of all the famous constellations.
3. First she points to the Great Bear, or *Ursa Major.*
4. The Big Dipper's cup sits right on the rear hip of the bear.
5. The stars in the handle make the bear's tail.
6. Next she shows me the Little Dipper, or *Ursa Minor.*
7. The Little Dipper contains the most important star in the sky, the North Star.
8. The North Star always stays in the same location.
9. Navigators still use the North Star as an important guide.
10. Blanca's astronomy class teaches her so many amazing facts about the stars!

Future Tense

Know the Rule

Future-tense verbs show action that is going to happen in the future. Use the helping verb *will* to form the future tense.

Examples:
We **will get** a new dog this year.
We **will choose** the puppy we all like best.

Practice the Rule

Number your paper 1–10. Write the correct verb form in ( ) to make a future-tense sentence.

1. Dad and I will (adopt/adopted) a male beagle.
2. A beagle puppy will (needs/need) lots of attention from his owners.
3. A good-tempered beagle will (made/make) a good family pet.
4. He will (go/gone) with me for exercise on long walks around the neighborhood.
5. I will (name/named) him Otis.
6. My friends will (thought/think) that he is a fun pet to have.
7. My mom will (fed/feed) him while I am at school.
8. Maybe Otis will (like/liked) her best!
9. I will (count/counted) the days until we can bring Otis home.
10. My family and I will (worked/work) hard to be good beagle owners.

Helping Verbs

Know the Rule

Helping verbs come before the main verb in a sentence. They are forms of *may, be, do, should, have*, and *will*. They help the verb show different tenses. Helping verbs also start many questions. Some sentences have more than one helping verb.

Examples:

I **am** writing my report about Lucy Ware Webb Hayes.
Have you heard of her?
You **should** know that she **was** married to President Rutherford B. Hayes, our nineteenth president.
This **could be** the most interesting report I **have** ever written.

Practice the Rule

Number your paper 1–10. Write the helping word or words in each sentence. Remember that helping verbs are forms of *may, be, do, should, have*, and *will*.

1. You will like my report about Lucy Ware Webb Hayes.
2. You may know that she was the first president's wife to be called the First Lady.
3. Do you also know that she was the first president's wife to have a college degree?
4. You might enjoy learning how kindly she treated the American people.
5. She may have been the most popular First Lady.
6. I should also tell you that she had the first bathrooms with running water installed in the White House.
7. Did you know that she also had the first White House telephone?
8. You might have read that Lucy Ware Webb Hayes and her husband started the official Easter Egg Roll on the White House lawn.
9. I have learned a great deal from my report.
10. Now I might want to go to the Easter Egg Roll next year!

Adjectives

Know the Rule

An **adjective** describes, or tells about, a noun. Adjectives make sentences more interesting. *A, an,* and *the* are special adjectives called *articles.*

Examples:
My teacher read us **a tall** tale.
It was **a funny** story about Paul Bunyan.
He was **the biggest** baby ever born in **the** state of Maine.

Practice the Rule

Number your paper 1–10. Write the adjective or adjectives that describe each underlined noun.

1. Legend says that a giant stork delivered Paul Bunyan to his parents!
2. His loud voice scared all the fish out of the rivers and streams.
3. The frogs wore special earmuffs so they wouldn't go deaf.
4. His parents had to milk twenty-four cows morning and night to keep Paul fed.
5. He slept in a lumber wagon pulled by a team of horses.
6. Right after Paul was born, he wore adult-sized shoes.
7. You can see what a tall tale this is!
8. Paul's friend was a blue ox named Babe.
9. The story of Paul Bunyan tells about pioneer spirit.
10. It has been part of the American culture since 1910.

Grammar, Usage & Mechanics

Adverbs

Know the Rule

An **adverb** describes, or tells about, a verb. Adverbs often end with *-ly*.

Examples:

Ballet dancers practice their movements **carefully**.

"Move **gracefully** and don't go too **fast**," said the teacher.

Practice the Rule

Number your paper 1–10. Write the adverb that describes each underlined verb.

1. My sister recently started ballet classes.
2. She badly wanted to study ballet.
3. You should see how eagerly she chose her leotard and slippers!
4. My sister's classes meet often.
5. My mom and I wait patiently for classes to end.
6. We sometimes buy a bagel for a snack.
7. My sister finally has learned to do a *plié*.
8. A *plié*, which is a little like a knee bend, came naturally to her.
9. She always knows just where to place her hands and feet.
10. She is happy that she has learned this basic movement correctly.

Prepositions

Know the Rule

A **preposition** shows a relationship between one word in a sentence and the noun or pronoun that follows the preposition.

Examples:

Eleanor Roosevelt was the wife **of** President Franklin Delano Roosevelt, our 26th President.

She worked hard **for** Americans who needed her help.

She was born **in** New York City.

Practice the Rule

Number your paper 1–10. Write the preposition in each sentence.

1. Eleanor Roosevelt was born on October 11, 1884.
2. During her childhood, she was shy and lonely.
3. She married Franklin Delano Roosevelt and entered the world of politics.
4. Eleanor Roosevelt was greatly admired by Americans.
5. She brought many helpful ideas into the White House.
6. She helped create job-training programs for young Americans.
7. Her concern for people was greatly admired.
8. She believed all people should be provided with equal rights.
9. Eleanor Roosevelt was a good friend to the American people.
10. She lived her life with dignity and respect.

Grammar, Usage & Mechanics

Interjections

Know the Rule

An **interjection** is a word that expresses strong emotion. It can stand alone or be part of a sentence. When it begins a sentence, it is followed by a comma.

Examples:
Hurrah, we're reading about cowboys this week!
Great, I have been looking forward to this unit!
We're going to learn about the history of cattle drives. **Yes!**

Practice the Rule

Number your paper 1–10. Write the interjection in each sentence.

1. Hey, I just learned that *vaquero* is the Spanish word for cowboy!
2. Wow! I never knew that cowboys needed so much special equipment.
3. Well, our teacher brought in a few tools to help us understand cowboy life.
4. Gee! Did you see that lariat?
5. Absolutely, that word comes from the Spanish word *la riata,* which means "rope."
6. Whoopee! I would like to try on the leather chaps.
7. Yes, chaps are used to protect the cowboy's legs when he is working with cattle.
8. Yikes, they are heavy!
9. Oops, be careful not to drop them.
10. Awesome! I want to learn even more about cowboys now!

Grammar, Usage & Mechanics

Coordinating Conjunctions

Know the Rule

And, *but*, and *or* are called **coordinating conjunctions**. They are used to join words in sentences. Put a comma before a coordinating conjunction when it is used to make a compound sentence.

Examples:

I traveled to South America with my parents **and** grandparents.
Dad said we could visit Argentina **or** Brazil.
Both countries sounded interesting, **but** I wanted to visit Argentina.

Practice the Rule

Number your paper 1–10. Write the conjunction in each sentence.

1. Buenos Aires is the largest city in Argentina and the capital.
2. The climate is mild, but it might rain at any time of the year.
3. The architecture of the city is old and beautiful.
4. Sometimes you feel like you are in Italy or France!
5. The official language is Spanish, but many different languages are spoken.
6. Tango, the national dance, is fun and energetic.
7. There are many parks for taking walks, picnicking, or playing sports.
8. We also visited a museum just for kids, but my favorite spot was the zoo.
9. There are more than 350 species of animals at the zoo, and you wouldn't believe the size of the elephant house!
10. There are also white tigers, pumas, cheetahs, jaguars, and lions.

Compound Words

Know the Rule

A **compound word** is made up of two smaller words. *Airplane* is a compound word made up of *air* and *plane*.

Examples:

With practice, **anyone** can learn to play the piano.
My **grandfather** taught me how to play.

Practice the Rule

Number your paper 1–10. Write the compound word in each sentence.

1. The bookshelves in Mr. Turner's room at school are filled with music.
2. Mr. Turner, our schoolteacher, likes to share his love of music.
3. Sometimes he plays the piano for us.
4. He pulls his music out of a big, black briefcase.
5. We love to sit in the comfortable armchairs in his room.
6. Mr. Turner plays so well that his fingers fly across the keyboard.
7. First he usually has to find his eyeglasses!
8. His classroom is decorated with posters of famous composers like Beethoven and Bach.
9. He helps us get started on our homework.
10. We love that he plays background music during our tests.

Homophones

Know the Rule

Some words sound alike but have different spellings and meanings, like *pair* and *pear*. These words are called **homophones**.

Examples:

Do you know that your paper is **due** tomorrow?

Yes, I **knew** that it was a **new** assignment.

Practice the Rule

Number your paper 1–10. Write the correct homophone in ( ) to complete each sentence.

1. Please don't (groan/grown) about doing your homework.
2. My sister has (groan/grown) three inches taller this year.
3. A (beat/beet) is a plant with an edible root.
4. The drummer in the band has to keep the rhythm, or (beat/beet).
5. I needed some wheat (flower/flour) to make the pizza dough.
6. Mrs. Ling's favorite (flower/flour) for Chinese New Year is a red peony.
7. I bought a giant poster (board/bored) for my book report project.
8. People sometimes get (board/bored) if they aren't busy.
9. Please (right/write) your name at the top of your paper.
10. I left my books (right/write) here on my desk!

More Homophones

Know the Rule

Some words sound alike but have different spellings and meanings, like *road* and *rode*. These words are called **homophones**.

Examples:

My **aunt** stepped right in the middle of a giant **ant** hill!

She said, "I would rather **be** bitten by an ant than stung by a **bee**!"

Practice the Rule

Number your paper 1–10. Write the correct homophone in ( ) to complete each sentence.

1. When I sprained my ankle, I could only take one (stair/stare) at a time.
2. It is rude to (stair/stare) at other people.
3. Our school colors are (blew/blue) and gold.
4. The wind (blew/blue) so hard that my umbrella turned itself inside out!
5. I have to (chews/choose) a book to read for my report.
6. Katie (chews/choose) her food slowly for good digestion and overall health.
7. I will get my (hare/hair) cut tomorrow after school.
8. A (hare/hair) is usually larger than a rabbit and has longer ears.
9. Lighthouses send signals to ships at (sea/see).
10. Can you (sea/see) better with your new glasses?

Irregular Verbs

Know the Rule

Some verbs do not add *-ed* to talk about the past. Their past-tense forms are **irregular**.

Present	Past	With *have, has, or had*
begin	began	begun
strike	struck	struck
come	came	come
win	won	won
grow	grew	grown
pay	paid	paid
teach	taught	taught

Practice the Rule

Number your paper 1–10. Write the word in ( ) that completes each sentence correctly.

1. By the time she was three years old, Alta Weiss (begin/had begun) to show how well she could throw a baseball.
2. When she was sixteen, Alta (strike/had struck) out every boy in her town!
3. In 1907 she (begin/began) to play for a semi-pro men's baseball team in Ohio.
4. Large crowds (came/come) to watch her play.
5. She (win/won) attention from baseball fans everywhere!
6. Alta (strike/struck) out many players in every game!
7. As news of her success (grow/grew), her team became famous.
8. Alta and her team (win/won) many baseball games.
9. She (was paid/pay) enough money to put herself through medical school.
10. Alta (teach/taught) Americans about the many things women can achieve.

More Irregular Verbs

Know the Rule

Some verbs do not add *-ed* to talk about the past. Sometimes the present-and past-tense forms of these verbs are the same. Sometimes they are different. These verbs are called **irregular verbs**.

Present	**Past**	**With *have, has,* or *had***
cut	cut	cut
let	let	let
put	put	put
say	said	said
tell	told	told

Practice the Rule

Number your paper 1–10. Write the word in ( ) that completes each sentence correctly.

1. My grandmother, Litta, (let/have let) my cousin and me make a fruit salad for lunch.
2. Litta (putted/had put) all the ingredients on the kitchen counter for us.
3. "Now be sure you cut this fruit carefully," she (say/said).
4. I (let/letted) Litta show me how to use the knife and cutting board.
5. After we (cutted/had cut) the watermelon into slices, we were ready for the strawberries.
6. I (put/had putted) them under running water to wash them.
7. Once the strawberries were clean, my cousin Jorge (cut/have cut) them into small pieces.
8. "I (cut/have cut) the pineapple into chunks already," Litta said.
9. "Let's put everything in the big fruit bowl," she (tell/told) us.
10. Litta (let/have let) Jorge and me use her best china to enjoy our delicious fruit salad!

Using the Right Word

Know the Rule

Some words are often misused in writing. It is important to know how to **use the right word** so your readers will not be confused.

Examples:
I feel really **well** today.
Today might be a **good** day to take a walk.
May I go with you?
I **can** get some great exercise.
I must **leave** right away.
Please **let** me bring my dog, too.

Practice the Rule

Number your paper 1–10. Write the word in ( ) that completes each sentence correctly.

1. During World War II, the United States needed a (good/well) code that could not be broken by the enemy.
2. Military leaders hired a group of young Navajo men who served their country (good/well).
3. They had to (leave/let) their homes to study in California.
4. The military (leave/let) these young men use the Navajo language to create a secret code.
5. These "Navajo Code Talkers" did not (leave/let) their country down.
6. They used their Navajo language to do a (good/well) job to make communication secure.
7. (May/Can) you believe that this code is still the only unbroken code in modern military history?
8. It was certainly a job done (good/well)!
9. Last summer I met a Navajo Code Talker on a trip to Arizona. "(Can/May) I have your autograph?" I asked.
10. We should not (leave/let) ourselves forget their loyalty to their country.

Object Pronouns

Know the Rule

An **object pronoun** takes the place of one or more nouns. Object pronouns come after action verbs and prepositions such as *to, at, for, of,* and *with.* Singular object pronouns are *me, you, him, her,* and *it.* Plural object pronouns include *us, you,* and *them.*

Examples:

My dad took my brother and **me** to the aquarium to see the penguins.
He invited Aunt Nina to go with **us**.
He asked **her** to meet **him** at the front entrance.

me	it	him	us	you	her	them

Practice the Rule

Number your paper 1–10. Write the object pronoun from the box that could take the place of the underlined word or words in each sentence. You can use some pronouns more than once.

1. As soon as the female penguin lays the egg, she goes out to look for food and leaves the male to watch the nest.
2. When she returns, it is his turn to go out and look for food.
3. Once the chick hatches, it calls out loudly to its parents so they will know its voice.
4. At the aquarium, we watched a female worker feed the penguins.
5. She threw the penguins lots of shrimplike animals called krill.
6. Penguins drink salt water; their bodies can adjust to the salt water.
7. Penguins have wings for swimming, but they can't use the wings to fly.
8. Even though penguins can't fly, it looked to Dad and me like they can really leap out of the water!
9. They jump out of the water, take a big gulp of air, and dive right back into the water!
10. They love to play in the water by diving into the water over and over!

Pronoun Antecedents

Know the Rule

An **antecedent** is the word or words a pronoun refers to. When you write a pronoun, be sure its antecedent is clear. A pronoun must agree with its antecedent. An antecedent and pronoun agree when they have the same number (singular or plural) and gender (male or female).

Examples:

Oliver did an oral report on spiders. **He** made a good presentation.

His **classmates** and **teacher** enjoyed his report. **They** applauded when he finished.

Practice the Rule

Number your paper 1–10. Write the antecedent or antecedents for each pronoun in dark print.

1. Spiders are not insects. **They** have eight legs instead of six.
2. My sister is very frightened of spiders. **She** runs when she sees one!
3. There are many different spiders in North America, but only two of **them** are actually dangerous.
4. The brown recluse and the black widow are not friendly. **They** are poisonous.
5. Another type of spider is the house spider. **It** looks scary but is harmless.
6. The house spider is actually very timid and scurries away when **it** senses danger.
7. You may see garden spiders outside. Eating lots of bugs makes **them** big!
8. My sister is afraid of spiders but loves to look at **their** webs.
9. Dad and I were amazed at some of the complicated designs Rachel pointed out to **us**.
10. "The design of these spider webs is beautiful!" exclaimed Rachel. **Her** enthusiasm made me want to learn more about the webs, too.

Avoiding Extra Pronouns

Know the Rule

A **subject pronoun** takes the place of one or more nouns in the subject of a sentence. Do not use the subject pronoun right after the noun it stands for.

Correct: Elephants are the largest living land animals.
Incorrect: Elephants **they** are the largest living land animals.

Correct: A newborn elephant might weigh 260 pounds!
Incorrect: A newborn elephant **it** might weigh 260 pounds!

Practice the Rule

Number your paper 1–10. Rewrite each sentence to leave out the extra pronoun.

1. An elephant it is supposed to have a good memory.
2. A mother elephant she carries a baby for 22 months before giving birth.
3. An elephant it has very thick, tough skin.
4. Elephants they use their trunks to get food.
5. When elephants need a drink, water it gets sucked up right into their trunks.
6. The female elephant she likes to spend her time with other female family members.
7. The male he prefers to live alone.
8. Their diet it is mostly leaves, fruits, and grasses.
9. My little sister she loves the books about the elephant named Babar.
10. Our parents they take turns reading to her at night.

Capitalization

Know the Rule

Capitalize the first letter of holidays, historical periods, and special events.

Examples:

Ming read a book about the **Civil War** for his history class.

Next he wants to learn about the **Reconstruction Era** after that war.

Practice the Rule

Number your paper 1–10. Rewrite each sentence. Capitalize holidays, historical periods, and special events.

1. One of my favorite holidays is the fourth of July.
2. My town always celebrates an event called the Center City festival of lights.
3. Did you know presidents' day celebrates George Washington's birthday?
4. He lived during the colonial era, the time period when the United States was not yet a country.
5. One famous event of that time is called the boston tea party.
6. Other time periods have special names; for example, the middle ages is a period of time in the history of Europe.
7. My other favorite holiday is thanksgiving.
8. We always go downtown to watch the main street thanksgiving parade.
9. One holiday that's special to my family is veterans day.
10. We honor veterans like my grandfather, who served in world war II.

Book Titles

Know the Rule

Capitalize the first word, the last word, and all the important words in the **title** of a book. All verbs, even short ones such as *is* and *are*, are important words. Capitalize *the* only if it is the first word in a title. Always underline a book title, or use *italic type* if you are typing on a computer.

Examples:

Have you read *The Story of the Statue of Liberty*?

No, but I did just read <u>So You Want to Be President</u>? by Judith St. George.

Practice the Rule

Number your paper 1–10. Rewrite the book titles in each sentence correctly.

1. living color is one of my favorite books because it explains how animals use their color to survive.
2. In the library, I looked at a book with unusual facts called polar bears and the arctic.
3. I also found a book by Sandra Markle called great white sharks.
4. The book titled storms has colorful photos and tells how storms form.
5. I just read earthquakes, a book about how they happen and what you can do to keep yourself safe.
6. garbage and recycling is a good book about how to reuse glass, metal, and wood.
7. Allyson checked out a book with great photos called storm chasers.
8. The book volcanoes and earthquakes also has excellent photos.
9. I've been looking for the book mummies made in egypt.
10. The author Aliki also wrote fossils tell of long ago.

Commas in a Series

Know the Rule

A **series** is a list of three or more words. Use **commas** to separate words in a series.

Examples:

Morgan is interested in math**,** science**,** and engineering.
She likes to study numbers**,** codes**,** and inventions.

Practice the Rule

Number your paper 1–10. Rewrite the incorrect sentences and put commas where they are needed. Write **Correct** if the sentence is already correct.

1. GPS navigation tools were developed in 1978 and are now used in cars airplanes and boats.
2. Scientists have used these systems to track the movements of the earth locate glaciers and follow the migration of turtles.
3. Today many people use them to locate streets homes and businesses.
4. GPS stands for *global positioning system* and gives directions at any time and in any place.
5. If you want to know about using GPS on land, on the sea, or in the air, you should know the system uses satellites.
6. These satellites give information for making maps surveying land and other scientific uses.
7. GPS tools are helpful convenient and popular with drivers.
8. My brother just got a GPS he can carry in his car, on his bike, or on foot.
9. He needs it to get safely to school work and home.
10. Sometimes it is best to use the GPS and a map.

Commas in Direct Address

Know the Rule

Use **commas** to separate a noun of direct address from the rest of the sentence. A **noun of direct address** names a person who is being spoken to.

Examples:
Will, please read page 19.
Please read page 19, Will.
The correct page, Will, is 19.

Practice the Rule

Number your paper 1–10. Rewrite the incorrect sentences and put commas where needed. Write **Correct** if the sentence is already correct.

1. Sophia do you know who is called the *Father of American Education*?
2. His name was Horace Mann Mr. Torres.
3. Your answer, Sophia, is correct.
4. I also know that Horace Mann was born in Massachusetts Mr. Torres.
5. Do you have a comment Evan?
6. Mr. Torres Horace Mann worked to make sure that every child received an education.
7. I think Evan that you are correct.
8. Matt, would you like to add something?
9. I would like to say Mr. Torres that Horace Mann also pushed for free libraries in schools.
10. We are fortunate, Matt, that Horace Mann believed so strongly in education.

Punctuating Sentences

Know the Rule

Begin each sentence with an **uppercase letter**. Put a **period** at the end of a declarative or imperative sentence. Put a **question mark** at the end of an interrogative sentence. Put an **exclamation point** at the end of an exclamatory sentence.

Examples:

Laura Ingalls Wilder wrote the Little House series.

Did you know that her first book was called *Little House in the Big Woods*?

I can't believe that she was sixty-five years old when she published her first book!

Practice the Rule

Number your paper 1–10. Write each sentence and put correct punctuation where needed. Write **Correct** if the sentence is already punctuated correctly.

1. Laura Ingalls Wilder was born in 1867 in Wisconsin
2. She and her family moved several times before settling in South Dakota
3. Did you know that Laura received her teaching certificate when she was only fifteen
4. She wrote the Little House series about her family's experiences on America's new frontier.
5. Her first book about her childhood in Wisconsin was called *Little House in the Big Woods*
6. Have you read *Farmer Boy* about her husband's childhood in New York state
7. What an accomplishment it was when she finished the final Little House book
8. Wow, she was seventy-six years old when she completed that book
9. Laura Ingalls Wilder was ninety years old when she died.
10. Be sure you read her wonderful stories of adventure and hardship

Direct Quotations

Know the Rule

A **direct quotation** shows a speaker's exact words. Use a comma to separate the quotation from the rest of the sentence. Put **quotation marks** around a direct quotation. Add punctuation before the last quotation mark.

Examples:

"I need to go to the Post Office," said Mom.
"Do you need to mail a letter?" I asked.
Mom replied, "No, I need to buy some stamps."

Practice the Rule

Number your paper 1–10. Rewrite each sentence and use quotation marks correctly. Write **Correct** next to each sentence that is already correct.

1. "Did you know that the correct name for the Post Office is actually the United States Postal Service?" said Mom.
2. Well, I just always call it the mail, said Dad.
3. Even though our country had mail delivery for many years, Benjamin Franklin officially started it, said Grandpa.
4. I said, Yes, we learned in school that he started it in Philadelphia in 1775.
5. Dad asked, "Did you also learn how many people are employed by the U.S. Postal Service?"
6. I think it employs over 600,000 people today, I replied.
7. "I am amazed at how many things you can do at the Post Office besides buy stamps," said Mom.
8. Grandpa added, "I sometimes go in to get a money order."
9. Last year I got help with my passport there, too, said Dad.
10. Mom said, "When I went in to buy my stamps, I was surprised that I could also buy colorful packaging materials and tape!"

More Practice

Simple Sentences

Read each group of words. Write **S** if the words make a complete simple sentence. Write **X** if the group of words is not a complete sentence.

1. Harry Houdini was a famous escape artist.
2. Did daring feats of escape.
3. He became one of the highest paid performers in show business.
4. Could escape from handcuffs, water tanks, or packing crates.
5. Born as Ehrich Weiss.

Compound and Complex Sentences

Identify each sentence as either **compound** or **complex.**

1. Elephants are very large, and they are thought to be intelligent.
2. African and Asian elephants are similar, but the African elephant has larger ears.
3. African elephants usually have larger bodies than Asian elephants, and they also have less hair on their bodies.
4. Because African elephants are endangered, they need protection.
5. If you get in the way of an angry elephant, you might get injured!

Imperative and Exclamatory Sentences

Write an exclamation point at the end of each exclamatory sentence. Put a period at the end of each imperative sentence.

1. Look at William's juggling show
2. Wow, he's juggling four balls at once
3. Oops, he just dropped all of them
4. Be sure to practice all of your new tricks
5. To learn one trick, William practiced for two whole months

More Practice

Nouns

Decide which of the underlined words is a noun. Write each noun. Also write whether it is **abstract** or **concrete**.

1. Beech trees are my favorite trees.
2. They have a smooth, gray trunk.
3. Wood from a beech tree is very hard.
4. Beech trees can live for hundreds of years.
5. My yard has both beech trees and maple trees.

Plural Nouns

Change each underlined singular noun to a plural noun. Write the plural nouns.

1. Roald Dahl's book are famous.
2. He wrote many interesting children's story.
3. All my friend love *James and the Giant Peach.*
4. My two favorite are *The BFG* and *The Twits.*
5. Some of Dahl's book have been made into movies.

Possessive Pronouns

Write the possessive pronoun or pronouns in each sentence.

1. My family traveled to China last year.
2. Our trip was amazing!
3. My dad said his favorite sight was the Great Wall of China.
4. Its construction began more than two thousand years ago.
5. The Chinese built the wall as a defense against their enemies.

More Practice

Action Verbs

Decide which of the two underlined words is a verb. Write that word.

1. John and I wanted to make tacos.
2. First we chopped up tomatoes and lettuce.
3. Then we browned some meat in a skillet.
4. We put everything in taco shells for a delicious treat.
5. I hope we make tacos again soon!

Past Tense

Write the correct verb form in ( ) to make a past-tense sentence.

1. Dinosaurs (roam/roamed) Earth for over 150 million years!
2. Enormous herbivores (ate/eat) huge amounts of leaves from treetops.
3. Carnivores like T-rex (attacked/attack) other animals as their prey.
4. We (learn/learned) that *dinosaur* means "terrible lizard."
5. Sir Richard Owen (invent/invented) the word *dinosaur* in the 1800s.

Present Tense

Write the verb in each sentence.

1. The giant panda looks much like a black and white bear.
2. Giant pandas live in mountain ranges in central China.
3. Their thick, woolly coats keep them warm in the cool forest.
4. Pandas eat as much as 40 pounds of bamboo every day.
5. Pandas climb trees very skillfully.

More Practice

Future Tense

Write the correct verb form in ( ) to make a future-tense sentence.

1. Tomorrow we will (go/went) to the farmers' market.
2. I will (bought/buy) some fresh carrots and potatoes.
3. My mom will (shop/shopped) for collard greens and tomatoes.
4. We will (came/come) home and cook a healthy vegetable feast!
5. After dinner I will (wash/washed) the dishes.

Helping Verbs

Write the helping word or words in each sentence.

1. You will like reading my book report on *Charlotte's Web.*
2. You may know that the author is E. B. White.
3. Do you know that Charlotte is the most famous spider in literature?
4. Her friend Wilbur could be known as a famous pig.
5. Will you read *Charlotte's Web*?

Adjectives

Write the adjective or adjectives that describe each underlined noun.

1. *Charlotte's Web* tells about a small, lonely <u>pig</u> named Wilbur.
2. A spider named Charlotte soon becomes his best <u>friend</u>.
3. Charlotte's clever <u>plan</u> saves Wilbur's life.
4. With the help of Templeton the rat, Wilbur also wins a prize at the county <u>fair</u>.
5. At the end of the story, Wilbur discovers a wonderful <u>surprise</u>.

More Practice

Adverbs

Write the adverb that describes each underlined verb.

1. My brother started tennis lessons yesterday.
2. The coach patiently taught him how to serve the ball.
3. He got the ball over the net often.
4. I was happy that he has learned this basic move so easily.
5. His skill will improve if he plays tennis frequently.

Prepositions

Write the preposition in each sentence.

1. I watched Venus Williams play in a professional tennis match.
2. She is the older sister of Serena Williams.
3. The Williams sisters have no trouble getting the ball over the net!
4. They are both greatly admired by many tennis fans.
5. What is it like to play professional tennis with your sister?

Interjections

Write the interjection in each sentence.

1. Wow! Did you know that Texas is the second-largest state?
2. Yes, Texas was also once an independent republic.
3. Right! That is why it is known as the Lone Star State.
4. Oh, I guess that's why the state flag has just one star.
5. Hey, do you think we could go there sometime?

More Practice

Coordinating Conjunctions

Write the conjunction in each sentence.

1. My favorite apples are Braeburn and Golden Delicious.
2. Braeburn apples make great applesauce or pies.
3. Golden Delicious apples are so juicy and sweet.
4. I like all apples, but these two types are definitely my favorites.
5. Now I have to decide whether to make some applesauce or a pie!

Compound Words

Write the compound word or words in each sentence.

1. I ate a bowl of sweet grapefruit for breakfast.
2. My cousin ate honeydew melon and pineapple.
3. "Would anyone like pancakes?" asked Aunt Ruby.
4. "I think I'll just have a big glass of buttermilk," said Grandfather.
5. "Do we have any cornbread?" asked Uncle Leo.

Homophones

Write the correct homophone to complete each sentence.

1. Let's plan to have a picnic on the (beech/beach).
2. (Beech/Beach) trees can live for many, many years.
3. Isaac learned to play a (cord/chord) on his guitar.
4. Be sure to tie a colorful (cord/chord) around the package.
5. I dropped my popcorn in the (I'll/aisle) at the movie theater.
6. (I'll/aisle) clean up the mess!

More Practice

More Homophones

Write the correct homophone to complete each sentence.

1. Be sure to use the hand (break/brake) to stop your bike.
2. I didn't mean to (break/brake) the delicate glass.
3. My family is very (deer/dear) to me.
4. Be careful to watch for (deer/dear) on the highway.
5. Did you (sea/see) all the different types of salt in the grocery store?
6. The crystals in (sea/see) salt are very coarse.

Irregular Verbs

Write the word in ( ) that completes each sentence correctly.

1. Thomas Jefferson (became/become) the third president of the U.S.
2. By the time he was thirty-three years old, he (wrote/had written) the Declaration of Independence.
3. Later in his life, he (begin/began) to design the University of Virginia.
4. Jefferson (grow/grew) many varieties of vegetables in his garden.
5. When you eat macaroni and cheese, you should (thought/think) of its inventor, Thomas Jefferson!

More Irregular Verbs

Write the word or words in ( ) that complete each sentence correctly.

1. Have you ever (hear/heard) how a pedometer works?
2. I (got/gotten) one for my birthday and (put/putted) it on my belt.
3. I (has kept/keep) it on all day.
4. It (have let/lets) me count each step I take.
5. It even counts the steps when I (run/ran)!

More Practice

Using the Right Word

Write the word in ( ) that completes each sentence correctly.

1. (May/Can) I go to the concert with you?
2. Yes, the outdoor concert should be really (well/good) this year.
3. I (may/can) meet you at the park.
4. Let's sit close to the stage so that we can hear (well/good).
5. We will not (leave/let) ourselves forget to bring an umbrella this time!

Object Pronouns

Write the object pronoun or pronouns in each sentence.

1. My aunt took my sister and me to the Texas Rose Festival.
2. She invited us to go on a special trip to this famous flower show.
3. The roses were all beautiful, and we enjoyed looking at them.
4. Aunt Anna's favorite was a red rose; it did not surprise her that it means "I love you."
5. Before we left, Aunt Anna bought us souvenirs at the gift shop.

Pronoun Antecedents

Write the antecedent or antecedents for each pronoun in dark print.

1. Mount Rushmore National Memorial features huge sculptures of four presidents. **It** is a symbol of freedom and hope.
2. Many people visit Mount Rushmore every year. **They** come to learn about the history of our country.
3. When Uncle Jorge saw these lifelike sculptures for the first time, **he** was amazed at their beauty!
4. Mom and I traveled to South Dakota to visit Mount Rushmore. **We** were thrilled to see such an important American memorial.
5. Mom took a lot of pictures at Mount Rushmore. She uploaded **them** to her travel blog.

More Practice

Avoiding Extra Pronouns

Rewrite each sentence to leave out the extra pronouns.

1. Books they are often called a window to the world.
2. Reading it is a way to both learn and be entertained.
3. My teacher he reads to our class every day.
4. Shana she is going to choose the next book.
5. Our class we thinks listening to him read is one of our best assignments!

Capitalization

Rewrite each sentence. Capitalize holidays, historical periods, and special events.

1. For me, memorial day is the official beginning of summer.
2. A town nearby puts on a show called the memorial day fireworks extravaganza.
3. Hey, do you think they had fireworks during the colonial period?
4. When labor day arrives, summer is almost over.
5. We will go to town day on the last Saturday in September.

Book Titles

Rewrite the book title in each sentence correctly.

1. stellaluna is a great book about a baby fruit bat.
2. Mia likes best friends for frances by Russell Hoban.
3. Another good book about friendship is george and martha.
4. My very favorite book about friendship is because of winn-dixie.
5. pink and say by Patricia Polacco is a book about two unusual friends.

Grammar, Usage & Mechanics

More Practice

Commas in a Series

Rewrite the sentences and put commas where they are needed.

1. There are many types of landforms, such as canyons deserts plains and glaciers.
2. Landforms are made by action of wind water or ice against the earth.
3. Movement inside the earth also creates mountains sinkholes and volcanoes.
4. A butte is a flat-topped landform with steep sides. You can see buttes in New Mexico Colorado Utah and other states in the Southwest.
5. The Appalachian Mountains are made up of several smaller ranges, including the Catskills the Blue Ridge Mountains and the Green Mountains.
6. Three of the world's most famous landforms are the Sahara Desert the Grand Canyon and Mount Everest.

Commas in Direct Address

Rewrite the sentences and put commas where they are needed. Write **Correct** if the sentence is already correct.

1. Miguel what is the capital of California?
2. The capital Mrs. Jones is Sacramento.
3. Sacramento, Miguel, is also home to the California State Railroad Museum.
4. I have been to that museum Mrs. Jones!
5. Is it an interesting place to visit Miguel?
6. Mrs. Jones, it is a great museum that honors the "iron horse" for connecting California to the rest of the nation.

More Practice

Punctuating Sentences

Write each sentence and put correct punctuation where needed.

1. Have you ever visited the Great Smoky Mountains National Park
2. It is the most visited national park in the United States
3. Many visitors come hoping to see one of the 1,500 bears that live there
4. I would like to see some of the beautiful wildflowers that grow in the Great Smoky Mountains National Park
5. Are the Great Smoky Mountains along the border of Tennessee and North Carolina

Direct Quotations

Rewrite each sentence and use quotation marks correctly. Write **Correct** if the sentence is already correct.

1. "Did you know that the Statue of Liberty was a gift of friendship from the people of France?" asked Dad.
2. Yes, it is a symbol of freedom and democracy, said Grandpa.
3. I said, "We learned in social studies that the statue is sometimes called Lady Liberty."
4. Last summer we walked all 354 steps up the statue to the crown, added Mark.
5. "You must have had a great view of New York City from the top of her crown!" exclaimed Dad.

Temporal and Linking Words and Phrases

Temporal (Time-Order Words) tell the reader what happened first, next, and last. These words help us organize our reading and writing.

first	next	then
before	during	later
last	soon	after
finally		

Cause-Effect Words give the reader a signal that one thing caused another thing to happen.

because	if	then
since	so	led to
as a result	therefore	on account of

Compare-Contrast Words give the reader a signal that two or more things are either similar or different.

Comparison Words signal the reader that things are similar.

each	similarly	like
too	same	as well as
both	another	also
in the same way		

Contrast Words signal the reader that things are different.

but	however	despite
unless	differ	instead
in contrast	on the other hand	whereas
on the contrary	although	for example

Prepositions

Prepositions link nouns, pronouns, and phrases to other words in a sentence. There are many prepositions in the English language. These are some of the most common ones:

after	beside	over
against	between	past
among	beyond	through
around	from	underneath
at	inside	upon
before	into	within
below	onto	

Appendix B
Rubrics

Narrative Writing Rubric

	4	3	2	1
Ideas	The topic is just the right size—not too big or too small. Descriptive details introduce and develop the setting, narrator, characters, and plot. Carefully selected ideas completely satisfy the needs of the reader.	The topic is the right size. Details introduce and develop the setting, narrator, characters, and plot. The ideas selected by the author frequently meet the needs of the reader.	The topic is too big or too small. Some details develop the setting, narrator, characters, and plot. The ideas selected by the author sometimes meet the needs of the reader.	The writing is not a narrative. Details are unrelated or not included.
Organization	The narrative unfolds logically and naturally. Temporal words and phrases help sequence the events. A strong beginning leads to a satisfying conclusion.	Some events are not connected or are out of order. Temporal words and phrases are needed to help sequence the events. The beginning and the conclusion work, but may not be strong.	The narrative does not unfold logically and naturally. Events are out of order. Temporal words and phrases are confusing or missing. The beginning or the conclusion is weak.	The writing is disorganized and very difficult to follow. Temporal words and phrases are not used. No beginning or conclusion is evident.
Voice	The voice, mood, and tone are just right for the purpose. Dialogue, if used, reveals each character's voice clearly.	The voice, mood, and tone are just right in places, but inconsistent. Dialogue, if used, somewhat reveals the characters' voices.	The voice sounds disinterested. Mood and tone are weak. Dialogue, if used, does not uniquely distinguish the characters' voices.	Voice is flat. Mood and tone are absent. Dialogue, if used, does not sound right for some of the characters.
Word Choice	Words and phrases consistently help the reader "see" the characters and "experience" the events. Nouns and verbs are clear and precise, supported by a few carefully selected modifiers.	Some words and phrases help the reader picture characters and events, but some are too general. Certain nouns and verbs are weak, requiring too much help from modifiers. Modifiers are satisfactory.	Many words and phrases are too general. They keep the reader from picturing the characters and events clearly. Nouns and verbs lack clarity or precision. Too many or too few modifiers are used, and many of them are weak.	Many words are not used correctly. They distract the reader.
Sentence Fluency	Varied sentence beginnings, lengths, and patterns make the writing flow smoothly. Several particularly well-crafted sentences add style and interest. The paper is effortlessly read aloud with inflection or feeling.	There is some variation in sentence beginnings, lengths, and patterns. The sentences are correct, and one or two sentences add style. The paper can be read aloud with inflection or feeling.	Many sentences have the same beginnings, lengths, and patterns. This interrupts the flow of the writing. The sentences are mostly correct but ordinary. It is difficult to read the paper with inflection.	Sentences are poorly written or incorrect. The writing does not flow.
Conventions	Spelling, grammar, punctuation, and capitalization are correct. The narrative contains no errors.	There are a few grammatical errors that may cause the reader to pause momentarily, but meaning is clear.	Many errors are present, and some confuse the reader.	The writing has not been edited. Serious errors make the narrative hard to understand.

Informative/Explanatory Writing Rubric

	4	3	2	1
Ideas	The topic is introduced clearly. Information and examples develop the main idea(s). Carefully selected ideas completely answer the reader's main questions.	A topic is introduced. Most of the information and examples develop the main idea(s). The ideas chosen by the author frequently answer the reader's main questions.	A topic is introduced, but little of the information or examples develops the main idea(s). Some of the reader's questions are answered.	A topic is not introduced. Information and examples are incomplete or unrelated to the topic.
Organization	Information is organized into a strong and thoughtful introduction, a body, and a satisfying conclusion. Varied and appropriate linking words and phrases connect the ideas.	Information is organized into an introduction, a body, and a conclusion. More or better linking words and phrases are needed.	Information is not well organized. The introduction, body, and conclusion may be poorly developed. Linking words and phrases are confusing or not helpful.	The writing is not organized. Introduction and conclusion may both be missing. Linking words and phrases are not used.
Voice	The voice sounds interested and informative. It fully connects with the audience and conveys the writer's purpose well.	The voice sounds informative and mostly connects with the audience. It conveys the purpose some of the time.	The voice sounds informative in places. It conveys the purpose, but often fades out.	Voice is weak or absent. It does not connect with the audience or convey the writer's purpose.
Word Choice	Precise language and domain-specific vocabulary are used. Definitions are complete and helpful. Nouns and verbs are clear and precise, supported by a few carefully selected modifiers.	Some precise language, domain-specific vocabulary, and definitions are used. Some nouns and verbs are weak, requiring help from modifiers. Modifiers are satisfactory.	Little precise language and domain-specific vocabulary is used. Definitions are missing or incorrect. Nouns and verbs lack clarity or precision. Too many or too few modifiers are used, and many of them are weak.	Precise language and domain-specific vocabulary are not used.
Sentence Fluency	Clear, concise sentences make the text flow smoothly. Sentence beginnings, lengths, and patterns are varied for effect. The paper is effortlessly read aloud with inflection.	One or two sections of the writing do not flow smoothly. In these sections, several sentences may have the same beginnings, lengths, or patterns. The paper can be read with inflection.	In many places, the writing does not flow smoothly due to repetitive sentence beginnings, lengths, and patterns. It is difficult to read the paper with inflection.	Sentences are incomplete or incorrect.
Conventions	The text contains no errors. Spelling, grammar, punctuation, and capitalization are correct.	The text contains some errors in spelling, grammar, punctuation, and capitalization. One or two errors may cause the reader to pause momentarily, but meaning remains clear.	Many errors are present. Some errors are basic or repeated. The errors interfere with meaning in places.	The writing has not been edited. Serious errors make the writing hard to understand.

Opinion Writing Rubric

	4	3	2	1
Ideas	The writer states a clear opinion. The perfect details and facts are chosen to support the writer's reasons.	The writer states an opinion. Some details and facts are well chosen to support the writer's reasons.	The writer states an opinion, but few details are well chosen to support the writer's reasons.	The writer does not state an opinion. Reasons are not provided.
Organization	The text is organized logically and creatively. Helpful, appropriate, even unique linking words connect the writer's opinion and reasons. A compelling conclusion clearly supports the opinion statement.	The text is organized logically. More or better linking words are needed to connect the opinion and reasons. The beginning and the conclusion are functional. The conclusion relates to the opinion statement.	The text is not organized logically. Linking words may not show how the writer's ideas are related. Either the beginning or the conclusion is weak. The conclusion may not relate to the opinion statement.	The text is not organized as an opinion. Linking words are not used. Ideas are hard to follow. No beginning or conclusion is evident.
Voice	The voice is clearly convincing and totally fits the writer's purpose. The mood and tone are appropriate and engage the audience.	The voice is convincing and fits the writer's purpose. The mood and tone are engaging some of the time.	The voice is convincing in some places. The mood and tone are incorrect or inconsistent. They lose the audience.	The voice is weak or absent. The tone is not appropriate.
Word Choice	Precise words and fair language convey the writer's opinion. No biased words or phrases are used. Nouns and verbs are clear and precise, supported by a few carefully selected modifiers.	Some words are too general. One biased word or phrase may be used. Some nouns and verbs are weak, requiring help from modifiers. Modifiers are satisfactory.	Most words are weak. A few biased words or phrases may be used. Nouns and verbs lack clarity or precision. Too many or too few modifiers are used, and many of them are weak.	Words are weak, biased, or used incorrectly.
Sentence Fluency	A variety of sentence patterns adds interest and style. Great variation in sentence beginnings and lengths makes the writing flow very smoothly. The paper is effortlessly read aloud with inflection.	Some sentence patterns are varied and add interest. Some variation in sentence lengths and beginnings is evident. The writing flows smoothly in some places, but not in others. The paper can be read with inflection.	Too many sentences share the same pattern. The writing does not flow smoothly due to a lack of variation in sentence lengths and/or beginnings. It is difficult to read the paper with inflection.	Sentences are poorly written or incomplete. The writing is hard to follow.
Conventions	The text contains no errors. Spelling, grammar, punctuation, and capitalization are correct.	There are some errors in spelling, grammar, punctuation, and capitalization. One or two of these errors may cause the reader to pause momentarily, but meaning remains clear.	Many errors are present. Some errors are basic or repeated. The errors interfere with meaning in places.	The writing has not been edited. Serious errors make the writing hard to understand.

Descriptive Elements in the Text Types Rubric

	4	3	2	1
Ideas	The topic is clear, focused, and complete. Sensory details and examples are related to and develop the main ideas. The description helps the reader experience what is being described very clearly.	The topic is clear but may not be focused or complete. Sensory details and examples develop most of the main ideas. The description sometimes helps the reader experience what is being described.	The topic is not clear or focused. Details and examples develop some of the main ideas. The reader cannot always experience what is being described.	The topic is not clear. Details and examples are unrelated or missing. The reader cannot experience what is being described.
Organization	The description is well organized into a strong introduction, body, and conclusion. Details support the topic. Appropriate linking words connect the ideas and guide the reader.	Most of the description is organized. The introduction, body, and conclusion are functional. Most of the details support the topic. More or better linking words are needed to connect the ideas and guide the reader.	Some of the description is organized. The introduction, body, or conclusion may be weak. Few of the details support the topic. More and better linking words are needed to connect the ideas and guide the reader.	The description is not organized and does not have an introduction or conclusion. Details are missing. Linking words are not used.
Voice	The writer's voice connects strongly with the audience. The mood and tone match the purpose perfectly.	The writer's voice connects with the audience in places. The mood and tone match the purpose, but are inconsistent.	The writer's voice does not fit the purpose or the audience well. The mood and tone are inappropriate or inconsistent.	The writer's voice is weak or absent. It does not connect with the audience.
Word Choice	Precise, descriptive language and creative comparisons create a clear picture of the subject. Nouns and verbs carry the descriptive load with help from a few carefully chosen modifiers.	Some of the language is precise, but some is vague. Some of the comparisons create a clear picture of the subject. Many nouns and verbs depend upon modifiers for specificity. Modifiers are satisfactory.	Most of the language is not descriptive. Comparisons are ineffective. Nouns and verbs lack clarity or precision. Too many or too few modifiers are used, and many of them are weak.	The language is very basic and limited. Comparisons are not used.
Sentence Fluency	A variety of sentence beginnings, lengths, and patterns keeps the description interesting. It is effortless to read aloud with inflection or feeling. The writing flows very smoothly.	Some sentences share the same beginnings, lengths, or patterns. Some of the writing flows smoothly. The paper can be read aloud with inflection or feeling.	Several sentences in a row have the same beginnings, lengths, or patterns. The flow of the writing may slow or stall in parts. The paper is difficult to read aloud with inflection or feeling.	Sentences are not varied or interesting. The writing does not flow. The description is very difficult to read.
Conventions	The description contains no errors. Spelling, grammar, punctuation, and capitalization are correct.	The description contains some errors in spelling, grammar, punctuation, and capitalization. One or two of these errors may cause the reader to pause momentarily, but meaning remains clear.	Many errors are present. Some errors are basic or repeated. The errors interfere with meaning in places.	The writing has not been edited. Serious errors make the writing hard to understand.

Narrative Writing Rubric

	5	4	3	2	1
Ideas	The topic is just the right size—not too big or too small. Descriptive details introduce and develop the setting, narrator, characters, and plot. Carefully selected ideas completely satisfy the needs of the reader.	The topic is the right size. Most details introduce and develop the setting, narrator, characters, and plot. Carefully selected ideas satisfy most of the reader's needs.	The topic is the right size. Some details introduce and develop the setting, narrator, characters, and plot. The ideas selected by the author frequently meet the needs of the reader.	The topic is too big or too small. Some details develop the setting, narrator, characters, and plot. The ideas selected by the author sometimes meet the needs of the reader.	The writing is not a narrative. Details are unrelated or not included.
Organization	The narrative unfolds logically and naturally. Temporal words and phrases help sequence the events. A strong beginning leads to a satisfying conclusion.	One or two events in the middle are not connected or are out of order. Temporal words and phrases help sequence most of the events. The beginning or the conclusion is strong.	Some events are not connected or are out of order. Temporal words and phrases are needed to help sequence the events. The beginning and the conclusion work, but may not be strong.	The narrative does not unfold logically and naturally. Events are out of order. Temporal words and phrases are confusing or missing. The beginning or the conclusion is weak.	The writing is disorganized and very difficult to follow. Temporal words and phrases are not used. No beginning or conclusion is evident.
Voice	The voice, mood, and tone are just right for the purpose. Dialogue, if used, reveals each character's voice clearly.	The voice, mood, and tone are just right most of the time. Dialogue, if used, reveals the characters' voices.	The voice, mood, and tone are just right in places, but inconsistent. Dialogue, if used, somewhat reveals the characters' voices.	The voice sounds disinterested. Mood and tone are weak. Dialogue, if used, does not uniquely distinguish the characters' voices.	Voice is flat. Mood and tone are absent. Dialogue, if used, does not sound right for some of the characters.
Word Choice	Words and phrases consistently help the reader "see" the characters and "experience" the events. Nouns and verbs are clear and precise, supported by a few carefully selected modifiers.	Words and phrases frequently help the reader "see" most of the characters and "experience" most of the events. Nouns and verbs are mostly clear and precise. Most modifiers are carefully selected.	Some words and phrases help the reader picture characters and events, but some are too general. Certain nouns and verbs are weak, requiring too much help from modifiers. Modifiers are satisfactory.	Many words and phrases are too general. They keep the reader from picturing the characters and events clearly. Nouns and verbs lack clarity or precision. Too many or too few modifiers are used, and many of them are weak.	Many words are not used correctly. They distract the reader.
Sentence Fluency	Varied sentence beginnings, lengths, and patterns make the writing flow smoothly. Several particularly well-crafted sentences add style and interest. The paper is effortlessly read aloud with inflection or feeling.	Most sentence beginnings, lengths, and patterns are varied. One or two sentences add style. The paper is easily read aloud with inflection or feeling.	There is some variation in sentence beginnings, lengths, and patterns. The sentences are correct but ordinary. The paper can be read aloud with inflection or feeling.	Many sentences have the same beginnings, lengths, and patterns. This interrupts the flow of the writing. The sentences are mostly correct but ordinary. It is difficult to read the paper with inflection.	Sentences are poorly written or incorrect. The writing does not flow.
Conventions	Spelling, grammar, punctuation, and capitalization are correct. The narrative contains no errors.	There are a few minor errors, but they do not make the narrative difficult to read.	There are a few grammatical errors that may cause the reader to pause momentarily, but meaning is clear.	Many errors are present, and some confuse the reader.	The writing has not been edited. Serious errors make the narrative hard to understand.

Informative/Explanatory Writing Rubric

	5	4	3	2	1
Ideas	The topic is introduced clearly. Information and examples develop the main idea(s). Carefully selected ideas completely answer the reader's main questions.	The topic is introduced clearly. Most of the information and examples develop the main idea(s). Almost all of the reader's main questions are answered.	A topic is introduced. Some of the information and examples develop the main idea(s). The ideas chosen by the author frequently answer the reader's main questions.	A topic is introduced, but little of the information or examples develops the main idea(s). Some of the reader's questions are answered.	A topic is not introduced. Information and examples are incomplete or unrelated to the topic.
Organization	Information is organized into a strong and thoughtful introduction, a body, and a satisfying conclusion. Varied and appropriate linking words and phrases connect the ideas.	Information is organized into an introduction, a body, and a conclusion. Most linking words and phrases are varied and appropriate.	Information is organized into an introduction, a body, and a conclusion. More or better linking words and phrases are needed.	Information is not well organized. The introduction, body, and conclusion may be poorly developed. Linking words and phrases are confusing or not helpful.	The writing is not organized. Introduction and conclusion may both be missing. Linking words and phrases are not used.
Voice	The voice sounds interested and informative. It fully connects with the audience and conveys the writer's purpose well.	The voice sounds informative and mostly connects with the audience. It conveys the purpose fairly well.	The voice sounds informative and connects with the audience somewhat. It conveys the purpose some of the time.	The voice sounds informative in places. It conveys the purpose, but often fades out.	Voice is weak or absent. It does not connect with the audience or convey the writer's purpose.
Word Choice	Precise language and domain-specific vocabulary are used. Definitions are complete and helpful. Nouns and verbs are clear and precise, supported by a few carefully selected modifiers.	Precise language and domain-specific vocabulary are used. Most definitions are complete and helpful. Nouns and verbs are mostly clear and precise. Most modifiers are carefully selected.	Some precise language, domain-specific vocabulary, and definitions are used. Some nouns and verbs are weak, requiring help from modifiers. Modifiers are satisfactory.	Little precise language and domain-specific vocabulary is used. Definitions are missing or incorrect. Nouns and verbs lack clarity or precision. Too many or too few modifiers are used, and many of them are weak.	Precise language and domain-specific vocabulary are not used.
Sentence Fluency	Clear, concise sentences make the text flow smoothly. Sentence beginnings, lengths, and patterns are varied for effect. The paper is effortlessly read aloud with inflection.	Most of the sentences flow smoothly. The sentence beginnings, lengths, and patterns are varied. The paper is easily read aloud with inflection.	One or two sections of the writing do not flow smoothly. In these sections, several sentences may have the same beginnings, lengths, or patterns. The paper can be read with inflection.	In many places, the writing does not flow smoothly due to repetitive sentence beginnings, lengths, and patterns. It is difficult to read the paper with inflection.	Sentences are incomplete or incorrect.
Conventions	The text contains no errors. Spelling, grammar, punctuation, and capitalization are correct.	The text contains very few errors in spelling, grammar, punctuation, or capitalization. The meaning remains clear.	The text contains some errors in spelling, grammar, punctuation, and capitalization. One or two errors may cause the reader to pause momentarily, but meaning remains clear.	Many errors are present. Some errors are basic or repeated. The errors interfere with meaning in places.	The writing has not been edited. Serious errors make the writing hard to understand.

Opinion Writing Rubric

	5	4	3	2	1
Ideas	The writer states a clear opinion. The perfect details and facts are chosen to support the writer's reasons.	The writer states a clear opinion. Most details and facts are well chosen to support the writer's reasons.	The writer states an opinion. Some details and facts are well chosen to support the writer's reasons.	The writer states an opinion, but few details are well chosen to support the writer's reasons.	The writer does not state an opinion. Reasons are not provided.
Organization	The text is organized logically and creatively. Helpful, appropriate, even unique linking words connect the writer's opinion and reasons. A compelling conclusion clearly supports the opinion statement.	The text is organized logically. One or two more linking words are needed to connect the opinion and reasons. The beginning is strong, and the conclusion supports the opinion statement.	The text is organized logically. More or better linking words are needed to connect the opinion and reasons. The beginning and the conclusion are functional. The conclusion relates to the opinion statement.	The text is not organized logically. Linking words may not show how the writer's ideas are related. Either the beginning or the conclusion is weak. The conclusion may not relate to the opinion statement.	The text is not organized as an opinion. Linking words are not used. Ideas are hard to follow. No beginning or conclusion is evident.
Voice	The voice is clearly convincing and totally fits the writer's purpose. The mood and tone are appropriate and engage the audience.	The voice is convincing and fits the writer's purpose. The mood and tone are appropriate and engaging most of the time.	The voice is somewhat convincing and fits the writer's purpose. The mood and tone are engaging some of the time.	The voice is convincing in some places. The mood and tone are incorrect or inconsistent. They lose the audience.	The voice is weak or absent. The tone is not appropriate.
Word Choice	Precise words and fair language convey the writer's opinion. No biased words or phrases are used. Nouns and verbs are clear and precise, supported by a few carefully selected modifiers.	Most words are precise and fair. No biased words or phrases are used. Nouns and verbs are mostly clear and precise. Most modifiers are carefully selected.	Some words are too general. One biased word or phrase may be used. Some nouns and verbs are weak, requiring help from modifiers. Modifiers are satisfactory.	Most words are weak. A few biased words or phrases may be used. Nouns and verbs lack clarity or precision. Too many or too few modifiers are used, and many of them are weak.	Words are weak, biased, or used incorrectly.
Sentence Fluency	A variety of sentence patterns adds interest and style. Great variation in sentence beginnings and lengths makes the writing flow very smoothly. The paper is effortlessly read aloud with inflection.	Most sentence patterns are varied and add interest. Variation in sentence beginnings and lengths makes the writing flow smoothly. The paper is easily read aloud with inflection.	Some sentence patterns are varied and add interest. Some variation in sentence lengths and beginnings is evident. The writing flows smoothly in some places, but not in others. The paper can be read with inflection.	Too many sentences share the same pattern. The writing does not flow smoothly due to a lack of variation in sentence lengths and/or beginnings. It is difficult to read the paper with inflection.	Sentences are poorly written or incomplete. The writing is hard to follow.
Conventions	The text contains no errors. Spelling, grammar, punctuation, and capitalization are correct.	The text contains very few errors in spelling, grammar, punctuation, or capitalization. The meaning remains clear.	There are some errors in spelling, grammar, punctuation, and capitalization. One or two of these errors may cause the reader to pause momentarily, but meaning remains clear.	Many errors are present. Some errors are basic or repeated. The errors interfere with meaning in places.	The writing has not been edited. Serious errors make the writing hard to understand.

Descriptive Elements in the Text Types Rubric

	5	4	3	2	1
Ideas	The topic is clear, focused, and complete. Sensory details and examples are related to and develop the main ideas. The description helps the reader experience what is being described very clearly.	The topic is clear and focused. Most sensory details and examples are related to and develop the main ideas. The description helps the reader experience what is being described most of the time.	The topic is clear but may not be focused or complete. Sensory details and examples develop most of the main ideas. The description sometimes helps the reader experience what is being described.	The topic is not clear or focused. Details and examples develop some of the main ideas. The reader cannot always experience what is being described.	The topic is not clear. Details and examples are unrelated or missing. The reader cannot experience what is being described.
Organization	The description is well organized into a strong introduction, body, and conclusion. Details support the topic. Appropriate linking words connect the ideas and guide the reader.	Most of the description is organized, featuring an introduction, body, and conclusion. Most details support the topic. One or two more linking words are needed to connect the ideas and guide the reader.	Most of the description is organized. The introduction, body, and conclusion are functional. Some of the details support the topic. More or better linking words are needed to connect the ideas and guide the reader.	Some of the description is organized. The introduction, body, or conclusion may be weak. Few of the details support the topic. More and better linking words are needed to connect the ideas and guide the reader.	The description is not organized and does not have an introduction or conclusion. Details are missing. Linking words are not used.
Voice	The writer's voice connects strongly with the audience. The mood and tone match the purpose perfectly.	The writer's voice connects with the audience most of the time. The mood and tone match the purpose.	The writer's voice connects with the audience in places. The mood and tone match the purpose, but are inconsistent.	The writer's voice does not fit the purpose or the audience well. The mood and tone are inappropriate or inconsistent.	The writer's voice is weak or absent. It does not connect with the audience.
Word Choice	Precise, descriptive language and creative comparisons create a clear picture of the subject. Nouns and verbs carry the descriptive load with help from a few carefully chosen modifiers.	Most of the language is precise. Most comparisons create a clear picture of the subject. Nouns, verbs, and modifiers are mostly strong.	Some of the language is precise, but some is vague. Some of the comparisons create a clear picture of the subject. Many nouns and verbs depend upon modifiers for specificity. Modifiers are satisfactory.	Most of the language is not descriptive. Comparisons are ineffective. Nouns and verbs lack clarity or precision. Too many or too few modifiers are used, and many of them are weak.	The language is very basic and limited. Comparisons are not used.
Sentence Fluency	A variety of sentence beginnings, lengths, and patterns keeps the description interesting. It is effortless to read aloud with inflection or feeling. The writing flows very smoothly.	Most of the sentences feature varied beginnings, lengths, and patterns, making the writing interesting. Most of the writing flows smoothly. The paper is easy to read aloud with inflection or feeling.	Some sentences share the same beginnings, lengths, or patterns. Some of the writing flows smoothly. The paper can be read aloud with inflection or feeling.	Several sentences in a row have the same beginnings, lengths, or patterns. The flow of the writing may slow or stall in parts. The paper is difficult to read aloud with inflection or feeling.	Sentences are not varied or interesting. The writing does not flow. The description is very difficult to read.
Conventions	The description contains no errors. Spelling, grammar, punctuation, and capitalization are correct.	The description contains very few errors in spelling, punctuation, or capitalization. Grammar is correct, and meaning is clear.	The description contains some errors in spelling, grammar, punc–tuation, and capitalization. One or two of these errors may cause the reader to pause momentarily, but meaning remains clear.	Many errors are present. Some errors are basic or repeated. The errors interfere with meaning in places.	The writing has not been edited. Serious errors make the writing hard to understand.

Narrative Writing Rubric

	6	5	4	3	2	1
Ideas	The topic is just the right size—not too big or too small. Descriptive details introduce and develop the setting, narrator, characters, and plot. Carefully selected ideas completely satisfy the needs of the reader.	The topic is the right size. Most details introduce and develop the setting, narrator, characters, and plot. Carefully selected ideas satisfy most of the reader's needs.	The topic is the right size. Some details introduce and develop the setting, narrator, characters, and plot. The ideas selected by the author frequently meet the needs of the reader.	The topic is too big or too small. Some details develop the setting, narrator, characters, and plot. The ideas selected by the author sometimes meet the needs of the reader.	The topic is undeveloped. Too few details develop the narrative. Some details are unrelated. The author did not consider the needs of the reader.	The writing is not a narrative. Details are not included.
Organization	The narrative unfolds logically and naturally. Temporal words and phrases help sequence the events. A strong beginning leads to a satisfying conclusion.	One or two events in the middle are not connected or are out of order. Temporal words and phrases help sequence most of the events. The beginning or the conclusion is strong.	Some events are not connected or are out of order. Temporal words and phrases are needed to help sequence the events. The beginning and the conclusion work, but may not be strong.	The narrative does not unfold logically and naturally. Events are out of order. Temporal words and phrases are confusing or missing. The beginning or the conclusion is weak.	The narrative does not unfold logically. Events are out of order. Temporal words and phrases are not used. The beginning or the conclusion is missing or problematic.	The writing is disorganized and very difficult to follow. No beginning or conclusion is evident.
Voice	The voice, mood, and tone are just right for the purpose. Dialogue, if used, reveals each character's voice clearly.	The voice, mood, and tone are just right most of the time. Dialogue, if used, reveals the characters' voices.	The voice, mood, and tone are just right in places, but inconsistent. Dialogue, if used, somewhat reveals the characters' voices.	The voice sounds disinterested. Mood and tone are weak. Dialogue, if used, does not uniquely distinguish the characters' voices.	The voice, mood, and tone are not consistent. Dialogue, if used, does not sound right for some of the characters.	Voice is flat. Mood and tone are absent. Dialogue is not used.
Word Choice	Words and phrases consistently help the reader "see" the characters and "experience" the events. Nouns and verbs are clear and precise, supported by a few carefully selected modifiers.	Words and phrases frequently help the reader "see" most of the characters and "experience" most of the events. Nouns and verbs are mostly clear and precise. Most modifiers are carefully selected.	Some words and phrases help the reader picture characters and events, but some are too general. Certain nouns and verbs are weak, requiring too much help from modifiers. Modifiers are satisfactory.	Many words and phrases are too general. They keep the reader from picturing the characters and events clearly. Nouns and verbs lack clarity or precision. Too many or too few modifiers are used, and many of them are weak.	Most words do not help the characters and events come alive for the reader. Nouns and verbs are vague, unclear, or confusing. Modifiers may be missing entirely.	Many words are not used correctly. They distract the reader.
Sentence Fluency	Varied sentence beginnings, lengths, and patterns make the writing flow smoothly. Several particularly well-crafted sentences add style and interest. The paper is effortlessly read aloud with inflection or feeling.	Most sentence beginnings, lengths, and patterns are varied. One or two sentences add style. The paper is easily read aloud with inflection or feeling.	There is some variation in sentence beginnings, lengths, and patterns. The sentences are correct but ordinary. The paper can be read aloud with inflection or feeling.	Many sentences have the same beginnings, lengths, and patterns. This interrupts the flow of the writing. The sentences are mostly correct but ordinary. It is difficult to read the paper with inflection.	All or almost all the sentences follow the same pattern. Lengths and beginnings do not vary, making the writing robotic or rambling.	Sentences are poorly written or incorrect. The writing does not flow.
Conventions	Spelling, grammar, punctuation, and capitalization are correct. The narrative contains no errors.	There are a few minor errors, but they do not make the narrative difficult to read.	There are a few grammatical errors that may cause the reader to pause momentarily, but meaning is clear.	Many errors are present, and some confuse the reader.	Several serious errors make the narrative hard to understand.	The writing has not been edited.

Informative/Explanatory Writing Rubric

	6	5	4	3	2	1
Ideas	The topic is introduced clearly. Information and examples develop the main idea(s). Carefully selected ideas completely answer the reader's main questions.	The topic is introduced clearly. Most of the information and examples develop the main idea(s). Almost all of the reader's main questions are answered.	A topic is introduced. Some of the information and examples develop the main idea(s). The ideas chosen by the author frequently answer the reader's main questions.	A topic is introduced, but little of the information or examples develops the main idea(s). Some of the reader's questions are answered.	A topic is introduced, but information and examples do not develop the main idea(s). The author did not think about what questions the reader might have.	A topic is not introduced. Information and examples are incomplete or unrelated to the topic.
Organization	Information is organized into a strong and thoughtful introduction, a body, and a satisfying conclusion. Varied and appropriate linking words connect the ideas.	Information is organized into an introduction, a body, and a conclusion. Most linking words are varied and appropriate.	Information is organized into an introduction, a body, and a conclusion. More or better linking words are needed.	Information is not well organized. The introduction, body, and conclusion may be poorly developed. Linking words are confusing or not helpful.	Information is only partly organized. The introduction or the conclusion is missing. Linking words are not used.	The writing is not organized. Introduction and conclusion may both be missing. Linking words are not used.
Voice	The voice sounds interested and informative. It fully connects with the audience and conveys the writer's purpose well.	The voice sounds informative and mostly connects with the audience. It conveys the purpose fairly well.	The voice sounds informative and connects with the audience somewhat. It conveys the purpose some of the time.	The voice sounds informative in places. It conveys the purpose, but often fades out.	The voice consistently sounds flat. It may sound uninformed or uninterested. It does not convey the purpose.	Voice is weak or absent. It does not connect with the audience or convey the writer's purpose.
Word Choice	Precise language and domain-specific vocabulary are used. Definitions are complete and helpful. Nouns and verbs are clear and precise, supported by a few carefully selected modifiers.	Precise language and domain-specific vocabulary are used. Most definitions are complete and helpful. Nouns and verbs are mostly clear and precise. Most modifiers are carefully selected.	Some precise language, domain-specific vocabulary, and definitions are used. Some nouns and verbs are weak, requiring help from modifiers. Modifiers are satisfactory.	Little precise language and domain-specific vocabulary is used. Definitions are missing or incorrect. Nouns and verbs lack clarity or precision. Too many or too few modifiers are used, and many of them are weak.	Some domain-specific vocabulary is used incorrectly. Clarification and definition are not provided for the reader. Nouns and verbs are vague, unclear, or confusing. Modifiers may be missing.	Precise language and domain-specific vocabulary are not used.
Sentence Fluency	Clear, concise sentences make the text flow smoothly. Sentence beginnings, lengths, and patterns are varied for effect. The paper is effortlessly read aloud with inflection.	Most of the sentences flow smoothly. The sentence beginnings, lengths, and patterns are varied. The paper is easily read aloud with inflection.	One or two sections of the writing do not flow smoothly. In these sections, several sentences may have the same beginnings, lengths, or patterns. The paper can be read with inflection.	In many places, the writing does not flow smoothly due to repetitive sentence beginnings, lengths, and patterns. It is difficult to read the paper with inflection.	All or almost all the sentences have similar beginnings, lengths, or patterns. The writing sounds robotic or rambling.	Sentences are incomplete or incorrect.
Conventions	The text contains no errors. Spelling, grammar, punctuation, and capitalization are correct.	The text contains very few errors in spelling, grammar, punctuation, or capitalization. The meaning remains clear.	The text contains some errors in spelling, grammar, punctuation, and capitalization. One or two errors may cause the reader to pause momentarily, but meaning remains clear.	Many errors are present. Some errors are basic or repeated. The errors interfere with meaning in places.	Serious errors stop the reader frequently and make the writing hard to understand.	The writing has not been edited.

Opinion Writing Rubric

	6	5	4	3	2	1
Ideas	The writer states a clear opinion. The perfect details and facts are chosen to support the writer's reasons.	The writer states a clear opinion. Most details and facts are well chosen to support the writer's reasons.	The writer states an opinion. Some details and facts are well chosen to support the writer's reasons.	The writer states an opinion, but few details are well chosen to support the writer's reasons.	The writer's opinion is not clear. Facts are inaccurate or unrelated to the writer's reasons.	The writer does not state an opinion. Reasons are not provided.
Organization	The text is organized logically and creatively. Helpful, appropriate, even unique linking words connect the writer's opinion and reasons. A compelling conclusion clearly supports the opinion statement.	The text is organized logically. One or two more linking words are needed to connect the opinion and reasons. The beginning is strong, and the conclusion supports the opinion statement.	The text is organized logically. More or better linking words are needed to connect the opinion and reasons. The beginning and the conclusion are functional. The conclusion relates to the opinion statement.	The text is not organized logically. Linking words may not show how the writer's ideas are related. Either the beginning or the conclusion is weak. The conclusion may not relate to the opinion statement.	The text is not organized logically. Linking words are not used. Ideas are hard to follow. The beginning or the conclusion is missing.	The text is not organized as an opinion. No beginning or conclusion is evident.
Voice	The voice is clearly convincing and totally fits the writer's purpose. The mood and tone are appropriate and engage the audience.	The voice is convincing and fits the writer's purpose. The mood and tone are appropriate and engaging most of the time.	The voice is somewhat convincing and fits the writer's purpose. The mood and tone are engaging some of the time.	The voice is convincing in some places. The mood and tone are incorrect or inconsistent. They lose the audience.	The voice is flat and does not fit the writer's purpose. The mood and tone do not engage the audience.	The voice is weak or absent. The tone is not appropriate.
Word Choice	Precise words and fair language convey the writer's opinion. No biased words or phrases are used. Nouns and verbs are clear and precise, supported by a few carefully selected modifiers.	Most words are precise and fair. No biased words or phrases are used. Nouns and verbs are mostly clear and precise. Most modifiers are carefully selected.	Some words are too general. One biased word or phrase may be used. Some nouns and verbs are weak, requiring help from modifiers. Modifiers are satisfactory.	Most words are weak. A few biased words or phrases may be used. Nouns and verbs lack clarity or precision. Too many or too few modifiers are used, and many of them are weak.	Many words are overused and ineffective. Several biased words and phrases are used. Nouns and verbs are vague, unclear, or confusing. Modifiers may be missing.	Words are weak, biased, or used incorrectly.
Sentence Fluency	A variety of sentence patterns adds interest and style. Great variation in sentence beginnings and lengths makes the writing flow very smoothly. The paper is effortlessly read aloud with inflection.	Most sentence patterns are varied and add interest. Variation in sentence beginnings and lengths makes the writing flow smoothly. The paper is easily read aloud with inflection.	Some sentence patterns are varied and add interest. Some variation in sentence lengths and beginnings is evident. The writing flows smoothly in some places, but not in others. The paper can be read with inflection.	Too many sentences share the same pattern. The writing does not flow smoothly due to a lack of variation in sentence lengths and/or beginnings. It is difficult to read the paper with inflection.	Almost all sentences are alike. The writing is boring and does not flow smoothly.	Sentences are poorly written or incomplete. The writing is hard to follow.
Conventions	The text contains no errors. Spelling, grammar, punctuation, and capitalization are correct.	The text contains very few errors in spelling, grammar, punctuation, or capitalization. The meaning remains clear.	There are some errors in spelling, grammar, punctuation, and capitalization. One or two of these errors may cause the reader to pause momentarily, but meaning remains clear.	Many errors are present. Some errors are basic or repeated. The errors interfere with meaning in places.	Serious errors stop the reader frequently and make the writing hard to understand.	The writing has not been edited.

Descriptive Elements in the Text Types Rubric

	6	5	4	3	2	1
Ideas	The topic is clear, focused, and complete. Sensory details and examples are related to and develop the main ideas. The description helps the reader experience what is being described very clearly.	The topic is clear and focused. Most sensory details and examples are related to and develop the main ideas. The description helps the reader experience what is being described most of the time.	The topic is clear but may not be focused or complete. Sensory details and examples develop most of the main ideas. The description sometimes helps the reader experience what is being described.	The topic is not clear or focused. Details and examples develop some of the main ideas. The reader cannot always experience what is being described.	The topic and main ideas are not clear. Few sensory details and examples are included. The reader has to work to experience what is being described.	The topic is not clear. Details and examples are unrelated or missing. The reader cannot experience what is being described.
Organization	The description is well organized into a strong introduction, body, and conclusion. Details support the topic. Appropriate linking words connect the ideas and guide the reader.	Most of the description is organized, featuring an introduction, body, and conclusion. Most details support the topic. One or two more linking words are needed to connect the ideas and guide the reader.	Most of the description is organized. The introduction, body, and conclusion are functional. Some of the details support the topic. More or better linking words are needed to connect the ideas and guide the reader.	Some of the description is organized. The introduction, body, or conclusion may be weak. Few of the details support the topic. More and better linking words are needed to connect the ideas and guide the reader.	The description is not well organized. The introduction or conclusion is problematic. Details are missing. Linking words are misused or missing.	The description is not organized and does not have an introduction or conclusion. Details are missing. Linking words are not used.
Voice	The writer's voice connects strongly with the audience. The mood and tone match the purpose perfectly.	The writer's voice connects with the audience most of the time. The mood and tone match the purpose.	The writer's voice connects with the audience in places. The mood and tone match the purpose, but are inconsistent.	The writer's voice does not fit the purpose or the audience well. The mood and tone are inappropriate or inconsistent.	The writer's voice does not fit the purpose or the audience. The mood and tone are inappropriate.	The writer's voice is weak or absent. It does not connect with the audience.
Word Choice	Precise, descriptive language and creative comparisons create a clear picture of the subject. Nouns and verbs carry the descriptive load with help from a few carefully chosen modifiers.	Most of the language is precise. Most comparisons create a clear picture of the subject. Nouns, verbs, and modifiers are mostly strong.	Some of the language is precise, but some is vague. Some of the comparisons create a clear picture of the subject. Many nouns and verbs depend upon modifiers for specificity. Modifiers are satisfactory.	Most of the language is not descriptive. Comparisons are ineffective. Nouns and verbs lack clarity or precision. Too many or too few modifiers are used, and many of them are weak.	The language is not descriptive. Comparisons are confusing. Nouns and verbs are vague, unclear, or confusing. Modifiers may be missing.	The language is very basic and limited. Comparisons are not used.
Sentence Fluency	A variety of sentence beginnings, lengths, and patterns keeps the description interesting. It is effortless to read aloud with inflection or feeling. The writing flows very smoothly.	Most of the sentences feature varied beginnings, lengths, and patterns, making the writing interesting. Most of the writing flows smoothly. The paper is easy to read aloud with inflection or feeling.	Some sentences share the same beginnings, lengths, or patterns. Some of the writing flows smoothly. The paper can be read aloud with inflection or feeling.	Several sentences in a row have the same beginnings, lengths, or patterns. The flow of the writing may slow or stall in parts. The paper is difficult to read aloud with inflection or feeling.	Many sentences have the same beginnings, lengths, or patterns. The writing does not flow smoothly.	Sentences are not varied or interesting. The writing does not flow. The description is very difficult to read.
Conventions	The description contains no errors. Spelling, grammar, punctuation, and capitalization are correct.	The description contains very few errors in spelling, punctuation, or capitalization. Grammar is correct, and meaning is clear.	The description contains some errors in spelling, grammar, punctuation, and capitalization. One or two of these errors may cause the reader to pause momentarily, but meaning remains clear.	Many errors are present. Some errors are basic or repeated. The errors interfere with meaning in places.	Serious errors stop the reader frequently and make the writing hard to understand.	The writing has not been edited.

Index